Solidarity and Organization

Philippe Eynaud
Genauto Carvalho de França Filho

Solidarity and Organization

Toward New Avenues for Management

palgrave
macmillan

Philippe Eynaud
Sorbonne Business School
University Paris 1 Panthéon Sorbonne
Paris, France

Genauto Carvalho de França Filho
Federal University of Bahia
Salvador-Bahia, Brazil

ISBN 978-3-031-27567-8 ISBN 978-3-031-27568-5 (eBook)
https://doi.org/10.1007/978-3-031-27568-5

This Palgrave Macmillan imprint is published by the registered company Springer Nature Switzerland AG.
The registered company address is: Gewerbestrasse 11, 6330 Cham, Switzerland

To Alice, Léa, Lis, Pedro, Quentin, Silvana, and Virginie

Foreword

The book *Solidarity and Organization: Toward New Avenues for Management* is part of a research work initiated between two countries: France and Brazil. Thus, it is the opportunity to create a dialogue between two literatures, two cultures, two hemispheres (North and South). The authors open the debate about the prevalence of Anglo-Saxon approach on the field of management sciences and claim that solidarity has been forgotten. Based on the work of solidarist authors, they open new avenues for management by highlighting the relevance of concepts such as solidarity economy, democratic governance, organizational pluralism, social movements, emancipation, global South, postcolonialism, and gender. The authors aim to propose a conceptual framework that can recognize the plurality of organizations and the social diversity of our economic systems. The contribution of the book is to draw on another management in the face of major social and environmental challenges and to open up possibilities for the transition to more sustainable models.

Contents

List of Figures

List of Tables

1

A Double Unsustainability

> Act so that the effects of your action are compatible with the permanence of genuine human life. (Hans Jonas, 1984, page 11)

> The means may be likened to a seed, the end to a tree; and there is just the same inviolable connection between the means and the end as there is between the seed and the tree.
> Gandhi

Scientists have already given us all the facts needed to anticipate and respond to the major global crisis that is looming. Their findings clearly demonstrate that our standard economic model is not sustainable. It is not sustainable because of the many negative externalities it produces and its major impact on global warming (IPCC, 2022) and biodiversity (IPBES-IPCC, 2021). It is unsustainable for the inequalities it feeds (Piketty, 2015) and which weaken the very foundations of our democracies (Servet, 2010; Juan, 2011). Its two unsustainabilities unfortunately combine. Global warming reinforces economic inequalities by triggering climate migrations that are difficult to manage. Economic inequalities make large sections of the population more precarious, condemning them to not being able to afford the equipment and clean technologies

P. Eynaud, G. Carvalho de França Filho, *Solidarity and Organization*,
https://doi.org/10.1007/978-3-031-27568-5_1

needed to face the climate challenges. This scissor effect is detrimental to the ecological and social transition because it complicates important decisions based on consensus (Chancel, 2017). If the transition does not involve a violent rupture, it does indeed presuppose a shared desire for change (Chabot, 2015). The question now is how to generate and organize it.

At the beginning of the twenty-first century, we must face up to the inevitability of catastrophe, and not to its mere possibility (Dupuy, 2002). The maintenance of our level of civilization will depend on our collective capacity to respond quickly and appropriately to the problems we face. As Diamond (2005) shows, the collapse of a society can never be attributed to ecological damage alone. Other aggravating factors add up, including the responses (or nonresponses) to the problem. It is therefore necessary to be vigilant beyond environmental factors to all social issues and practices. We are currently going through a collective existential crisis (Klein, 2015).

The seriousness of climate change and the loss of diversity challenges the traditional distinction between the history of nature and human history, leads us to think about the Anthropocene (Beau & Larrère, 2018), and requires us to consider ways of acting with nature and not against it (Larrère & Larrère, 2015). This implies moving away from "technological progressivism (…) which has become the major figure of contemporary nihilism" (Gras, 2003; p. 293) and refusing economic models "at war with life on earth" (Klein, 2015). We must abandon a development model that endangers natural resources and "ruins the possibilities of living a human life" (Rey, 2014, p. 44). The finitude of the world is not sufficiently taken into account, trapped as we are in the illusions of an infinite development of techniques.

The actors aware of the challenges to be met are in the same position as Cassandra announcing to the Trojans the threat weighing on their city. Nobody seems really ready to listen to them. The radical decisions that need to be made are struggling to be taken. We seem to be collectively stunned and in a way weakened by our own power (Gras, 2003). There is indeed a glaring and dangerous gap between the level of capitalization and technological mastery reached by humanity and its level of political maturity.

1.1 A Need for Solidarity

Faced with these threatening perils, one and the same solution—which is both "of the order of the sign and of the technique" (Musso, 2015, p. 107)—can be called upon: solidarity. The defense of a solidarity between humans and nature (understood as all living beings: animals and plants) is indeed the most direct way to respond to the challenges of climate change and biodiversity loss. The development of solidarity between humans themselves is also a sustainable response to the inequalities that divide them. But if the answer is easy to state, its implementation is particularly difficult. It is confronted with numerous obstacles, not least of which is the lack of reflection on the concepts that can be mobilized to organize this solidarity as closely as possible to the actors and their economic activity. There is indeed an important paradox to be noted as a preliminary to this book. Solidarity has never been so necessary to implement at the national and international levels, and reflection on it has never been so eluded, misunderstood, if not discredited. Although solidarity thinking is rich and nourished by a significant body of thought, notably from nineteenth-century French authors (Blais, 2007), it is still largely absent from thinking about organizational models and their sustainability. While questions of solidarity are not absent from current discourse, they are generally confined to societal horizons or to debates related to the defense of rights. Solidarity does not seem to be able to claim a direct entry into the economy and management. It always has to take a detour.

1.2 Management at the Heart of Contemporary Problems

Yet the story could have been different. Burnham's attempt (1941) was in line with this inflection. The managerial revolution that this author called for was in fact accompanied by two announcements. The capitalist economy would disappear in favor of a managerial economy supposed to correct its defects. At the same time, the state was to merge with the economy, thanks to the development of managerial techniques in both fields. Today, we can see that the capitalist economy has survived the managerial revolution perfectly well. It has even used it to gain an advantage over the states. The latter have indeed weakened in the face of the major economic actors of the globalized world (Dowbor, 2017; Chomsky, 2017). Management has merged with the commercial entrepreneurial vision to spread in the modern world. The alchemy worked so well that it allowed it to compete with and then oust other models and to combat alternative models. From then on, management presented itself "as a tutelary, hypertrophied and dominating rationality, dwarfing and delegitimizing in the process all other models of government (public services, cooperation, self-management, family model)" (Chauvière, 2007; p. 9). The inability of management to transform itself in depth according to a perspective of solidarity has thus made it dangerous for the many nonmarket fields in which it has invested without reforming itself. The state has not escaped this. The state bureaucracy has been discredited. It now seems legitimate to most people that business leaders or fervent followers of the entrepreneurial vision can reach the highest level of political power. This extension has been possible because "the historical, ideological, and political dimensions of the discourse" that accompany it have been "obscured through an enterprise of naturalization" (Naro, 2015; page 172). Under the guise of pragmatism, management techniques designed for the commercial world have thus spread to the public arena, to administrations, and to ministries, perverting in the process the modes of regulation initially built around the general interest. In the 1970s, they took the form and the name of "new public *management.*" The irruption of new public management in public services was accompanied by an insistent discourse referring "constantly to the idea of modernity—the modernization of public services—which must inevitably involve the implementation of good business management practices" (Naro, 2015; page 172). Even though the aporia of these solutions is demonstrated and new models now need to be formulated (Fábián, 2010), the new public management still remains the dominant reference. In the case of associations, the method has been the same. Under the guise of professionalization, associations have been led to adopt the management and evaluation methods of companies (Eynaud, 2015). This change took place gradually. It was made possible by the transition from the tutelary regulation of the welfare state to a competitive regulation where the state adopts the Anglo-Saxon model and market logic. The tutelary regulation has been questioned "on the grounds that it would maintain the disempowerment of beneficiaries and clientelism" (Laville & Salmon, 2016, p. 148). Thus, in France, subsidies have seen their share gradually reduced while at the same time the volume of public orders has increased (Tchernonog & Prouteau, 2019). Calls for tender pitting associations and companies against each other have appeared. The declared intention was to use these competitive mechanisms to choose between service providers without taking into account their action project or their legal nature. The management of associations has been modified as a result. Managerial professionalization has resulted in an "organizational downsizing" (Laville & Salmon, 2016, p. 149) and a functionalist vision of the associative project (Bernet et al., 2016). By spreading a culture of performance accompanied by its own modes of evaluation, this instrumentalist management has endangered our sick societies (Gaulejac, 2005).

1.3 From Solidarity Economy to Solidarity Management

Yet Burnham's announcement was not without its fair share of insights. One could have expected something else from the development of management. It could have been built around a questioning of the incompleteness of capitalism. This missed appointment with the past is not, however, incompatible with a future reorientation. The aporias of the capitalist model have in fact left a free field for the strengthening of social and solidarity economy organizations. With the latter, the development of management based on other principles is possible. Change can be "achieved by changing the way we act" (Chabot, 2015; p. 51). Articulated with solidarity, this Other Management is able to respond to the two unsustainabilities mentioned earlier. Solidarity refers by its etymology to "the solidity of society" and "what holds it together" (Musso, 2015, p. 107). It is more useful than ever to combine the pessimism of intelligence with the optimism of will, as Gramsci wrote in his prison diaries. To do this, we need to develop a different imaginary that breaks with the dominant ideology of competition and financial performance. Indeed, "revolt begins in the imaginary: it is that which opens our eyes" (Gras, 2003; p. 292). This book starts from the idea that managers have a decisive role to play in the production of this new imaginary. The naturalization of a Darwinian vision of the world in which management is exercised in a context of generalized competition must be put into perspective (Aktouf, 2000). The search for maximum profit is above all a factor of vulnerability. A system that is too efficient becomes highly fragile (Ulanowicz et al., 2009). The natural world itself does not only obey the law of the strongest. There is another law in the jungle of the living world (Servigne & Chapelle, 2017). Kropotkin foresaw this at the beginning of the twentieth century (Kropotkine, 1902). It is about mutual aid. This law of the living has of course corollaries in human activity (Sennett, 2013) that can be read in the economic space. The academic production in the field of solidarity economy (Laville, 2017) intends to account for these phenomena. If there is a solidarity economy, there is also a management related to it. The project of this book is to open up the reflection on the managerial spirit (Ogien, 1995) in order to bring out the theoretical foundations of a solidarity-based management. Indeed, there is a lack of reflection in organizational theory with regard to solidarity. Following the example of what has been done in the solidarity economy, a major theoretical analysis must be conducted and pursued in management sciences (Béji-Bécheur et al., 2018; Bayle & Dupuy, 2012; Bernet et al., 2016; Quéinnec & Igalens, 2004; Laville & Glémain, 2010). This book aims to revisit certain authors who are unfortunately not widely used in management science and management in order to lay the foundations for a new science of organizations within the framework of a North-South dialogue as proposed by Guerreiro Ramos (1981). In this perspective, the economic purpose cannot be distinguished from the means chosen to serve it.

To follow this project, the book is articulated in four parts. In the first part, we will look for references to solidarity in the body of organizational theory. For this, a detour through the history of thought will be necessary. It will lead us to ask why solidarity has appeared for so long as an unthought of organization, and how another history of ideas and practices could have been possible. In the second part, we will begin to order the two terms in order to identify perspectives. We will first look at the conditions necessary for the organization of solidarity. We will see in particular that such a project cannot succeed without first questioning the nature and definition of the economy itself. By mobilizing Polanyi, we will be able to distinguish between the formal economy and the substantive economy and to consider their transposition from the conceptual framework to the management space. In the third part, we will reverse the perspective and think about the prerequisites necessary to solidify the organization. We will thus be led to focus on democratic solidarity and to see in what way and how solidarity-based management can have the ambition of democratizing management. In order to do this, we will have to discuss the problems of managing multi-stakeholder organizations, inclusiveness, and solidarity-based territories, reconciling the economic and the social. In the fourth part, we will return to the double unsustainability mentioned in the introduction to our paper, and we will detail the analysis of two proposals that are rich in terms of solidarity and sustainable management. The first is South American. It is the Brazilian school of thought on solidarity-based management. A rich and ancient debate animates it. It can be seen as a conceptual and practical response from a country that has long been characterized by strong inequalities. The second is North American. It is about the management of the commons. This school of thought is in line with the work of Ostrom and initially starts from the problems of preserving natural spaces but is not limited to them. We will see how these two schools of thought differ and complement each other. Finally, we will conclude on the epistemological aspects by seeking to see what the project of another management can be. We will discuss the methodological and operational implications of such a project, and we will reflect on the links between solidarity management and the possible renewal of public action.

References

Aktouf, O. (2000). *Management entre tradition et renouvellement*. Gaëtan Morin. 710 pages.

Bayle, E., & Dupuy, J. C. (2012). *Management des entreprises de l'économie sociale et solidaire : identités plurielles et spécificités*. Editions De Boeck. 334 pages.

Beau, R., & Larrère, C. (2018). *Penser l'Anthropocène*. Presses de Sciences Po. 554 pages.

Béji-Bécheur, A., Codello, P., & Château-Terrisse, P. (2018). *Gestion des entreprises sociales et solidaires*. Editions Ems, Management et société. 259 pages.

Bernet, J., Eynaud, P., Maurel, O., & Vercher, C. (2016). *La gestion des associations*. Eres édition.

Blais, M. C. (2007). *La solidarité : histoire d'une idée*. NRF, Editions Gallimard.

Burnham, J. (1941). *The managerial revolution: What is happening in the world?* John Day Company.

Chabot, P. (2015). *L'âge des transitions*. Puf.

Chancel, L. (2017). *Insoutenables inégalités : pour une justice sociale et environnementale*. Editions Les petits matins.

Chauvière, M. (2007). *Trop de gestion tue le social : Essai sur une discrète chalandisation*. Alternatives sociales. Editions La Découverte.

Chomsky, N. (2017). *Who rules the world?* Penguin Books Ltd. 336 pages.

Diamond, J. (2005). *Collapse: How societies choose to fail or survive*. Penguin Books.

Dowbor, L. (2017). *A era do capital improdutivo - Autonomia Literária*. Outras Palavras.

Dupuy, J. P. (2002). *Pour un catastrophisme éclairé : quand l'impossible est certain*. Editions Points, Collection Essais. 216 pages.

Eynaud, P. (2015). *Gouvernance entre diversité et normalisation*. Collection Hors Série Juris Association, Editeur Dalloz.

Fábián, A. (2010). New public management and what comes after. *Current Issues of Business and Law, 5*, 41–56.

Gaulejac, V. D. (2005). *La société malade de la gestion : idéologie gestionnaire, pouvoir managérial et harcèlement social*. Editions Points.

Gras, A. (2003). *Fragilité de la puissance : se libérer de l'emprise technologique.* Editions Fayard.
Guerreiro Ramos, A. (1981). *The new science of organizations: A reconceptualization of the wealth of nations.* University of Toronto Press. 210 pages.
IPBES-IPCC. (2021). *Scientific outcome of the IPBES-IPCC co-sponsored workshop on biodiversity and climate change (report).*
IPCC. (2022, September). *AR6 synthesis report: Climate change.*
Jonas, H. (1984). The imperative of responsibility. In *Search of ethics for the technological age (translation of Das Prinzip Verantwortung).* University of Chicago Press. 255 pages.
Juan, S. (2011). *La transition écologique* (3e ed.). Eres éditions. Juris editions. 372 pages.
Klein, N. (2015). *Everything can change: Capitalism and climate change.* Actes Sud/Lux. 623 pages.
Kropotkine, P. (1902). *Mutual aid: A factor of evolution.* McClure Phillips and Co.
Larrère, C., & Larrère, R. (2015). *Penser et agir avec la nature : une enquête philosophique.* Editions la Découverte. 330 pages.
Laville, J. L. (2017). *L'économie sociale et solidaire.* Seuil.
Laville, J. L., & Glémain, P. (2010). *L'économie sociale et solidaire aux prises avec la gestion.* Desclée de Brouwer. 480 pages.
Laville, J. L., & Salmon, A. (2016). Les associations et leur contribution à la démocratie : un défi contemporain. In R. Lafore (Ed.), *Refonder les solidarités : les associations au cœur de la protection sociale* (pp. 147–162).
Musso, P. (2015). La solidarité : généalogie d'un concept sociologique. In A. Supiot (Ed.), *La solidarité : enquête sur un principe juridique* (pp. 93–107). Collège de France, Edition Odile Jacob.
Naro, G. (2015). Le new public management ou la gestion malade de la société. In Dietrich, Pigeyre, & Vercher-Chaptal (Eds.), *Dérives et perspectives de la gestion : échanges autour des travaux de Julienne Brabet.* Septentrion, Presses Universitaires. 180 pages.
Ogien, A. (1995). *L'esprit gestionnaire : une analyse de l'air du temps.* Editions de l'EHESS. 226 pages.
Piketty, T. (2015). *The economics of inequality.* Belknap Press. 160 pages.
Quéinnec, E., & Igalens, J. (2004). *Les organisations non gouvernementales et le management.* Editions Vuibert. 319 pages.
Rey, O. (2014). *Une question de taille.* Les essais.
Sennett, R. (2013). *Together: The rituals, pleasures and politics of cooperation.* Penguin. 336 pages.

Servet, J. M. (2010). *Le grand renversement : De la crise au renouveau solidaire.* Desclée de Brouwer. 264 pages.

Servigne, P., & Chapelle, G. (2017). *L'entraide, l'autre loi de la jungle.* Editions Les liens qui libèrent.

Tchernonog, V., & Prouteau L. (2019). *Le paysage associatif français - Mesures et évolutions.*

Ulanowicz, R. E., Goerner, S. J., Lietaer, B., & Gomez, R. (2009). Quantifying sustainability: Resilience, efficiency and the return of information theory. *Ecological Complexity*, 27–36.

2

Solidarity: An Unthought in Organizational Theory?

At the beginning of the twenty-first century, the economic equation could no longer be reduced to opposition and/or simple complementarity between the market and the state. At the institutional level, many countries have yet to recognize the importance of another field through framework laws and specific public policies (Chaves & Demoustier, 2015): the social and solidarity economy. This emergence of a third actor in the field is the result of numerous tensions and a double incompleteness. On the one hand, the states are no longer able to play the regulatory role of the social state of the Thirty Glorious Years. The weakening of regulations in terms of fiscal policy, worker protection, and public services has been "a decisive factor in explaining the rise in inequality"' (Chancel, 2017, p. 67). On the other hand, market logics are not able to guarantee the sustainability of their economic model. Consequently, there is a need for new solidarities to refound public action.

However, our organizational models are not adapted to serenely envisage this refounding. First, they suffer from a high degree of porosity in the face of the logic of the market economy. The strong link between management sciences and the dominant economy is problematic. By the primacy it gives to methodological individualism, the market economy is indeed incapable of thinking about solidarity. Moreover, the market logic

P. Eynaud, G. Carvalho de França Filho, *Solidarity and Organization*,
https://doi.org/10.1007/978-3-031-27568-5_2

is extensive, and its implicit doctrine is "that of crowding out: any extension of the public sphere quantitatively reduces the extent of the private sphere; any regulation decided by the legislator reduces the efficiency of the market" (Fitoussi, 2004, p. 17). As Rosanvallon ironically notes, "It is no longer politics, law and conflict that must govern society, but the market" (Rosanvallon, 1979, p. 3). In so doing, market logics pervert our organizational models and spread beyond the market sphere. The organizational model of the firm is in a way "exported" to public institutions, social organizations, and domestic economies. This context tightens the public sphere, weakens our regulatory capacity, and endangers the logics, institutions, and organizations that serve solidarity. To reverse these trends, it seems to us that we need to do some fundamental work to reexamine the history of organizational thinking. In particular, we need to question the assumption that allows some authors to assert that management sciences are "inseparable from the history of companies" (David et al., 2012, p. 21). This assumption is detrimental because it overshadows cooperative, mutualist, and associative forms and their history. The conceptual approach to solidarity-based management certainly requires a return to the foundations of the economy and the historical production of knowledge. Are management sciences only support sciences for managers trained in market logic? Can they be critical and have the legitimacy to be reflective sciences on management (Huault, 2008)? Can they serve emancipation and the reversal of mechanisms of power and domination (Enriquez, 2003; Herreros, 2012)? Can they accompany a heterodox economy in cross-cutting approaches to reconsider the nature of wealth and encourage the production of new indicators (Renault, 2011; Viveret, 2004)? After reviewing the birth and history of management, we will consider the possibility of a counter-history. This consideration will lead us to reveal the main lines of organizational reflection articulated around the issue of solidarity.

2.1 Solidarity and the History of Management: Missed Appointments

Although management is a young science, it already has a history. Historians are working on its analysis and understanding, and although the history of management—as a management discipline—is often ignored or neglected (Nikitin, 2003), it is nonetheless a valuable source for defining and studying concepts. A notable point is that the history of management is not univocal. There are several competing histories that can account for the birth of the discipline. However, among these histories, one dominates North American history. Consequently, diversion via the North American continent is essential to understand the current logics at work in managerial thought.

2.1.1 The Prevalence of Anglo-Saxon Literature and Its Consequences

Anglo-Saxon researchers (Cummings et al., 2017) have carried out some very interesting research based on the best known and most widely read journals in the history of organizational and management sciences. They collected approximately two thousand articles published over the last sixty years in these journals. They then coded them according to the geographical location of their field of observation. Their results speak for themselves. Over this period, the scientific production of these leading journals focused nearly exclusively on English and North American cases. Continental Europe, Asia, Africa, and South America are mostly absent from published works. One might think that this phenomenon of the dominance of the English language and culture is general and that it illuminates nothing in particular about the field of knowledge in organization and management theory. The second part of the study refutes this hypothesis. It shows, in fact, through a cross-analysis of three historical knowledge objects (medicine, architecture, and management), that the history of management looks the least toward external (non-Anglo-Saxon) experiences. It also has the least historical depth (ibid.). Management historians did not begin their thinking until the early nineteenth century. This timeline suggests that this discipline considers that there were no organizational problems in premodern civilizations, which is surprising, to say the least.

Beyond the language barrier, there is of course a cultural filter that renders invisible experiences in non-English speaking countries. This effect might be permissible if these were academic journals with a national focus. However, given the major role now played by Anglo-Saxon academic journals through international rankings, such a prism is highly damaging to the development of knowledge. The consequences of this truncated history are felt far beyond the geographical area covered. By reducing the history of thought to a narrow cultural and geographical thread, our collective ability to understand the present and creatively address the future is impaired. The performative power of this dominant model of thinking should not be overlooked (Callon, 2006).

In educational terms, organizational theory is often approached and described chronologically in textbooks. Therefore, the official history of organizational theories has a strong potential impact on the training of managers and decision-makers and on their future cognitive abilities. However, Anglo-Saxon textbooks (and many others) situate the birth of organizational questioning with Smith's thinking on the division of labor. In particular, they retain the idea of the "invisible hand" that values individual egoism. They see Weber as the one who opened the way to the development of the theory of organizations by bringing to light the bureaucratic phenomenon. They associate the emergence of the scientific approach to management with Taylor and criticize his mechanistic vision of the organization. Mayo is credited with having identified the importance of the human factor in pursuing this same scientific management. Behind this neat and perfectly chronological portrait, which values individual initiative and the market enterprise, there seems to be little room for solidarity. In fact, the reality is somewhat different. Presented in this way, the history of management is reduced to the thinking of the authors mentioned. It overlooks the complexity of their contributions and tends to assert the idea of linear time in which organizational theory has only progressed.

With Guerreiro Ramos, it can be argued that organizational theory, as it has been formed in the managerial vulgate, is above all an expression of market ideology (Guerreiro Ramos, 1981). A critical reflection on the history of management is more necessary than ever if we want to cultivate a richer imagination and develop the potential of the discipline. This narrowing of the spectrum of analysis in time and space is of course detrimental to the richness of academic research and determines a certain reading of the history of organizational thought. We will now follow the arrowed path of this official history made in the USA in search of missed appointments with solidarity issues. We will distinguish between the initiators of the discipline of European origin and the pioneers, essentially North Americans.

2.1.2 The Truncated Reading of the Work of the Initiators of the Discipline

Although Smith cannot be classified as an organizational theorist, he is nevertheless identified as the originator of thinking in the organizational field. He is credited with being the first to clearly analyze the issue of the division of labor and its consequences. He was the one who understood and anticipated the emerging need for control in the economic space and the need to train professional managers. However, the Smithian idea that has stuck most is that of the "invisible hand." This well-known metaphor generally accompanies the explanation of the economic doctrine of generalized laissez-faire and equates Smith's work with the valorization of selfish behavior. For Smith, these would be likely to contribute—if encouraged—to the wealth of a nation. We are using the conditional tense here because a critical reading of the same story can, however, shed completely different light on organizational theories. A first simple and objective observation can be made about Smith's work. The expression "invisible hand" is used only three times in all of his writings and in different ways, which is a noticeably low occurrence for a concept that is supposed to be central to his work. In fact, the assimilation between the "invisible hand and market can [...] be considered as an extrapolation that has no real basis in Smith's texts" (Dellemotte, 2009, p. 34).

Indeed, "Smith did not carry in his heart, unlike to certain preconceived ideas, the big entrepreneurs and merchants" (ibid., p. 36). For him, "the order that emerges from the free expression of private interests is thus far [...] from being necessarily consistent with the general interest" (ibid., p. 37). In the struggle between capitalists and workers, Smith explicitly takes the side of the latter. The former are described "as plotters, supported by law and order, who do not hesitate to starve the mass of the population to increase their profits" (ibid., p. 36). Smith assigns to the sovereign the duty of "erecting and maintaining certain public works and institutions which are beneficial to the community, but whose profitability is not immediate enough to be taken over by the private sector" (p. 37). Finally, Smith favors progressive taxation. He states: "The subjects of a state should contribute to the support of the government, each as much as possible in proportion to his faculties, that is, in proportion to the income he enjoys under the protection of the state" (Smith, 2013, p. 240). Smith is therefore in favor of a redistributive tax. On this position, he is very close to Bourgeois (1896), a French author known for his defense of solidarism. If we consider a societal current in organizational theories, we understand that "some of Adam Smith's ideas about the importance of citizen involvement in promoting well-being in society could be considered as the origin of this current" (Vaujany et al., 2016, p. 15). Why, then, have most management studies adopted a reductive vision of Smith's work, erasing everything that falls within the register of redistribution and solidarity?

Weber, for his part, is often cited in Anglo-Saxon literature as the author who opened up two perspectives: that of broadening the questioning of companies to organizations and that of taking into account the bureaucratic phenomenon (Cummings et al., 2017). The first idea implies a chronological development of knowledge in organization theory from Smith to Weber. This view of history is criticizable and problematic because it assumes a teleology in the production of knowledge. The second idea, on the other hand, oversimplifies Weber's work. While Weber did analyze and describe the bureaucratic phenomenon, his thinking is much broader. In particular, he discusses at length the question of "sociation," which he defines as a social relationship based on a compromise or on a rationally motivated coordination of interests (in value or in finality). He therefore takes into account the association and uses it to broaden the framework for considering rationality that can be expressed in value. His work paints a precise picture of all the rationalities at work in the variety of organizational forms, whether they are in the market or outside the market. Why, then, has management research given such prominence to Weber's reference to the market and to his writings on bureaucracy?

Like Smith, Weber seems to be appreciated in management science by authors who have only partially read his writings. Part of the misunderstanding can be explained by difficulties in accessing the work and issues with translation (Weiss, 1983). In reality, Weber makes nuanced statements about bureaucracy. He is fully aware of its pros and cons. He notes that the bureaucratic phenomenon is characteristic of the evolution of modern society and should be analyzed as such. By focusing on the negative side of bureaucratic phenomena, management studies can both value market organizational forms (because they are not subject to them) and criticize the organization of public administrations. The extension of firms to organizations is in fact accompanied by a concomitant invalidation of nonmarket organizational forms. This partial double reading (Smith, Weber) has ideological coherence: the focus on Smith's invisible hand legitimizes market logics based on private initiative, while the focus on Weber's bureaucracy disqualifies nonmarket modes of organization. From these truncated premises of the European literature, the American management literature can take off.

2.1.3 Nonsolidarity American Pioneers

Based on Smith's division of labor, Taylor developed a rational approach to control and introduced performance and efficiency objectives to management. Taylor is also recognized as the first to have produced a "scientific" approach to management. This scientific dimension is retained by Drucker and Maciarielo (2008) to affirm that the discipline was born with Taylor. This assertion implicitly invalidates previous organizational knowledge. For Duncan, in fact, considering the existence of management before Taylor is utopian. According to him, there were managers and organizations before Taylor (they cite the construction of the pyramids in ancient Egypt), but the discipline could not exist because no one before Taylor had sought to systematize, codify, and prescribe solutions for managing more effectively (Duncan, 1989). No historical analysis supports this argument, but the supremacy of the North American managerial approach is thus preserved. History is definitely not welcome in management studies. Not only is managerial thinking captured by the Anglo-Saxon world, but it is above all a matter of men, and, more precisely, white men. As Laurent points out, there is probably nothing a priori "intrinsically racist in the classical philosophical-economic theory of the free market," but it cannot be ignored that "liberal thought and the exploitation of people of color have advanced together" (Laurent, 2016; p. 182). One cannot understand the expansion of capitalism without colonialism. In its amorality, management seems to ignore the issue of slavery, no doubt to reinterpret it. By naturalizing Darwinism, liberal management validates the existing systems of domination, especially that of racial domination. The way for Taylor's scientific management is open.

By saying that management was born with Taylor, the advent of the discipline is associated with the rise of the market economy. In fact, the scientific quality of Taylor's approach is questionable. As in the work of Cummings et al. (2017), Taylor himself had no ambition to qualify his work as scientific. The term was in fact proposed to him by Pinchot, a member of Roosevelt's cabinet, who looked to him for support in promoting the idea of nature-conscious management. For Pinchot, scientific management took into account the general interest. The collaboration between the two people did not last, but Taylor retained the term "scientific management,' which made him popular. If Taylor had accepted Pinchot's proposal, the management story would have been very different. Indeed, Pinchot had in mind a management approach geared toward ecological sustainability that would offer the greatest good, for the greatest number, and for the longest term (quoted by Cummings et al., 2017, p. 324). In this proposition, Pinchot was a visionary.

While the scientificity of Taylor's approach is rarely contested, there is nearly unanimous criticism of his method. In particular, he is criticized for neglecting the human dimension of the organization and for remaining trapped in a cold and mechanistic approach to work. Taylor therefore underestimated the importance of the human factor. From then on, the figure of Mayo appeared attractive, and it is in fact a counterpoint to Taylor's work. Mayo would thus have intuited the absence of the human dimension in Taylor's analysis. The story goes that Mayo's discovery was the result of serendipity. In an experimental approach deployed at Hawthorne, Mayo and his team were said to have realized by chance that productivity gains could be obtained by paying greater attention to workers. Mayo's insight would therefore constitute both a break with and a continuation of Taylor's thinking: a break through the refusal of a cold vision of the organization, a continuation through the pursuit of scientific work on management. Here, again, such a historical vision does not stand up to the test of facts. In fact, Mayo does not hesitate to generalize his conclusions without seeking to substantiate them. Mayo has a fixed idea: he despises unions. Paying attention to the workers is therefore for him a lesser evil since it undermines the constitution and/or growth of unions. Contrary to what one might have thought, the Hawthorne company he studies is not a company like any other. Even before Mayo came to observe it, it was known to have developed an entire policy of support and assistance for its workers. In fact, it is a pioneer in human resources policy. Interestingly, this company hosts communities of foreign workers. By financially supporting each of these communities, the company manages to prevent the establishment of trade unions. Mayo does not study a company that provides insufficient attention to employees but, on the contrary, a company that is very attentive to their fate. The scope of the work presented by Mayo is therefore greatly reduced. Samson and Daft (2012) are categorical in their analysis and shatter the scientificity of Mayo's work. According to them, money is the best hypothetical explanation for the increased productivity observed by Mayo. The case is closed, but that does not prevent misconceptions from continuing to be set forth.

Thus, the opposition we have just highlighted between Taylor and Mayo is partly related to that of Smith and Weber. Taylor sought to rationalize the work chain and refused to be sentimental. In this attempt, he wanted to be amoral. He thus claimed to be able to provide answers to the challenges posed to the companies of his time by a new organization of work. Workers must accept the consequences; today's sacrifices are tomorrow's profits. The Taylorian proposal thus found its natural extension and its hour of glory in Fordism. By postulating the possibility of a reversal of evil into good, Taylor takes up the figure of speech of the invisible hand, which intends to transform selfishness into virtue. However, Taylor does not envisage any solidarity other than that which is coldly expressed on the work line. Mayo, on the other hand, differs from Taylor in his method. His work emphasized the need for immediate attention to workers and provided the first arguments for the emergence of a theory of human resources. However, Mayo joins Taylor in an amoral perspective. According to Mayo, it was not a question of company managers participating in the emancipation of workers but rather of preventing the risks of confrontation that would disrupt the production of goods and services. Mayo thus joined Taylor in a certain form of cynicism and in the refusal of strong solidarity between social classes. It is true that both authors consider the enterprise to be a closed and self-sufficient system. They do not seem to see that management is the bearer of issues that extend beyond the narrow boundaries of the company and that it is potentially revolutionary.

2.1.4 Can the Managerial Revolution Be Mutually Supportive?

When Burnham published a book titled *The Managerial Revolution* in 1941, he immediately linked management to national and international economic policy. In the period of the emerging Cold War between the two East–West blocs, Burnham relied on management to ease tensions and reduce the risk of conflict. He saw management as a way of overcoming the shortcomings of both the command economy and the capitalist economy. He puts forward the idea that there seems no reason to believe that managerial economy will be subject to the capitalist type of economic crisis, since the factors involved in this type of crisis, which are related to the profit requirement of capitalist economy, will be done away with (Burnham, 1941). He thus sees management as a means of preventing crises. For him, the advent of the managerial revolution is a guarantee of a fusion between the state and the economy and of the overcoming of the systems formed at the beginning of the twentieth century. From then on, the managerial revolution augured a different form of problem-solving, one that was likely to encompass the technical, economic, and political dimensions in a single approach. The intuition is not incorrect, but history, unfortunately, will not prove Burnham correct. The managerial revolution is taking place, but, alas, it is not proving to be the expected guarantee of a peaceful world.

Burnham observes that the growth in the size of companies has favored the development of management. At the same time, bureaucratic methods have developed strongly in administrations and in the political arena. For Burnham, these developments reflect the same phenomenon. Bureaucracy and management are part of the same organizational thinking. Their convergence heralds the merger of the economic and political fields. As this phenomenon can be observed on both sides of the Berlin Wall, Burnham sees a revolutionary dimension. He says, "If political problems were settled by scientific reasoning, we should, most probably, expect that the political system of managerial society would take the form of a single world-state. In this way the anarchy necessarily following from conflicting sovereignties would be wholly eliminated. World production could be organized on the most efficient plan with the maximum utilization of world resources and the most effective division of labor. Unnecessary duplications could be avoided, and land, climate, peoples, and resources could be exploited in the most fruitful way" (ibid., p. 165). This fortunate change for Burnham occurred during World War II. For him, "the war of 1914 was the last great war of capitalist society, and the war of 1939 the first great war of managerial society" (ibid., p. 168).

Burnham's book has been a success in the United States. It is said to have inspired Orwell to write *1984*. However, this success conceals an important biographical element in the author's life. Until 1940, Burnham was a communist. More precisely, he was a Trotskyist. He naively saw in the rise of the "organizers" an emerging regulatory capacity between the bourgeoisie and the proletariat. In abandoning the communist revolution for the managerial revolution, Burnham makes the mistake of all new converts: he lends slightly too many virtues to the revolution he joins. By placing realism at the center of thinking, the managerial revolution does not pacify the world, nor does it solidify it; it only gives it a smooth form that does not offer any room for criticism. However, Burnham's work has left its mark on people's minds and provides two key ideas for understanding the modern world: management has become widespread, and it is a vector of regulation. In this sense, it has an institutional dimension.

2.1.5 The Firm as an Institution

Compared to the pioneering authors, neo-institutional theory shifts the balance. It abandons the postulate of perfect instrumental rationality. The institutional economics of Coase and Williamson considers the firm an open system (Coase, 1937; Williamson, 1985). The firm is thought of as an institution in its relationship to other institutions such as the market. Information is central to this conceptual framework. If access to market information is easy and suppliers are numerous, it is profitable to outsource one's activity. Otherwise, transaction costs may be high and favor the choice of internal hierarchical control of the activity within a company. Thus, institutional economics justifies the need for nonmarket institutions by the market. This thinking legitimizes the existence of hierarchically organized companies. The individual, on the other hand, arbitrates between the pursuit of profit as an independent worker and the pursuit of a wage as an employee in a hierarchical system (Douglas, 1986). By separating the firm from the market into two institutions, neo-institutionalist authors recognize, like Simon (1955), that human rationality has its limits and that it is now common to regard institutional organization as a means of compensating for the limits of rationality (Douglas, 1986).

They also recognize that there are institutional arrangements that may be more relevant than the market. Indeed, in his article, "The nature of the firm" (1937), Coase seeks to understand why firms exist. He proposes a reflection that articulates the logic of the market and the internal hierarchical logic of firms. It is the institution that manages and stores information. In this way, it reduces uncertainty. We could continue the history of thought and argue that by showing the importance of the firm between the market and the hierarchy in a neo-institutional vision, Williamson and Coase finalized the thinking on organizations. They made the link between Smith and Weber. For Bonnafous-Boucher, the institutional approach of Coase and Williamson is a step forward in that it allows the firm to be considered a system without being rooted in a scientistic model, whether biological or cybernetic (Bonnafous-Boucher, 2005). However, it is important to consider the definition of the concept of institutions. As Douglas points out, economists' interest in the structures of institutions says virtually nothing about legitimation, although the issue of authority is sometimes mentioned (Douglas, 1986). Mary Douglas understands an institution as a legitimized social grouping. For anthropologists, it is a question of not only whether an organization is an institution but also "under what conditions it is" (Bonnafous-Boucher, 2005, p. 108). Thus, anthropology adopts "social and cultural symbolism, which is nothing other than the analysis of institutions" (ibid.) and is often neglected by the theory of organizations. This opening up of the institutional question in the economic field does, however, inaugurate a broader reflection on the enterprise as a social institution. It allows the possibility of a first consideration of solidarity in the framework of a firm that is now described as "social."

2.1.6 The Firm as a Social Business

The international debate on social enterprises is largely dominated by North American literature. The first definition of the concept was put forward in the United States in the 1990s by researchers at Harvard Business School. For them, a social enterprise is capable of setting and working toward a dual economic and social objective. This type of enterprise exists because it is run by altruistic social entrepreneurs. They are driven by the desire to combine a profitable business project with the defense of a social cause. In line with this movement of thought, Yunus (2007) proposed the concept of social business to designate enterprises that could redefine the face of capitalism. The idea he defends is to favor the evolution toward a new capitalism where companies would have a double objective: profit and a social cause. For this author, companies can set social objectives for themselves and achieve them if they are supported by groups that are aware of their social responsibilities. This idea may seem attractive for indebted states facing increasing social needs. By addressing the aporias of the market economy, this social entrepreneurship could tackle the problem of poverty. Proponents of social business believe that this new capitalism can operate according to the management principles of a conventional business (Ibid) and can be guaranteed to cover both its own costs and social costs. There is therefore no need to change management methods or adopt a different rationality: it is enough to adapt to the constraints and find the most effective solutions within the chosen framework. Social business is thus in line with David Cameron's idea of a "Big Society" presented in 2010. Social entrepreneurship, venture philanthropy, and libertarian paternalism are combined to form an ideal neoliberal society (Corbett & Walker, 2013). This perspective shows how much capitalism—although it denies it—shares an undeniably utopian dimension with the other doctrines (Rosanvallon, 1979).

If, among the authors we have just mentioned, Yunus offers with his concept of social business the most accomplished version of humanist entrepreneurship, we cannot affirm that the aim is truly solidarity-based. Social business appears above all as an attempt to moralize capitalism (Thompson, 1966). In this respect, it cannot be taken as a reference for those seeking to rethink management using the principle of solidarity. While this type of enterprise often expresses the need to fight poverty, its entrepreneurs rarely seek to defend an alternative mode of governance and to correct inequalities at their source. The virtuous discourse of the social is akin to the rhetoric of vaccinia, which consists of confessing the accidental evil of a class society in order to better mask its main evil. The collective imagination is immunized by a small inoculation of the recognized evil, and it is thus defended against the risk of a generalized subversion (Barthes, 2013). The social enterprise (in its Anglo-Saxon definition) therefore remains a market enterprise with classic management and governance. The social enterprise in fact draws its strength from the achievements and experience accumulated in the managerial revolution.

2.1.7 Forgetting Solidarity and Its Consequences

To conclude this historical development, let us draw a parallel between the opposition of Smith and Weber, on the one hand, and that of Taylor and Mayo, on the other. Whereas Smith sought to produce a theory that would "demoralize" economic policy by bringing out the "natural" laws of the market, Weber's ambition was to nurture a broader vision. For him, the market is only one of the forms of rationality at work. Taylor, for his part, followed in Smith's footsteps and sought to translate the laws of the market into a management method. In search of natural laws, his vision of the organization was amoral and intended to break from a paternalistic consensus. This intention is not the case with Mayo. In his ambition to reduce the internal conflict in companies exacerbated by the Taylorian vision, Mayo proposes, on the contrary, a moralization of management. In this choice, he affirms the possibility of a popular consensus on a form of moral economy described by Thompson, namely, justifying paternalism and establishing a moral economy of the poor.

Burnham, on the other hand, is one of the first management writers to seek to link Smith's and Weber's visions. For Burnham, the link is not simple. According to him, the management announced by Smith and the bureaucracy of Weber are part of the same movement to pacify the world. The rationality that is expressed in both spaces implements procedures that link the political to the economic. Burnham's approach is similar to that of the institutional economic school, in that Coase and Williamson also seek to link the work of Smith and Weber. However, the latter see the market and the hierarchical firm as two institutions that need to be articulated. If Burnham's vision is naive, Coase and Williamson's is technical. The question of the articulation between the two institutions is resolved by estimating transaction costs.

Consequently, the link established between Taylor's approach and Mayo's does not make it possible to escape a cold or paternalistic vision of social relations within the hierarchical organization. The attempt to overcome this issue by the social enterprise (which shows a concern for integrating the social issue) is, however, hampered by the absence of any questioning of traditional management. We have seen that the history of management could have been very different on the basis of the same premises if the pioneering authors had made other analytical choices. Both Smith's and Weber's writings lent themselves to a broad vision of organizational issues in which the question of solidarity was present. If Taylor had followed Pingeot's proposals, scientific management could have been put in the service of environmental sustainability. If Mayo had truly wanted to explore the question of attention to the workers in the firm, he would have studied the emergence of the cooperative forms of organization of which he was a contemporary. The partial reading of Smith and Weber and the partial vision of the pioneer authors have led management down a path that avoids the question of the solidarity of human beings with each other and human beings with nonhuman beings. This concern to avoid any reference to a higher value, such as the preservation of nature or respect for people, has had two important consequences: the disappearance of the subject and the flight into a culture of perpetual change.

As Boltanski shows, "one of the most relevant properties of managerial domination is [...] to be without a subject" (Boltanski, 2015, pp. 201–202). The absence of a subject is decisive in that it prevents the resistance of the actors involved in the collective action. It is indeed each time "necessity, in the sense of causal necessity, that dictates the measures taken, and provides an explanation rather than a justification" (ibid., p. 202). There is no need, therefore, to exercise threat or live in a climate of terror to maintain domination: it is enough to demand that all actors be realistic and accept the economic constraints presented to them, "not because they would be good or right in themselves, but because they cannot be other than they are" (ibid., p. 204); this is the TINA[1] system dear to Thatcher.

It is therefore understandable how the managerial revolution announced by Burnham could have fueled a widespread feeling of powerlessness, with the consequence of "withdrawal from the spheres of political action and, at the end of the day, a disinterest, not only in activism but even in that minimal form of political activity that consists in going to vote" (ibid., p. 204). A second important point for

[1] TINA: There is no alternative.

understanding the strength of the managerial regime is its apology for change. Deprived of an external reference, managers constantly value change and theorize its implementation. One of the main tasks of the team leader is thus to break down resistance to change, which prompts Boltanski to say, "This connection, strange when one thinks about it, of will—that is to say, freedom—and necessity, which has often been associated with totalitarian regimes claiming a deterministic philosophy of history, is nevertheless a commonplace of the modes of governance of advanced capitalism" (ibid., p. 207). The desire for permanent change is the source of a continuous recomposition of reality that maintains and feeds what Bauman (2000) calls the "liquid society," that is, a society where consumption and disposability reign. To maintain this race to the top, the managerial society relies "on a form of authority—that of the experts—which intends to be located at the point of indistinction between reality and the world" (Boltanski, 2015, p. 210).

In an environment characterized by uncertainty, experts compose and recompose grids for reading the world. They are therefore always one step ahead of their opponents. Critics of experts can only be experts in turn. The legitimacy of speech is thus taken away from ordinary nonexpert citizens. Criticism is trapped in a logic of domination and in "quarrels between expertise and counter-expertise, in which counter-expertise is necessarily dominated, and more often than not loses out, since it can only try to reach expertise, i.e. to make itself admissible or simply audible, by submitting to the test formats set up by the latter" (ibid., p. 212). Thus, the managerial drift described by Boltanski blocks any consideration of solidarity. To eliminate this system of domination, a return through a counter-history is necessary.

2.2 From History to Counter-History

After showing how the history of management has been built—despite many missed opportunities—outside the question of solidarity, we focus here on the forgotten authors of solidarity. Although neglected, these authors are numerous, and they form a rich framework of thought for deconstructing the official version of management and considering a critical reflection, likely to favor the emergence of a school of organizational thought on solidarity. First, although the great authors of management have always refused to put solidarity at the heart of their analysis, they have not succeeded in eliminating it. It remains deep in the manager's unconscious as a repressed thought. From Taylor to Mayo, from Williamson to Yunus, the question of solidarity is eluded. How can the freedom that is their guiding principle be reconciled with the "rigidities" caused by the human factor and by nature? This confrontation gives rise to endless problems that cannot be avoided for long. Marx himself pointed out the problem when he showed that capitalism at the same time exhausts "the two sources from which all wealth springs: the earth and the worker" (quoted by Coutrot, 2018, p. 65). The evolution of managerial thought clearly shows the return of the repressed. Burnham sees management as a possible link between the market and communism.

In a more polite version, Williamson and Coase recognize the institutional dimension of the economy and make a link between the market and the organization. In doing so, they take management out of the pantheistic utopia of the market and try to move closer to the living world. However, their approach is formal. In the end, they only recognized the company as an institution to better convert it to the market. Transaction costs were thus used to outsource company activities and to develop subcontracting. This worldwide phenomenon will lead to the weakening of all national systems of collective solidarity. The emergence of the concept of social business is a belated and timid response to this weakening. Here again, the response is insufficient. Although the social business recognizes the presence of a living world and the need to take it into account in an economic context, it does not deduce from this recognition the idea of a transformation of management. Yunus' social business uses the classic management methods inherited from Taylor and Mayo to fight poverty. The social business thus appears to be more an extension of the market toward the social (and a commodification of the latter) than a genuine consideration of the social for the purposes of market reform. From this concept, it can be deduced that liberal ideas are now progressing by taking over the social (Chauvière, 2007). To escape the aporia of this thinking, we will therefore call on other authors.

2.2.1 Solidarity and Organization Are Compatible

From this perspective, Burnham's hypothesis of a managerial revolution is interesting because it lies at the crossroads of a market logic and a state logic. It is theoretically weak because it does not construct anything precise at this junction. It is therefore clear that the authors who can help us to define a management system based on solidarity are those who simply put forward the hypothesis of another economy, that is, an economy that is neither a market nor a planned economy controlled by the state. The idea is that "the market and the state alone are no longer able to provide employment, activity, dignity and self-esteem for all. Hence the need for the emergence, alongside them and in interaction with them, of a third pillar, at once economic, ethical and political, society itself in short, whose spearhead would be the associations" (Caillé & Laville, 1998, p. 6).

The first author who helps us to define the solidarity organization is Leroux. He tackles "the difficult problem of the social link by starting to draw a triangle of which the state, the market and the association, i.e. society itself, are the three vertices" (Viard & Vaillancourt, 2000, p. 26). Leroux sees in solidarity a "renewed metaphysics" (Leroux, 1860, p. 62) that makes it possible to overcome the dichotomous vision of society (given over to egoism on the one hand and to charity on the other). As Viard points out, Leroux has a binocular vision that attempts to link methodological individualism and holism (Viard & Vaillancourt, 2000). For Leroux, "absolute individualism consists in taking without giving, while absolute socialism consists in giving without receiving. This leads to the two complementary utopias, liberal and statist" (ibid., p. 24). At the dawn of modern society, Leroux sets out "the anthropological and political principles likely to inspire a regeneration of the present social bond on a basis of solidarity and association" (ibid., p. 8). Leroux himself is part of the rich filiation of other important authors: "To Saint Simon, the teacher, Leroux gives credit for having foreseen the new era by reversing the Rousseauist formula and for having proposed a new organization of humanity based on industry. The discovery of Saint Simon is association. Saint Simon's discovery is association. [...] In Fourier, Leroux salutes the one who pushed utopian speculation the furthest [...] As for Owen, he announced the reign of machines and the end of social islandism" (Abensour, 2013, p. 123).

Robespierre had the three terms "*liberté, égalité, fraternité*" inscribed on the tricolor flag of the French national guard as early as December 1790, but not until the French revolution of 1848 did this expression become the official motto of the French Republic (Viard & Vaillancourt, 2000). Examining these three principles of the French Republican motto, Leroux notes that the third term—fraternity—is often neglected. He notes that freedom is associated with the market and equality with the state. However, what about fraternity? Often mocked, including by Marx (ibid., p. 20), Leroux intends to rehabilitate this concept. He thus wanted to "reconcile liberty and equality by placing fraternity between them" (ibid.). In 1842, in a speech to politicians, he wrote: "I put fraternity at the center of the formula because it is the link between the freedom of each and the freedom of all" (quoted in ibid., p. 24).

According to Leroux, it is necessary that "man finally renounces a long error, which has made him seek an imaginary paradise outside the world, outside nature, and outside life" (Leroux, 2016). For Leroux, a return to the living world involves solitude. It allows us to put aside Christian charity, which is of the order of pity and commiseration, and the market, which is a matter of individualism and selfishness. In doing so, Leroux authorizes a renewal of thought. Indeed, unlike charity and egoism, solidarity belongs fully to the domain of the organizable. Leroux even states that "solidarity alone is organizable" (ibid.). For a manager, this idea is interesting and will inspire other authors.

2.2.2 Solidarity Is Based on a Quasi-contract

Bourgeois is probably the author who has most influenced solidarist thinking. His book *Solidarité* was widely read in France, and the author enjoyed a significant aura during his lifetime (Bourgeois, 1896). Moreover, his thinking remains highly topical in the way that it is based on the observation that human well-being has not increased to the same extent as the immense progress of science and technology. Despite the accumulated wealth, inequalities persist and grow. Bourgeois believes that there is a moral necessity to correct this state of affairs. However, the strength of his argument is that he leaves aside the moral question and focuses on what he regards as a universal law: solidarity. He states that "men are placed and held in bonds of mutual dependence" (ibid., p. 50). From then on, people must organize themselves to recognize these bonds of solidarity that link them in time and space.

This organization has an accounting aspect. Bourgeois speaks of debt. Man, when he is born and grows up, is in debt to his contemporaries. Thus, "from the very day of his birth, he is obliged. Man is born a debtor to human association. By entering into association, he takes his share of an accumulated heritage" (ibid., p. 116). From then on, "it is towards all those who will come after us that we have received from our ancestors the responsibility of discharging the debt we have received" (ibid., p. 124). Solidarity is transgenerational. For Bourgeois, "it is a legacy from the whole past to the whole future" (ibid.). To recognize the debt of each individual to other generations is to recognize the collective nature of our social organization. Man cannot "withdraw materially or morally from human association. Man in isolation does not exist" (ibid., p. 137).

The strength of Bourgeois' proposal is that it can be operationalized. The debt of which he speaks translates not into a questioning of current rights but into their moderation according to a universal principle. Thus, for him, "to recognize a debt is not to abandon a right, it is to recognize the true limit of that right" (ibid., p. 103). To this end, he coined the concept of "quasi-contract." This quasi-contract binds all men without their being aware of it. The intellectual breakthrough proposed by Bourgeois lies precisely in the awareness and operationalization of this quasi-contract. Its purpose is to translate into the collective organization "the equitable evaluation of the services exchanged, that is to say, the equitable distribution of profits and expenses, of social assets and liabilities, which is the legitimate object of social law" (ibid., p. 138). As the debt is intergenerational, there is "for each living man a debt to the following generations because of the services rendered by the past generations" (ibid.).

By proposing a quasi-contract between men, Bourgeois uses a management concept to link economic and noneconomic criteria. Thus, Bourgeois recognizes that "man does not only have economic interests, he has physiological, psychological and moral interests" (ibid., p. 144). By means of his proposal for an acknowledgment of debt, he intends that "the definition of the rights and duties of men can no longer be sought outside the relationships that bind them jointly to each other in space and time" (ibid., p. 80). The notion of quasi-contract would therefore be nothing more than the gift itself (Chanial, 2010), that is, the need to have a link (Caillé, 1994). The quasi-contract can be seen as another conception of the social contract (Laville & Roustang, 1996).

2.2.3 Solidarity and Self-interest Rightly Understood

Although Tocqueville is a liberal who excludes all economic equality from the equalization of conditions (Menger, 2002), he does not subscribe to the notion of the invisible hand attributed to Smith. In his view, the addition of egoisms cannot be the source of the wealth of nations. This view is nonsensical. However, recognizing the problem raised by Smith, he proposed the concept of enlightened self-interest as a way of resolving the tensions between individuals and the collective. This concept offers each citizen of a democracy the prospect of working for the happiness of all while defending his or her own individual advantage. Tocqueville thus puts forward a theory of interest in democracies, where the addition of particular interests makes it possible to identify more or less the skeleton of the general interest. He seeks to understand how the democratic balance can guarantee the necessary coincidence between the interests of those in power and those of the people. To this end, Tocqueville aims to identify what makes people interested in public affairs. He observes associative life and sees it as a means of fostering civic engagement (Chanial, 2010; Cefaï & Chanial, 2000). Tocqueville was the first author to highlight associations as the main vehicles of solidarity in the social and economic sphere. In this respect, he is an innovative author. He believes that association should be the object of all attention and states that in democratic countries, the science of association is the mother science; the progress of all others depends on the progress of this one (Tocqueville, 2002).

This proposition places the question of solidarity at the heart of his analysis. While his proposal is relevant, Tocqueville's voice unfortunately carries little weight when compared to Smith's. Indeed, he is denied any competence as an economist, which discredits and invalidates his response to Smith. By pointing out the importance of individual participation, Tocqueville nevertheless emphasizes a crucial point: the danger inherent in democracies when the absence or lack of civic and associative involvement is the breeding ground for dictatorships. Although he is concerned with economic development, he is particularly clear-sighted about the civilizational dimension of solidarity. Thus, if we want men to remain civilized or to become civilized, the art of association must develop and be perfected among them in the same ratio as equality of conditions increases (ibid.). This question is more topical than ever.

2.2.4 Solidarity at the Heart of Organizational Thinking

Tönnies helps us to think about the nature of the bond of solidarity by distinguishing between the lasting personal bonds that arise in the primary spaces of sociality (family, neighborhood, friends, etc.) and the more ephemeral impermanent bonds that are formed in the wider space of modern society. For Tönnies, the former are nourished by the affective and spatial proximity of individuals and determine a community of place, of blood, and of spirit (Tönnies, 2021). Society, on the other hand, is a place of unbridled individualism, of generalized competition between men, the reign of personal interest. The man in society arbitrarily chooses his relationships according to the financial interest he can expect from them. The dissolution of community ties, which were the basis for strong forms of mutual aid in favor of new forms of socialization, impoverishes social ties. Tönnies criticizes Smith, for whom society is the state in which "every man is a merchant." This economic view of society is precisely what threatens authentic and disinterested social bonds, according to Tönnies.

Durkheim tries to overcome Tönnies' vision, which, according to him, shows nostalgia for a bygone golden age. Specifically, Tönnies' ideal was "the restoration of community—not however by returning to the pre-industrial stage of society, but by advancing to a higher form of community that would follow upon our present civilisation. He thought of it as a kind of cooperative phase of civilisation, that would retain the advantages of technological progress and individual freedom, while restoring the wholeness of life. His position resembled, to some extent, that of Robert Owen or, among modern thinkers, that of Lewis Mumford" (Polanyi, 1977, p. 49). Durkheim criticized this vision, which he considered to be partisan: "It can be seen that, in sum, the society that Tönnies is currently depicting is the capitalist society of the socialists; and indeed, the author often borrows from Marx and Lassalle the dark colours in which he represents it to us" (Durkheim, 1975). For Durkheim, modern societies are just as natural as less extensive traditional societies. He therefore refused to privilege one over the other.

Where Smith sees a natural law that leads men to divide labor as production increases, Durkheim questions a paradox: how can a society adapt to the development of individualism within it without calling into question the principles on which it is based? Durkheim solves the apparent contradiction by analyzing the transformation of solidarity. To this end, he distinguishes two types of solidarity in his demonstration. The first, which he describes as mechanical solidarity, functions by similarity. It refers to traditional societies where individuals are not very different from each other in terms of activity and where there is a great amount of homogeneity between the members who make up a society. The second, described as organic solidarity, characterizes modern societies. It gives everyone a precise social position and a differentiation in the tasks to be performed. This solidarity offers less social control because it empowers its members.

Durkheim shows that traditional societies have a strong collective consciousness. This fact results in maintaining group cohesion through the absorption and homogenization of individuals. In modern societies, in contrast, collective consciousness weakens. It is this very weakening that, for Durkheim, encourages the development of the division of labor. However, if society resists this weakening of collective consciousness, it does so because the division of labor unites as well as opposes (Durkheim, 2014). It is not univocal and converges the activities it differentiates; it brings together what it separates. Durkheim then adds a decisive argument. Since competition cannot have determined this rapprochement, it must have preexisted. The individuals between whom the struggle is engaged must already be in solidarity and feel it, that is, belong to the same society. Durkheim thus shows that the division of labor can only occur within a preexisting society, meaning that there must first be moral ties between them. The author thus invites us to consider that society is a prerequisite for the division of labor, not the other way around. The demonstration is elegant. Collective life is not born of individual life, but it is, on the contrary, the latter that is born of the former. Only on this condition can we explain how the personal individuality of social units could be formed and grow without disintegrating society. This view is in line with the Maussian interpretation of Durkheim (Cefaï & Chanial, 2000).

However, Durkheim's demonstration stumbles on one point. It presupposes that the division of labor concerns increasing not only the output of the divided functions but also the solidarities between these functions. For Durkheim, all productive action presupposes both a differentiation of tasks through the division of labor and an integration into a human whole to achieve collective ends (Laville, 2017). The main result of the division of labor is therefore not in the "sphere of economic interests but in the establishment of a sui generis social and moral order. Individuals are not independent, they have to work together. The division of labor, far from dividing men, reinforces their complementarity to cooperate" (Paugam in Durkheim, 2016, p. 15). For this statement to hold, however, a condition is necessary. Durkheim himself recognizes this. The division of labor presupposes that "the worker, far from remaining bent on his task, does not lose sight of his collaborators, acts on them and receives their action. He is not, therefore, a machine which repeats movements whose direction he does not see, but he knows that they tend somewhere, towards a goal which he perceives more or less distinctly" (ibid., p. 365).

This issue is where the problem lies. While Durkheim's scheme is particularly relevant, it comes up against somewhat different realities on the ground. In its prosaic version, the division of labor can contribute to drying up the integrating force of solidarity. Durkheim is not fooled. He devotes the last part of his book to what he calls "abnormal forms." He admits that the "repetition of the same movements with monotonous regularity has the effect of turning the worker into an inert machine"

(Paugam in ibid., p. 25). He recognizes that workers can harbor great bitterness at being forced into enduring inferiority. The point of Durkheim's demonstration is to know whether these forms, which he designates as abnormal, are exceptional. The degree of exceptionality depends on social law and the collective protections that the social state can provide. The question of solidarity in the context of the division of labor thus incidentally leads not only to the regulatory relationship between the market and the state but also to the possibility of a different economy.

2.2.5 Solidarity and Rationality

Weber, like Durkheim, uses Tönnies' categories to distinguish between two forms that are essential for sociological analysis: communalization, which he considers to be guided by the subjective feeling of the participants of belonging to the same community, and sociation, which he defines as a social relationship based on a rationally motivated compromise of interests. Communalization can be expressed in a family community, a group of friends, and a nation. Sociation can take the form of a free market exchange agreement, the pursuit of material interests, and a conviction-based association organized to serve a cause. However, behind this first classification proposal, Weber immediately points out that the great majority of social relations have partly the character of a communalization, partly that of a sociation. Thus, communalization is not immune to the violence that might be expressed within it, and the coldest sociation imaginable is never completely free of sentimental values.

Weber sees bureaucracy as a rational and efficient system that prevents the excesses of those in charge by placing them within a binding regulatory framework. He thus speaks of legal-rational domination to refer to a system that regulates the potentially liberticidal practices of political power. The formal rules supported by the bureaucracy are in fact a means of recourse against arbitrariness, which at the same time conditions the predictability of administrative behavior (Crozier, 1964). Bureaucracy therefore has undeniable advantages. It can be understood as the unseen shadow of mass democracy (Weber, 2019).

At the same time, however, Weber recognizes that bureaucracy can have an oppressive dimension, resulting in what he calls a "steel cage," which closes in on individuals as a trap and an oppressive factor (Weber, 2002). Bureaucracy is incidentally based on the specialized knowledge whose absolute need is determined by modern technology and the economy of goods production (Weber, 2019). As such, bureaucracy is indeed at the heart of the growth of capitalism and cannot be reduced to the figure of the civil servant. While Weber posits that the capitalist entrepreneur is the only instance really immune (at least relatively) to the inevitability of rational bureaucratic domination of knowledge (ibid), he also emphasizes, as Colliot-Thélène points out, that "modern forms of domination share with the capitalist economic system the character of impersonality [...]. The formula without consideration of the person is the watchword of the market, and it is also the watchword of pure bureaucratic domination" (Colliot-Thélène, 2011; p. 18). In fact, commercial and bureaucratic logics share the same desire to implement a centralized management scheme based on a standardized approach. This goal manifests the vector of a system of domination and a certain number of pathologies (Scott, 1998). Far from opposing the market, bureaucracy would therefore be at the heart of its extension logic (Graeber, 2015a, b), suggesting that contrary to the common ideas of liberal ideology, market enterprises are not immune to bureaucracy. It can therefore be assumed that there are several forms of bureaucracy.

To distinguish between these different forms (i.e., those that protect and those that oppress), Weber gives us some keys. He distinguishes between two types of rationality: the first, which he describes as formally rational (Zweckrationalität), is expressed in monetary values through numerical or accounting reasoning (Weber, 2019); the second, which he describes as substantive rationality (Wertrationalität), is not confined to the formal aspect but takes into account other requirements: ethical, political, utilitarian, hedonistic, class-based, or egalitarian. This second rationale is expressed in terms of value and is substantively oriented in terms of purpose. Because of the diversity of motives on which it can be based, material rationality is by nature plurivocal (Colliot-Thélène, 2011).

Notably, Weber's work is a "comprehensive sociology, since the object of his study is human action and it has meaning" (Mazuir, 2004, p. 122).

While his approach is in line with his time, it is not truly congruent with the modern concept of organization developed by the sociology of organizations (Mayntz, 1965). For Weber, the grouping of domination itself is considered in the context of a larger whole, namely that of the political and social order of a given society (Ibid). Weber's focus is not so much on organizational efficiency as on the organizational or processual characteristics that determine organizational activity. This view represents an interesting perspective on the evolution of thinking. As Mayntz points out, it is necessary to develop an analysis oriented in such a way that it necessarily combines reflection at the organizational level with reflection at the level of society as a whole. Moreover, Weber's thinking does not focus only on the logics of domination. Thus, for Weber, groups can also strive to reduce the powers of domination associated with executive functions (Weber, 2019). Direct democracy without domination is possible in these groupings as long as the parties do not set themselves up as permanent structures, do not fight each other, and do not seek to appropriate the functions. Otherwise, the party leader who fights and triumphs—no matter what the means—becomes, with his administrative leadership, an instrument of domination, despite the maintenance of all the forms of the previous administration (ibid). Here, we see that Weber prefigures the iron law of the oligarchy of Michels, one of his students (Michels, 2016).

Weber describes as "notables" people who possess two characteristics: they are in an economic situation that allows them to engage in the action of the association without monetary compensation in the form of a salary; they enjoy a social esteem that is conducive to gaining the trust of the other members. Weber thus points out that notables can live for politics without having to live from it and that their situation presupposes a social esteem which is not only a source of trust, but also a source of confidence (Weber, 2019). For these reasons, Weber believes that every direct democracy tends to become an administration of notables—from the ideal point of view, because it is considered especially qualified by experience and objectivity, and from the material point of view, because it is inexpensive or, in some cases, entirely free (ibid).

Finally, while Weber points out that smaller groups are better able to avoid the risks of internal domination, he believes that larger groups can also achieve this, provided they take a few precautions, which he lists (ibid, page 433):

(a) brief periods of office, if possible only in between consecutive assemblies;
(b) standing right of recall;
(c) the principle of appointment to posts by turn or by lot, so that each "has their turn"; hence, avoidance of power accumulating with those possessing specialist or secretarial knowledge;
(d) a strict imperative mandate for the conduct of office (substantive, not general, competence), as determined by the assembly;
(e) strict accountability to the members' assembly;
(f) the obligation to bring to the assembly (or to a committee) any special or unforeseen question;
(g) a number of associated posts assigned to special issues, hence
(h) the part-time character of the appointment.

In speaking of groups that seek to reduce the powers of domination, Weber refers to a field of knowledge that will develop in France under the name of social economy.

2.2.6 The Emergence of Social Economy

The social economy has its theorists. In asserting the existence of several approaches to the economy, Walras stands out among economists. He distinguishes between pure economics, which is the science of "social wealth considered in itself," applied economics, and moral economics (Dockès, 2005, p. 8). Although these three theoretical approaches refer to different truths, all three, according to him, have the character of science. This observation leads him to approach human actors in two dimensions: *homo economicus* and *homo ethicus* (Walras, 1992, p. 406). As such, justice is a criterion "as scientific as the criterion of efficiency for production or pure economic truth for the theory of prices" (Lallement, 2012, p. 63). Walras thus delivers what he sees as "the rational society that will be realised and which presents itself as a conciliation of the just and the useful" (Dockès, 2005, p. 18). Walras emphasizes the dynamics of productive forces. He is idealistic when he notes that "steam and machines have done away with slavery and serfdom" and that "modern industry will do away with injustice" (ibid., p. 19). Nevertheless, the Walrasian man is characterized by "three major psychological faculties: sensibility, intelligence and will" (Lacan, 2006, p. 72).

This characterization leads him to consider the question of poverty in a radical way compared with other economists. According to him, if there are poor people, it is because of an "initial unjust distribution of social wealth among individuals, which contradicts the equality of conditions" (Lallement, 2012, p. 58). It is therefore necessary to intervene in this initial distribution and propose that land should not be subject to private appropriation because, according to him, it belongs to humanity and therefore cannot be subject to private appropriation (Dockès, 2005). Furthermore, Walras was convinced of the value of mutual insurance companies. He noted that without seeking any profit, they provide their members with risk cover according to a logic of reciprocity and in a free and optional framework (Lallement, 2012, p. 59). Charles Gide was in the intellectual neighborhood of Walras. Like Walras, he rejects competition as a sufficient principle for thinking about the organization of economic life (Gide, 2010), and, like Walras, he believes that the solution to the social problem "consists in reconciling justice with freedom" (Pénin, 2006, p. 78). He emphasizes solidarity and cooperation as fundamental principles of the economic approach (ibid., p. 76). For Gide, solidarity and cooperation are embodied in the professional association, the mutualist association, and the consumer cooperative (of which he is a specialist). Gide highlights "the institutions of social economy that he wished to see developed" (ibid., p. 80). In this vision, he echoes the work of Bourgeois and aims to go beyond natural solidarity.

2.2.7 The Organizational Innovation of the Social Economy

If the work of Walras and Gide is moving the lines in the field of ideas, it is indeed in the field of action that innovations arise and give a practical translation of the benefits of a moral economy guided by a sense of justice. The basic components of the social economy are cooperatives, mutuals, and associations with a management vocation (Vienney, 1994). As Musso points out, the problematization of solidarity "emerges with the industrial revolution, which on the one hand assigns everyone his or her place in the factory through the division of labor, and on the other hand engenders pauperism and exclusion" (Musso, 2015: 94–95). Although the sources of inspiration for mutuality can be traced back to the companionships and guilds of the Ancien Régime, its rise is contemporary, starting in the nineteenth century. Mutuality managed to emerge in a very unfavorable legal context inherited from the French Revolution and Napoleon's legal code (Laborde, 2015, p. 111). Even though "the term solidarity did not enter the common vocabulary of the mutualist world until the end of the 19th century" (Toucas-Truyen, 2014, p. 98), it was the mutuals that translated it into reality through multiple experiments. These took different forms, "from the simple neutral insurance technique to the collective demonstration of compassion at member-policyholders' funerals" (ibid.). Beyond the concrete mechanisms of economic solidarity, the members "weave bonds of brotherhood among themselves according to the term used in mutualist writings" (ibid.). While mutuals focus on redistributive solidarity (ibid.), the cooperative form intends to give the same management power to the employee and the contributor of capital.

Although management techniques are at the heart of the birth of socioeconomic organizations, they have been little studied in this respect in the field of management sciences. However, without the implementation of innovative organizational methods, the first cooperative and mutual initiatives would not have been able to cope with the very difficult context in which they emerged. The pioneering experience of Rochdale in the early nineteenth century illustrates this requirement. From the outset, the experiment established the principle of the dual quality of actors, meaning that the beneficiaries are also members. The ambition is great, and the management complexity is high. The success of the first workers' collective experiments was therefore linked to the unfailing commitment of the actors involved. The workers who initiated them were indeed novices in terms of management skills. In the first place, they had to be inventive. Subsequently, the sustainability and spread of these experiments were the results of a long process of improving practices (ibid.). The great diversity of cooperative forms (agricultural, financial, production, consumption, etc.) that resulted from this process testifies to the relevance and strength of the organizational proposal. This diversity was also an invitation to compare. Thus, in 1893, Lassale established a hierarchy between production cooperatives and consumer cooperatives. For him, "the exploitation of which the workers are victims affects them as producers and not as consumers. It is therefore under the production regime that we must act if we really want to improve their lot." Behind this debate between the different forms of cooperation lies another: the opposition between neutral and socialist cooperatives (Vandervelde, 1913). The former tended to see the cooperative as a business, the latter as "an instrument of struggle, as a means of emancipation" (ibid., p. 79). Thus, the cooperative experience gives "the intelligent worker the means to create capital and to learn the handling of commercial affairs, and allows him to free himself from the bosses" (Audier, 2010, p. 45). This opposition reflects the pluralist origin of the social economy, which combines liberal influence, the values of social Christianity, and socialist affiliation (Parodi, 2008). It also reflects the initial contradictions at work in the definition and nature of the cooperative project.

2.2.8 The Managerial Professionalization of Cooperatives

Cooperatives are of course different from associations, which do not have shareholders. Importantly, however, management is cited as a strong criterion for membership in the social economy. Thus, associations that belong to the social economy are those that are "managerial," which means that their management needs are proven by the presence of employees (such as cooperatives). At the same time, associations have the power to attract cooperatives, and it is possible to envisage the cooperative as "the combination of an association and an enterprise" (Laville, 2010, p. 293). This capability opens up a range of possible forms (Draperi,

1998) where collective entrepreneurship plays a major role (Demoustier et al., 2003). However, one may wonder about the nature and objective of this collective management: should it serve the weakest by working to transform the economic field (as the emancipatory ambition of cooperatives invites)? Should it, on the contrary, focus on the sustainability of jobs and the organization through better integration into the market economy? The answer is not obvious because it puts the actors in Desroche's (1976) quadrilateral in tension: members, directors, managers, and employees. Older organizations that "identify with the social economy through the combination of their cooperative, mutualist or associative status and their management function [...] are experiencing contradictions that distance some of them from forms of democracy and solidarity" (Demoustier et al., 2003, p. 56). From the 1970s onward, capitalist intensity increased.

At the same time, the generalization of co-optation practices guaranteed that the leaders of cooperatives had virtually no counterpower. Economic integration into the market—a guarantee for these cooperatives of their ability to resist competition—is at the same time leading to a drift, with the adoption of standards and management practices from the commercial world. This development is all the more pronounced, as national and European legislation favors free competition and thus the progressive alignment of cooperative rules with those of companies. Consequently, the statutory difference between cooperatives and enterprises tends to diminish, as does the feeling of belonging to the social economy. This perspective leads cooperatives to favor the enterprise logic over the associative logic. In the financial and insurance field, large cooperatives are opening up to noncooperative investors, while others are creating commercial subsidiaries. The import of management tools and methods from commercial enterprises is thus part of a process of acculturation. The employees of these organizations no longer perceive the effects of the difference in status in their daily work. They do not or no longer recognize themselves as actors in the social and solidarity economy (Utting, 2015; Calvo & Morales, 2017).

2.2.9 Management and Recognition

The question of recognition is a question of primary importance. One author has particularly understood the issues at stake: Honneth. At the heart of his social analysis is the need for people to benefit from forms of recognition (Honneth & Joel, 1998). He postulates that the self is formed in the approval of others. Honneth distinguishes three forms of recognition: personal concern, which is linked to affect and love; cognitive consideration, which opens up moral responsibility and presupposes legal relations; and social esteem, which is manifested in a community of values. The social space is conflictual, and the concept of recognition is therefore inseparable from a struggle in which each person tries to secure access to esteem. As there are three forms of recognition, this struggle "leads from love to right and from right to solidarity" (Courtel, 2010: 11). For Honneth, the term solidarity primarily refers to a kind of interactional relationship in which subjects are interested in the personal itinerary of their fellow human beings, because they have established symmetrical bonds of esteem between them (Honneth & Joel, 1998). Recognition is at stake in the intersubjective relationship. Solidarity is present as soon as there is an ethical community that allows for the sharing of mutual esteem outside of love and law. According to him, solidarity is possible only if relations of mutual esteem develop between individuals and if this initial sympathy is translated into acts that extend this feeling. Solicitude can therefore be interpreted as a form of recognition; it is a performative act of confirmation by others of the moral qualities that individuals lend to each other. Hence, attention to solidarity is an attention to identities and to the wounds that can result from a deficit (or denial) of recognition. In terms of management, Honneth's analysis leads to placing self-esteem at the heart of conflict prevention. It refers to the preservation of identities and ancestral knowledge.

2.2.10 Managing the Good Life and Anti-colonial Thinking

A political revival has been expressed in Andean countries with the advent of constitutions conferring rights to nature and incorporating the notions of *buen vivir* in Ecuador (Acosta, 2014) and *bien vivir* in Bolivia (Martins, 2014). These notions are "Spanish translations of *sumak kawsay* or *suma qamaña*" (Cadalen, 2018: 79). The Bolivian Indians consider the land to be a *Pachamama*, "*madre tierra* or mother earth, the only legal basis for the collective ideal of *buen vivir*" (Martins, 2014, p. 77). The utopia of *Pachamama* moves away from a utilitarian vision rooted in private appropriation and selfish use to an anti-utilitarian vision of the good life, as it "values collective well-being" (ibid., p. 79). The good life invites us to understand "the limits of a model of domination based on private logic" and to oppose "the appropriation of material wealth by a small group at the expense of the majority" (ibid: 80). *Pachamama's* political contribution lies "in the originality of a postcolonial contestation led by an indigenous social movement that has been able to reverse coloniality to reintroduce the power of ethnic tradition into Western cosmology" (ibid.). The environmental approach to the good life is part of Amerindian practices. It is observed that the relationship between man and nature in the Amazon "is always based on the notion of gift, which reveals an important cultural ecology" (Viveiros de Castro, cited by Martins, 2014). Amerindians "insist on ritualising each tree felling and [...] feel obliged, by the force of the counter-gift, to plant another tree to restore the lost balance" (Martins, 2014, p. 80).

The Bolivian *Pasha Mamists* consider that "vital resources existed long before the arrival of colonisers, private companies, white ethnic politicians, long before man himself, and that they still constitute the basis of their material and spiritual survival" (ibid., p. 82). This image is a metaphor or symbol that gives meaning to collective movements and is "the watchword against the private appropriation of the collective conditions of community life" (ibid., p. 83). Interestingly, the good life inspires a new hierarchy by positing that the rights to life "are fundamental and universal because they are shared by every living being, and that capitalist rights to growth and accumulation are private rights that are not universal, they are minor rights" (ibid., p. 84). In effect, the market economy is re-embedded in the social environment. In this regard, the good life is a critique of the idea of unlimited economic growth (ibid; Gadrey, 2010). The idea of the *buen vivir* is "an anti-capitalist and communitarian contestation that seeks to value wealth outside the logic of accumulation, individualism and ethnocentrism" (Farah & Gil, 2012, p. 100).

2.2.11 Management and Popular Economy

In the North, organizational forms such as cooperatives, mutualist organizations, and associations have been modes of resistance to capitalism and its spearhead, private enterprise. In the South, especially Latin America, the relationship between solidarity and organizations has been different. Resistance comes from the social strata most excluded from the development process. It has been expressed through demonstrations linked to the organizational modes of traditional communities. In addition to the contribution of ancestral peoples of indigenous origin, there was resistance from communities of former slaves and their descendants. On the outskirts of the large cities where these populations have been relegated, families follow multiple strategies to survive. To analyze the management of solidarity within these communities, it is first necessary to understand how cooperation networks are formed and how individual life and career paths are constructed.

The relationship between solidarity and organization in the countries of the South can be illuminated using the notion of a popular economy. This notion allows the study of social life to be linked to the organization of work and to identify a heterogeneous reality characterized by the emergence and multiplication of numerous small productive and commercial activities in the poor and marginal sectors of large Latin American cities

(Razeto, 1991). This reality may take the form of small trades, autonomous professions, microenterprises, or associations. The popular economy draws its strength from the constitution of a set of reciprocal relations woven into the exercise of these multiple activities. This set of relationships extends the ordinary solidarity of everyday life, be it family or friendship. The work carried out within the framework of the popular economy is often carried out within the family (Kraychette et al., 2000). Although the popular economy echoes the information economy in responding to the problem of unemployment through survival strategies in urban areas (Lautier, 1994), it differs from it in that it is strongly anchored in a social base and in traditional knowledge. The popular economy thus proposes a specific articulation between needs and skills available at the local level (França Filho, 2002). In Brazil, this articulation is constructed in the form of *mutirão*, that is, a system of self-organization of a popular and community-based project, consisting of mobilizing and involving all the members of a community in executing a project (ibid.).

Although popular economic activities play an important role in the daily lives of excluded populations, they have little capacity to translate into institutional change. Therefore, the idea of building a popular and solidarity economy (PSE) appears to be a virtuous organizational strategy to emancipate the working classes (França Filho, 2006). The objective of the PSE is to move from a logic of survival to a logic of social transformation likely to improve the daily lives of excluded people (Coraggio, 2004). In this way, the PSE draws on the basic foundations of the popular economy to invent new forms of socioeconomic self-organization and new frameworks for public policy (França Filho, 2006).

A second perspective on solidarity is based on the analysis of life histories that have led to the breakdown of the walls of inequality. The study of the upward social mobility of the most disadvantaged people allows us to understand the nature of solidarity networks. These networks are complex and combine relationships between close relatives (extended family, friends, acquaintances) and relationships built within solidarity organizations. Although these organizations have always played a fundamental role in the history of solidarity with the most disadvantaged, they are little known in the field of management sciences. Two types of Brazilian organizations rooted in the tradition of the black Brazilian people are important to study: the *terreiros* and the *irmandades*. The *terreiros* are organizations run by traditional Candomblé religious communities (of African origin). These organizations have played a strong role in the working class. They appeared between the end of the nineteenth and the beginning of the twentieth century through the initiative of former slaves who sought to welcome people who had suffered discrimination.

As a place of solidarity, these organizations have promoted social support and the reintegration of excluded people. In the city of Salvador, a *terreiro* called *Tumba Junssara* is currently undergoing a process of institutional recognition to be included in the city's cultural heritage. This *terreiro* is defined as a *milonga*. This word, originating from the language of the *Banto* people, means mixing. The organization sees itself as the result of a mixture of all the cultural elements of the Brazilian nation. The *terreiro* recognizes the *Candomblé* tradition from Angola, the *Banto* tradition, and the indigenous cultures of *Iorubá, Jêje,* and *Ijexá*, among others. The *terreiros* have contributed to recreating strong forms of solidarity for enslaved populations, separated from their families, clans, or tribes.

There are two types of *irmandades*: *irmandades negras laicas* and *irmandades negras religiosas*. The former are secular societies for the management of social protection for the disabled (*sociedades protetoras dos desvalidos*), which appeared at the time of the abolition of slavery in 1888 in several regions of Brazil (Bahia, Minas Gerais, Rio de Janeiro, in particular). At the beginning, organizations took charge of purchasing *auforrias*, which were titles granting former slaves citizenship rights. Then, their mission rapidly evolved toward training, technical education, and professional integration. In the early years of the twentieth century, these organizations were major players in the professionalization of young people from working classes, training them in construction trades (masons, carpenters, blacksmiths, etc.). At a time when public schools were practically inaccessible to the descendants of slaves, the *irmandades negras laicas* played a leading role in improving the living conditions of black people in Brazil. *Irmandades negras religiosas* bring together Catholic populations of African origin. In Bahia, these organizations have offered places of welcome to the most discriminated people, such as single mothers.

2.2.12 From Practice to Ideals: Solidarity in Brazilian Critical Thinking

Solidarity is a strong element among some Brazilian intellectuals. Three names are worth mentioning: the educator and philosopher Paulo Freire, the geographer Milton Santos, and the sociologist Alberto Guerreiro Ramos. Freire was born on September 19, 1921, in the city of Recife. His family was middle class, but he experienced poverty during the 1929 crisis. Freire's work falls within the field of educational theory. His work consisted of developing teaching methods for the poorest. In particular, he developed innovative literacy methods. During the military dictatorship in Brazil, he was persecuted, accused of subversion, and exiled. This series of events led him to work in Chile for five years at the Chilean Institute for Agrarian Reform. It was during this period that he wrote his main work *Pedagogy of the Oppressed* (1968). From 1969, Freire taught at Harvard University in the United States, and over the next decade became a consultant to the World Council of Churches (WCC) in Geneva. He provided educational assistance to many poor African countries at the beginning of their independence. After spending sixteen years in exile, he returned to Brazil in 1980 and wrote two of his fundamental books: *Pedagogy of Hope* (1992) and *In the Shadow of the Mango Tree* (1995). Freire focuses on dialogicity and its central role in the educational process. For Freire, learning takes place in a process in which the actors must alternate the postures of educator and educated. Education is about learning from the life experience of the other. The theme of solidarity underlies all his work. It becomes explicit in one of his last works, *Pedagogy of Solidarity* (Freire et al., 2009). In this work, he argues for libertarian education and reaffirms the need for solidarity as the condition for a more democratic world.

Santos was born on May 3, 1926, in the town of Brotas de Macaúba in the state of Bahia. He obtained his doctorate in geography at the University of Strasbourg. At the end of the 1950s, he returned to Brazil and created the Regional Studies Laboratory. With the military coup, he returned to France, where he became a university professor. In 1977, Santos moved back to Brazil and taught human geography at the Federal

University of Rio de Janeiro (UFRJ). In 1994, he was awarded the Vautrin-Lud International Prize for Geography. Santos developed a critical approach to urban areas in which he denounces the living conditions on the outskirts of cities and advocates solidarity as a central element. According to him, solidarity makes it possible to enact the process of democratic citizenship in the city and to fight against what he calls mutilated citizenship (Santos, 1993).

Finally, Guerreiro Ramos was a black Brazilian sociologist and politician. He was born on September 13, 1915, in Santo Amaro da Purificação, Bahia State. He is considered a major figure in Brazilian social sciences. In addition to his intellectual career (a dozen books and numerous articles published in several languages), he had other experiences: he was a federal deputy for Rio de Janeiro and a member of the Brazilian delegation to the United Nations. He completed his academic career as a professor at the University of California. He died in Los Angeles in 1982. In recent studies, Guerreiro Ramos was described as a "peripheral intellectual" (Marcelo Maia, 2015). There are three reasons for this description: first, Guerreiro Ramos engaged as a Brazilian author in a critical dialogue with European and North American sociological and philosophical theories; second, his writing style is distinguished by a refusal to bend to the linguistic canons of his time; and third, his work is driven by a strong quest for intellectual autonomy. According to Lynch (2015), Guerreiro Ramos develops a postcolonial theory in which he asserts a critical posture in the field of social sciences. For Guerreiro Ramos, solidarity is implicit. This view can be deduced from the importance he attaches in his work to the notion of a "universal human community" (Flores, 2015), which he sees as a central notion for a human rights culture in Brazil. According to Flores, the concept of a universal human community is at the heart of Guerreiro Ramos' organizational thinking, and management is seen as a lever for substantive democracy and citizen governance. Guerreiro Ramos' emphasis on substantive rationality is consistent with his desire to refound organizational theory and his concern to give a new meaning to solidarity in organizational action.

2.3 Remaking the History of Management from a Solidarity Perspective

As we have seen in this chapter, the history of management includes a number of missed opportunities. Management seems to have failed to respond to demands for social transformation. Important political actors who wanted to implement solidarity-based economic policies looked to management methods for operational solutions without finding what they were looking for, as was the case with Roosevelt in the United States in the moment of the unproductive rapprochement between Pinchot and Taylor, and in France, when Herriot prefaced Casson's book on the science of business. On this occasion, Herriot forwarded the idea that "business must be directed by a true science whose laws must be discovered little by little" (Nikitin, 2003, p. 71). What, however, is this science? What principles guide it? How can solidarity provide the basis for a better understanding of collective action?

The fame encasing Taylor's work has ultimately overshadowed authors who do not share this vision. Taylor's triumphant America invented management and allowed itself not to take on board the (too) long European history or ancestral cultures. Without any qualms, it neglected the reflections and experiments of the organizations of the social economy. The popularity of Taylor's scientific management marginalizes old world managers. To achieve its aims, the new management dressed up in the clothes of scientificity. It is indeed "scientific" management that silences the solidarist authors. This attack is twofold and comes from both market thinkers and Marxist authors. Engels also claims a conceptual difference between scientific socialism and utopian socialism (Engels, 2015). It is thus under the guise of scientificity that liberal and Marxist authors seek to disqualify the solidarist current. The solidarity school differs "from the liberal school in that it repudiates the principle of competition and the struggle for life in favor of that of cooperation and union between opposing interests" and separates itself from the revolutionary school "in that it does not believe in the effectiveness of revolution and expropriation to transform man" (Audier, 2010, p. 68). In the absence of a vision of solidarity, formal management was put in the service of the moralization of the economy in Thompson's sense to "fill the ethical vacuum of capitalism from the moment it dissociated itself from the Protestant ethic that founded its legitimacy" (Gaulejac, 2005, p. 40). Consequently, organizational analysis developed from a functionalist perspective. Since functionalism is a theory "which tends to relate social phenomena to the functions they perform" (ibid., p. 73), political economy has been transformed into "a managerial economy in which business and financial considerations take precedence over human and social considerations" (ibid., p. 25).

It now seems necessary to develop the links between history and management from a critical perspective (Cailluet et al., 2013). The aim is for management to look at important and forgotten authors of its history to reopen perspectives of thought that are indispensable to the reflection on the sustainability of our economic systems. By taking an interest in the story of a counter-history of management, we have highlighted authors who seem useful for rethinking management. Leroux thus helps us to resituate solidarity in relation to the economic freedom of the market and the equality defended by the republican state in relation to its citizens. With the idea of a quasi-contract, Bourgeois places the solidarity equation in an organizational and transgenerational perspective. Tocqueville proposes the resolution of tensions between individuals and the collective through democracy within organizations guided by the principle of self-interest. Tönnies and Durkheim rethink the division of labor through a double characterization of solidarity. Weber envisages several forms of rationality. Walras and Gide outline the principles of an economy that is open to solidarity through its concern with the notion of justice. Honneth shows that solidarity is built on recognition. Freire invites us to reflect on the question of education from the perspective of emancipation. The Pachamamists refer us to ancestral organizational knowledge, which in turn opens the way to the good life. Finally, Guerreiro Ramos puts forward the concept of a universal human community to think about solidarity in the field of organizational thought outside of colonial domination.

Notwithstanding the perspectives opened up by these authors, there are unresolved tensions. The absence of a recognized theoretical framework for solidarity management has undoubtedly allowed a drift in organizations claiming to be part of the social and solidarity economy. Indeed, the adoption of a commercial management style and its usual instruments has introduced into these organizations an invisible technology in the sense of Berry (1983). This approach acted as a Trojan horse. Through an insidious and gradual shift, it has moved the cursor of solidarity toward that of market logic from within. There is no brutal rupture of the social pact, but the tools have created a "profound change in the representations of the social question and the legal and necessary means of dealing with it" (Chauvière, 2007, p. 14).

We can ask with Bonnafous-Boucher to what extent the firm (and its management), as a stabilized object, does not block organizational thinking? For this author, it is better to speak of "theories of organization rather than a theory of organizations" (Bonnafous-Boucher, 2005, p. 108). One can only agree with the idea. Rather than constructing a dominant management model that ends up imposing itself on all organizations (including those that do not claim to be market-based), is it not better to think of competing models that can be adopted by a diversity of organizations? Such a proposal amounts to reversing the order of values. Rather than defending the generalization of the general model of market enterprises and then adapting it to the organizations of the social and solidarity economy, can we not produce a management model that is intrinsically solidarity-based? By definition, it would be perfectly suited to the organizations of the social and solidarity economy (SSE) but could also be suited to market organizations seeking to free themselves from the market (Peters, 1993). It should not be forgotten that managing also means "inventing new systems of legitimacy" (David et al., 2012, p. 17) and that management doctrines "make reflexivity possible, and therefore the evolution of this action" (ibid., p. 33).

This inversion of the frame of thought can be translated for management authors by a societal turn. From then on, "organisational phenomena are no longer considered as autonomous objects in a given society, they make society" (Vaujany et al., 2016, p. 20). The societal turn questions "the emergence of organisational phenomena and their inextricable relations with the socio-economical and environmental dynamics that participate in the construction of society" (ibid., p. 14). Three propositions can thus be stated. First, the organization is a permanent movement, which means that it cannot be "circumscribed in a precise space or by the contracts that bind people together" (ibid., p. 15). In this case, the organization in the classical sense dissolves in favor of an organizational context that carries potentialities. "The organization is then an open place that can include different stakeholders without a priori restriction" (ibid., p. 16) and that is sensitive to the meaning given to collective action. Second, the organization is a situated system, that is, it is inseparable from the material, spatial, temporal, and cultural dimensions. Finally, the organization is a heterogeneous phenomenon made up of interacting actors and artifacts. With these principles and assumptions, it is possible to think about social transformation within organizations and to consider ways of reorganizing solidarity.

References

Abensour, M. (2013). *Le procès des maîtres rêveurs (followed by) Pierre Leroux et l'utopie*. Sulliver.

Acosta, A. (2014). *The Buen Vivir*. Utopia. 208 pages.

Audier, S. (2010). *La pensée solidariste : aux sources du modèle social républicain*. PUF.

Barthes, R. (2013). *Mythologies* (2nd ed.). Hill and Wang. 288 pages.

Bauman, Z. (2000). *Liquid modernity*. Polity.

Berry, M. (1983). *Une technologie invisible : l'impact des systèmes de gestion sur les comportements humains*. École polytechnique, report for the Ministère de la Recherche et de la Technologie. http://crg.polytechnique.fr/incunables.

Boltanski, L. (2015). Situation de la critique. In B. Frère (Ed.), *Le tournant de la théorie critique* (pp. 189–217). Desclée de Brouwer.

Bonnafous-Boucher, M. (2005). *Anthropologie et gestion*. Economica. 169 pages.

Bourgeois, L. (2015). *Solidarité*, Ed. originale A. Colin 1896. Bibebook Free Edition. 158 pages.

Burnham, J. (1941). *The managerial revolution: What is happening in the world?* John Day Company.

Cadalen, P. Y. (2018). Les temps conflictuels du commun en Equateur et en Bolivie. *Revista de economia solidaria, 11*, 79–97.

Caillé, A. (1994). In Coll. Recherches, Série Bibliothèque du Mauss (Ed.), *Don, intérêt et intéressement : Bourdieu, Mauss, Platon et quelques autres*. La Découverte.

Caillé, A., & Laville, J. L. (1998). Une seule solution, l'association ? Socio-économie du fait associatif. *Revue du Mauss, 11*.

Cailluet, L., Lemarchand, Y., & Chessel, M. E. (2013). *Histoire et sciences de gestion*. Vuibert, coll. Fnege.

Callon, M. (2006). *What does it mean to say that economics is performative?* Csi working papers, series 005.

Calvo, S., & Morales, A. (2017). *Social and solidarity economy: The world's economy with a social face* (1st ed.). Routledge. 384 pages.

Cefaï, D., & Chanial, P. (2000). Politique de l'association. Une généalogie de l'associationnisme civique en France. *La revue du GERFA, 1*.

Chancel, L. (2017). *Insoutenables inégalités : pour une justice sociale et environnementale*. Editions Les petits matins.

Chanial, P. (2010, January 30). La délicate essence du socialisme. *Revue du MAUSS permanente*.

Chauvière, M. (2007). *Trop de gestion tue le social : Essai sur une discrète chalandisation*. Alternatives sociales. Editions La Découverte.

Chaves, R., & Demoustier, D. (2015). *The emergence of the social economy in public policy: An international analysis*. edited by CIRIEC.

Coase, R. (1937). *The nature of the firm*. Blackwell Publishing.

Colliot-Thélène, C. (2011). Retour sur les rationalités chez Max Weber. *Les Champs de Mars, 22*(2), 13–30.

Coraggio, J. L. (2004). *La gente o el capital. Desarollo local y economia en trabajo*. Espacio Editorial.

Corbett, S., & Walker, A. (2013). The big society: Rediscovery of 'the social' or rhetorical fig-leaf for neo-liberalism? *Critical Social Policy, 33*(3).

Courtel, Y. (2010). La lutte pour la reconnaissance dans la philosophie sociale d'Axel Honneth. *Revue des sciences religieuses, 82*(1).

Coutrot, T. (2018). *Libérer le travail : Pourquoi la gauche s'en moque et pourquoi cela doit changer*. Edition Seuil. 303 pages.

Crozier, M. (1964). Le phénomène bureaucratique. Essai sur les tendances bureaucratiques des systèmes d'organisation modernes et sur leurs relations en France avec le système social et culturel. *Revue française de science politique, 14*(5), 991–997.

Cummings, S., Bridgman, T., Hassard, J., & Rowlinson, M. (2017). *A new history of management*. Cambridge University Press.
David, A., Hatchuel, A., & Laufer, R. (2012). *Les Nouvelles fondations des sciences de gestion : éléments d'épistemologie de la recherche en management*. Presses des mines Paris Tech.
Dellemotte, J. (2009). La main invisible d'Adam Smith : pour en finir avec les idées reçues. *L'économie politique, 44*, 28–41.
Demoustier, D., Rousselière, D., Clerc, J. M., & Cassier, B. (2003). L'entreprise collective : unité et diversité de l'économie sociale et solidaire. *Recma, 290*, 56–73.
Desroche, H. (1976). *Le projet coopératif*. Editions ouvrières.
Dockès, P. (2005). Léon Walras et la conciliation des vérités. *Cahiers du CERAS*. April, HS N°4.
Douglas, M. (1986). *How institutions think*. Syracuse University Press. 158 pages.
Draperi, J. F. (1998). L'économie sociale, un ensemble d'entreprises aux formes infiniment variées. *Recma, 268*.
Drucker, P., & Maciarielo, J. A. (2008). *Management* (revised ed. 1973). Collins.
Duncan, W. J. (1989). *Great ideas in management: Lessons from the founders and foundations of managerial practice*. Jossey-Bass.
Durkheim, E. (1975). *Textes. 1. Eléments d'une théorie sociale*. Collection Le sens commun, Paris Éditions de Minuit. 512 pages.
Durkheim, E. (2014). *The division of labor in society*. Free Press. 416 pages.
Durkheim, E. (2016). *De la division du travail social*. PUF.
Engels, F. (2015). *Socialism: Utopian and scientific* (1st ed.). CreateSpace Independent Publishing Platform. 70 pages.
Enriquez, E. (2003). *L'organisation en analyse*. PUF. 334 pages.
Farah, I., & Gil, M. (2012). Modernidades alternativas: una discusión desde Bolívia. In P. H. Martins & C. RoDrigues (Eds.), *Fronteiras abertas da América Latina*. Editora da UFPE.
Fitoussi, J. P. (2004). *La démocratie et le marché*. Biblio Essais, Le livre de poche.
Flores, E. C. (2015). O conceito de "comunidade humana universal" na obra de Guerreiro Ramos. *Cadernos Ebape.Br, 13*, 573–592.
França Filho, G. C. (2002). Terceiro setor, economia social, economia solidária e economia popular: traçando fronteiras conceituais. In *Bahia Análise e Dados* (Vol. 12). SEI/Governo da Bahia.
França Filho, G. C. (2006). Políticas públicas de economia solidária no Brasil. In França Filho, Laville, Medeiros, & Magnen (Eds.), *Ação Pública e econo-*

mia solidária - uma perspectvia internacional (pp. 259–267). EDUFBA/EDURGS.

Freire, P., de Oliveira, W. F., & Freire, N. (2009). *Pedagogia da solidariedade*. Paz e terra.

Gadrey, J. (2010). *Adieu à la croissance : Bien vivre dans un monde solidaire*. Les petits matins.

Gaulejac, V. D. (2005). *La société malade de la gestion : idéologie gestionnaire, pouvoir managérial et harcèlement social*. Editions Points.

Gide, C. (2010). *The works of Charles Gide* (Vol. XI). L'Harmattan. 273 pages. Texts presented and annotated by Patrice Devillers. Paris, Comité pour l'édition des œuvres de Charles Gide.

Graeber, D. (2015a). *Bureaucracy*. Editions Les liens qui libèrent. 300 pages.

Graeber, D. (2015b). *The utopia of rules: On technology, stupidity and the secret joys of bureaucracy*. Melville House. 272 pages.

Graeber, D. (2015b). *The utopia of rules: On technology, stupidity and the secret joys of bureaucracy*. Melville House. 272 pages.

Guerreiro Ramos, A. (1981). *The new science of organizations: A reconceptualization of the wealth of nations*. University of Toronto Press. 210 pages.

Herreros, G. (2012). *La violence dans les organisations : plaidoyer pour des organisations réflexives*. Eres Editions.

Honneth, A., & Joel, A. (1998). *The struggle for recognition: The moral grammar of social conflicts*. MIT Press.

Huault, I. (2008). Les approches critiques en management. In G. Schmidt (Ed.), *Le management*.

Kraychette, G., Lara, F., & Costa, B. (2000). *Economie dos setores populares - entre realidade e utopia*. Editora Vozes.

Laborde, J. P. (2015). La solidarité entre adhésion et affiliation. In A. Supiot (Ed.), *La solidarité : enquête sur un principe juridique* (pp. 109–123). Collège de France, Edition Odile Jacob.

Lacan, A. (2006). Léon Walras et les sociétés d'assurance mutuelles. *RECMA, 299*, 68–82.

Lallement, J. (2012). Les économistes et les pauvres : de Smith à Walras. *L'économie politique, 55*(3), 43–66.

Laurent, S. (2016). *La couleur du marché : Racisme et Néoliberalisme aux Etats Unis*. Editions Seuil.

Lautier, B. (1994). *L'économie informelle dans le tiers monde*. La Découverte. (Collection Repères).

Laville, J. L. (2010). *Politique de l'association*. Seuil. 350 pages.

Laville, J. L. (2017). *L'économie sociale et solidaire*. Seuil.
Laville, J. L., & Roustang, G. (1996). *Vers un nouveau contrat social*. Desclée de Brouwer.
Leroux, P. (1860). *Quelques Pages de vérités*. NTU Librairie Editeur.
Leroux, P. (2016). *De l'humanité, de son principe et de son avenir où se trouve exposée la vraie définition, Tome 1: de la religion & où l'on explique le sens, la suite & l'enchaînement du mosaïsme & du christianisme*. Hachette Livre BNF. Edition originale 1840. 508 pages.
Lynch, E. C. (2015, Jan./Apr). Teoria pós-colonial e pensamento brasileiro na obra de Guerreiro Ramos: o pensamento sociológico (1953-1955). *Cadernos CRH, 28*(73).
Marcelo Maia, J. (2015). História dos intelectuais no terceiro mundo: reflexões a partir do caso de Guerreiro Ramos. *Cadernos Ebape.Br, 13*, 550–559.
Martins, P. H. (2014). La nature symbolique des usages politiques du bien vivre. *Revue du Mauss, 43*, 75–87.
Mayntz, R. (1965). The Weberian ideal type of bureaucracy and the sociology of organizations. *Zeitschrift für Soziologie und Sozialpsychologie, 17*, 493–502.
Mazuir, F. (2004). Le processus de rationalisation chez Max Weber. *Sociétés, 86*(4), 119–124.
Menger, C. (2002). In O. Meuwly (Ed.), *Grandsätze der Volkwirtschaftslehre*. Liberté et société. Original edition 1923. 264 pages.
Michels, R. (2016). *Political parties: A sociological study of the oligarchial tendencies of modern democracy*. Martino Fine Books. 380 pages.
Musso, P. (2015). La solidarité : généalogie d'un concept sociologique. In A. Supiot (Ed.), *La solidarité : enquête sur un principe juridique* (pp. 93–107). Collège de France, Edition Odile Jacob.
Nikitin, M. (2003, Décembre). De la science des affaires aux sciences de gestion : un siècle de tâtonnements ? *Revue Gérer et Comprendre, 74*.
Parodi, M. (2008, Octobre). *L'économie sociale et solidaire, une alternative à l'économie capitaliste*. Colloque de l'Addes.
Pénin, M. (2006). Charles Gide est-il toujours d'actualité ? *Revue internationale de l'économie sociale*, (301), 65–81.
Peters, T. (1993). *L'entreprise libérée - Liberation management*. Dunod.
Polanyi, K. (1977). In H. W. Pearson (Ed.), *The livelihood of man*. Academic Press.
Razeto, L. (1991, Février). La veine populaire dans l'économie latino-américaine. *La Revue Nouvelle, 47*(2), 27–36.
Renault, M. (2011). Elaborer des outils pour construire une société plus conviviale : d'une expérience de terrain à un raisonnement théorique. In Caillé,

Humbert, Latouche, & Viveret (Eds.), *De la convivialité : dialogues sur la société conviviale à venir* (pp. 167–187). La Découverte.
Rosanvallon, P. (1979). *Le libéralisme économique*. Le Seuil.
Samson, D. & Daft, R. L. (2012). *Management* (4th Asia Pacific ed.). Cengage learning.
Santos, M. (1993). *O espaço do cidadão*. Nobel.
Scott, J. (1998). *Seing like a state*. MIT Press.
Simon, H. (1955). A behavioral model of rational choice. *The Quarterly Journal of Economics, 69*, 129–138.
Smith, A. (2013). *The wealth of nations*. CreateSpace Independent Publishing Platform. 426 pages.
Thompson, E. P. (1966). *The making of the English working class*. Vintage. 864 pages.
Tocqueville, A. D. (2002). *Democracy in America*. University of Chicago Press. 722 pages.
Tönnies, F. (2021). *Community and society* (1st ed.). Mockingbird Press. 320 pages.
Toucas-Truyen, P. (2014). Les différents âges de la solidarité mutualiste en France : un concept singulier, des pratiques évolutives. *Vie sociale, 7*, 95–107.
Utting, P. (2015). *Social and solidarity economy: Beyond the fringe* (1st ed.). Zed Books. 402 pages.
Vandervelde, E. (1913). *Coopération neutre et socialiste*. Librairie Felix Alcan.
Vaujany, F. X. D., Hussenot, A., & Chanlat, J. F. (2016). *Théorie des organisations : nouveaux tournants*. Economica.
Viard, B., & Vaillancourt, Y. (2000). *Pierre Leroux : socialiste associatif, Actualités de 1848*. Thierry Quinqueton Editeur.
Vienney, C. (1994). *L'économie sociale*. La Découverte.
Viveret, P. (2004). *Reconsidérer la richesse*. Editions de l'aube, Poche essai.
Walras, L. (1992). Etudes d'économie politique appliquée. In Auguste et Léon Walras (Ed.), *Œuvres complètes* (Vol. X). Economica. (collection of studies written between 1874 and 1898).
Weber, M. (2002). *The protestant ethic and the spirit of capitalism*. Penguin Books. translated by Peter Baehr and Gordon C. Wells.
Weber, M. (2019). *Economy and society: A new translation*. Harvard University Press. 520 pages.
Weiss, R. (1983). Weber on bureaucracy: Management consultant or political theorist? *Academy of Management Review, 8*(2), 242–248.
Williamson, O. E. (1985). *The economic institutions of capitalism*. Free Press.
Yunus, M. (2007). *Creating a world without poverty: Social business and the future of capitalism*. PublicAffairs.

3

(Re)organizing Solidarity

We saw in the previous chapter that the link between solidarity and organization was unthought of, but that at the same time other paths of thought would have been possible. These could have led to a very close relationship between the two concepts. Indeed, it appears that the classical and orthodox vision of a market economy centered on the question of market entrepreneurship has strongly influenced the conceptual formation of organization theory. The presuppositions of methodological individualism developed in this theory have in fact thwarted the possibility of any interdependent thinking within this field. In this second chapter, we propose to go beyond this simple observation by questioning the conditions of the rapprochement between the organizational question and the concern for solidarity. We will first address the economic question as a primary condition for this reinterrogation. We will see how Polanyi's conceptual framework offers the necessary elements to rethink theories of organization. This will lead us to deduce, with Guerreiro Ramos, the conceptual foundations of a new theory of organizations that fully allows the two terms to be combined: organization and solidarity.

P. Eynaud, G. Carvalho de França Filho, *Solidarity and Organization*,
https://doi.org/10.1007/978-3-031-27568-5_3

3.1 Organizing Solidarity by Rethinking Its Economy

The framework of dominant economic thought places market mechanisms at the heart of its analysis, thereby invalidating any approach that seeks to describe and fully understand solidarity relations. Before we can even attempt to organize solidarity, we must therefore overcome this invalidation by choosing a broader framework of analysis. Polanyi's conceptual proposal is relevant in this respect. By mixing history, anthropology, sociology, and economics, Polanyi developed an original transdisciplinary approach and made several particularly important contributions concerning our initial question. First of all, he broadened the field of observation of the economy in time and space to define his concept of the substantive economy. This led him to uncover the ideological construction that accompanies and favors the growth of self-regulating markets. Finally, from this, he deduced orientations in terms of analysis of the forces at play and the question of disembedding which for him was central.

3.1.1 The Economy Is Not Reduced to the Market

Polanyi shows first of all that the market is not the exclusive form of circulation of economic goods and services. He denounces what he calls an economic fallacy, the now common desire to reduce the economy to the market economy. For him, the importance that the market has attained in our societies tends to mask other forms that coexist with it: reciprocity, redistribution, and domestic sharing. Polanyi's historical analysis is particularly edifying in this respect. It shows that the domination of the market is historically dated, relatively recent, and that the present period is an exception in the history of humanity. Drawing on the work of Mauss, Malinovski, and Boas, Polanyi shows that reciprocity—relatively unnoticed today—and redistribution prevailed in the past. One can thus think of Mauss as being in line with Leroux. "Leroux and Mauss agree in thinking, one of calling it solidarity, the other calling it gift, that taking and receiving, far from being opposed, are complementary gestures that together constitute the only alternative to violence and the very definition of life, from the biological to the social level" (Viard & Vaillancourt, 2000, p. 24). In the premodern era, the setting of exchange rates on markets was the decision of the authorities and city officials. The functioning of markets was thus embedded in social and political control mechanisms. Polanyi shows that the rise of capitalism is associated with the emergence of self-regulated markets, that is, markets characterized by unconstrained price setting. In a self-regulated market, prices are in fact the result of the law of supply and demand and therefore do not depend (in the first analysis) on social, cultural, or political factors. Polanyi argues that the appearance of self-regulating markets was the triggering factor for the great transformation he observed (Polanyi, 1983). Without the multiplication of such markets, the market economy would not have been able to impose itself and the economic perception of the actors would not have changed.. The growth of the market economy is thus linked to a progressive disengagement of the economic from social relations. The rise in power of the market that we have naturalized today is therefore largely an ideological construction. The social and political disembedding of the market has valorized it and given it a new legitimacy. Capitalism has taken advantage of this shift to reverse the relationship of dependence. It is now society that is embedded in the market. Of course, this vision can be qualified. Market logics are not always reduced to a simple search for interest. From time to time, they are also subject to issues of recognition, power, or socialization (Granovetter, 2000). Granovetter thus asserts that Polanyi has in a way given an "over-socialized" version of non-modern economies and an "under-socialized" version of the market economy (Maucourant, 2005, p. 113). However, the observation remains that a large-scale changeover is underway, with the market logic taking over all modern societies.

3.1.2 The Proposal of a Substantive Economy

Based on the critic of economic fallacy, Polanyi puts forward the concept of substantive economy. For him, the economy historically finds its origin in man's dependence on nature and his fellow human beings, and he deduced the need for men to manage this dependence in order to ensure their survival. The substantive meaning thus comes from man's manifest dependence on nature and his fellow men to obtain his subsistence (Polanyi, 1977). Polanyi distinguishes two levels within the substantive economy: the interaction of humans with their environment and the institutionalization that follows. The latter aims to lift men out of their precariousness by not relying on a fragile chain of causality for their survival (Polanyi, 1977). It is this process of institutionalization that interests Polanyi and constitutes the strength of his proposal. Indeed, it is characteristic of Polanyi's thought to seek to place himself at the heart of the tension between actor and institution and to "hold fast to this intellectual requirement throughout his historical analyses, without falling back on one side (methodological individualism) or the other (holism or structuralism)" (Postel & Sobel, 2010, p. 31).

From then on, Polanyi will oppose the substantive economy to what he calls the formal economy. The latter neglects the institutional dimension by focusing solely on the process of the economy of means in a context of scarcity. To criticize this option retained by the formal economy, Polanyi refers to Menger (1923 [2002]) and highlights two economic perspectives mentioned in the last version of Menger's "Principles": one advocating an approach in terms of scarcity of means, the other emphasizing "the physical requirements of production without regard to the abundance or scarcity of means" (Polanyi, 1986).[1] From this second understanding, Polanyi builds his proposal of substantive economy. For him, it is a matter of paying attention to industry rather than business, technology rather than ceremonialism, the means of production rather than property titles, productive capital rather than finance, capital goods rather than capital, in a word, the substance of the economy rather than its market form and terminology (Polanyi, 1977). In doing so, the substantive economy is not built around scarcity. The substantive sense implies neither choice nor scarcity. Man's subsistence may or may not entail the need to choose. Custom and tradition in general eliminate choice and, if there is choice, it need not be caused by the limiting effects of any scarcity of means. Polanyi thus frees the economic decision from

[1] Quoted in Maucourant (2005), p. 71.

the sole reference to scarcity. He points out that the difficulty in making a choice can come as much from abundance as from scarcity of means (Polanyi, 1977). His intent is to construct an expanded view of economics that embraces the history of both modern and non-modern economies, and since the latter were not dominated by the market, scarcity was not the rule. Polanyi looks to Aristotle for arguments for his proposal, noting that Aristotle thinks that "the true riches of a household, or of a state, are the necessities of life that can be stored and will keep." And they are "nothing more than means to an end and like all means they are intrinsically limited and determined by their ends. In the household, they are means to life; in the polis, they are means to the good life. Human wants and needs are therefore not boundless" (Polanyi, 1977, p. 30). The substantive economy is then considered in reference to an ancient city defending the principle of a good life and thus limiting the space given to market relations.

Polanyi thus opposes head-on the foundations of the market economy: needs are not unlimited, and choices do not only concern questions of scarcity. Polanyi also criticizes the concept of property, which is central to the market economy, by putting it into perspective. He thus refers to Mead to remind us that in ancient societies it is the man who belongs to the plot of land, not the land to the man (Polanyi, 1977). Polanyi further points out that the range of human needs is greatly reduced when only those that can be translated into utilitarian value scales of isolated individuals acting in markets are retained (Polanyi, 1977).

3.1.3 The Question of Fictitious Goods

Another focus of Polanyi's work is to highlight the conditions of the rise of the market. Over the very long historical period in which reciprocity and redistribution predominated, trade, money, and markets did not constitute an integrated institutional whole (Polanyi, 1977). Markets existed, but they were socially regulated. The setting of prices in these markets was not beyond the control of the actors involved, as would be the case with the emergence of self-regulating markets.

It is therefore necessary to understand what made such a profound change possible. Polanyi hypothesizes a deliberate will to gradually transform three factors of production (labor, money, and nature) into commodities. These three factors are not chosen at random. They are indeed part of a possible limitation of the exercise of self-regulated markets. The market needs to assign to a price with raw materials, a price with the number of hours worked, and a price with the production goods financed by credit. The pressure is important because the "political construction of these three markets is the sine qua non for the appearance of a self-regulating market" (Postel & Sobel, 2010, p. 9).

For Polanyi, this transformation is a priori inconceivable. Labor, money, and nature are not commodities. At no time have these factors been produced to be sold. For Polanyi, therefore, there is an ideology at work that contributes to creating and maintaining a fiction that he considers to be the most powerful fiction ever imagined. The "commodification" of these factors has a double advantage: an unlimited supply of markets, thanks to the automated regulation of flows, and the weakening of social resistance to an anonymous system. The market economy thus needs these "fictitious goods" in order to establish its hegemony and to ensure its endless extension.

The process of commodification of labor, money, and nature has not been carried out in a linear way. Waves of commodification are seen to follow one another and deepen "as they move from labor to money and then to nature, with each wave incorporating the commodification of the previous period" to undermine with increasing force labor rights, then social rights (which include labor rights) and human rights that encompass all three types of rights (Burawoy, 2013). From then on, the point is clear. The development of the market works against democracy. On issues as important as well-being and fulfillment in work, trust in money, or the preservation of nature, the market economy installs its own devices to invalidate any social control. The detour through history is again very relevant because it shows us that this phenomenon of disembedding is not inevitable. In particular, it was reversible after World War II with the Treaty of Philadelphia and the victory against fascism (Supiot, 2012). Reversibility is expressed today in innovative organizational forms, as we shall see in the next chapter.

3.1.4 The Implications of Substantive Economics for Organizational Theory

The Polanyian grid carries many strong issues for the orientation of organization theory. We will now try to make an inventory of the main ones. First of all, Polanyi's approach underlines the importance of studying phenomena over the long term and the strength that the historical approach can have in breaking out of the prisms that block thinking. This confirms an element that we have already underlined in the previous chapter by referring to the work of management historians. This neglect of history is undoubtedly particularly acute for relatively young sciences such as organization theory, which may be tempted to neglect its own contribution. Moreover, Polanyi is very critical of an evolutionary and finalist vision of economic history. With Benjamin, he sees history outside a linear narrative and in a non-predictable series of continuities and discontinuities.

The second important point brought about by the concept of substantive economy is the autonomization of the economic sphere and its assimilation to the market. The great transformation of which Polanyi speaks is first of all the separation of politics and economics (Polanyi, 1983). This separation, concomitant with the birth of the organizational sciences, was not neutral. It has had the consequence of limiting organizational thinking to the framework of market enterprises and of limiting the exploration of the interaction between politics and the economy. For Polanyi, the rehabilitation of citizen power requires "a democratically controlled and socially embedded economy" (Birchfield, 2014). This embedding is indeed likely to give back to the citizen his power of decision on economic life while rehabilitating the political. Such an option has the consequence of repositioning organizational analysis. With substantive analysis, society and politics are not outside the field. They legitimately participate in the organizational study. This means that organizational theorists must decentralize and no longer consider the market enterprise as the only unit of measurement for their observations and the only reference for their studies and recommendations. The substantivist conceptual framework calls for the consideration of other territories of analysis (Hart et al., 2010).

The third contribution of the Polanyian grid is to allow a better account for the emergence and rise of organizations in the field of the social and solidarity economy (SSE). The result of the gathering of historical actors (associations, cooperatives, mutual societies) and new actors, the SSE was recognized in December 2014 by a framework law in France. It lays down the principle in Article 1 that SSE organizations recognize themselves in the pursuit of a goal that is not reduced to profit sharing and implement democratic governance. We can clearly see there the reintegration of which Polanyi speaks and the possibility of a democratization of the economy.

The fourth contribution is a different way of thinking about the space for exchanges between economic actors. In the case of a market exchange, the agreement is fixed at the moment when a contract is signed, supposedly guaranteeing the equilibrium of the transaction (through a price adjustment mechanism) and its completion (through the resulting payment). Everything is therefore played out in the here and now between any two actors who are only known to meet on a market. Polanyi's discovery of other economic logics, such as reciprocity and redistribution, contributes to an enrichment of the reading grid of interactions between actors. They make it possible to move away from contractuality, which has become a general social form "in the world of business, commercial or private, but just as much in the sphere of the social and the political" (Caillé, 2005, p. 143). Thus, reciprocity is freed from the contract. It is not bound by a need for equivalence or a formal approach. It will describe the movement of goods and services (or their elimination) between the points of a symmetrical arrangement (Polanyi, 1977). Redistribution, on the other hand, means the movement toward a center and then from the center outward, whether the objects are physically moved or merely changed in their arrangement. The center can be the village leader or the social state. Unlike market exchange, it is not resolved by a contract between two parties. We can therefore make a spatial reading of Polanyi's work where the forms of integration can be represented by diagrams illustrating the types of movements of goods and people: changes in location, appropriation, or both. If this spatial reading is coupled with a temporal reading, the logics of reciprocity and redistribution appear richer. The spatial figures are more complex and the logic of long-term prevails for they have a great socializing power, unlike market logics.

Polanyi's fifth contribution is related to the management decision. If the reference of organizational theories is no longer an economy based on scarcity but on an economy based on substance, the question of decision is profoundly transformed. The first consequence is that the decision does not necessarily result in an optimization calculation. It may be that the choice has to be made between equivalent options or solutions. It may also be that the choice is expressed in the face of sufficient means (or not). The abandonment of the principle of scarcity opens up the field of possibilities. The choice can be freely based on other criteria: moral, ethical. The choice loses its technical and inappropriate character to become political again. It can be shared, discussed, and chosen collectively.

Polanyi's sixth contribution to organization concerns the question of fictitious goods. Denouncing the commodity fiction maintained around work, money, and nature implies an awareness within organizations that calls for a precautionary approach. How can we engage management in the demarketing of fictitious goods? Three perspectives are open. The first is the valorization of work in relation to capital. This is expressed by mechanisms to protect the interests of workers, by the capacity to participate in decisions, by limitations on income differentials, and by the control of the power of capital providers. On all these aspects, the experience acquired by the historical actors of the social economy is rich and relevant. The second is the question of money. Polanyi shows that ancient societies had several currencies for several uses. The emergence of local currencies is part of this renewal of questions about the social appropriation of money outside the national currency. Finally, the question of nature refers to the negative externalities of companies in terms of the environment, and it refers to management methods that are built on the calculation of the ecological footprint and the preservation of biodiversity. In these three perspectives, Polanyi sees an opportunity to increase our freedom of creative adaptation and thus increase our chances of survival. All of this underscores the currency of Polanyi's thought for organizational thinking (Hillenkamp & Laville, 2014) and invites a rethinking of the very foundations of organization theory. This is the task that a Brazilian author, Guerreiro Ramos, has taken on.

3.2 Organizing Solidarity by Rethinking Its Rationality: The Contribution of Guerreiro Ramos

Guerreiro Ramos' work is ambitious in that it proposes the creation of a "new theory of organizations" (Guerreiro Ramos, 1981). The epistemological basis of his approach is substantive. In this he joins Polanyi whose contribution he recognizes. Guerreiro Ramos believes that "modern social science was conceived with the aim of freeing the market from the chains that, throughout human history until the rise of the commercial and industrial revolution, kept it confined within defined limits" (Ibid, p. 22). Guerreiro Ramos proposes in fact to complete and to extend to the organizational field the work initiated by Polanyi on the economic field. He refuses the orthodox economic theorists' claim to universality and with Polanyi affirms that the economy has always been embedded in society and that consequently capitalist society must be understood and approached as an exceptional case. Like Polanyi, he refers to classical thinkers such as Plato and Aristotle to affirm the primacy of politics over economics in order to guarantee a good life. He links his thinking on substantive organizational issues with the proposal of a number of original concepts. We will now address them.

3.2.1 Power and Conditioning of Formal Organizations

Guerreiro Ramos believes that formal organizations have too much power today. This idea may appear at first glance to be a common observation. Indeed, no one disputes the formidable rise in power of market organizations in today's world and many people criticize their power. The richness and profusion of academic literature in organization theory is a clear sign of this and reflects such debates. However, the originality of Guerreiro

Ramos' thinking is that he is not interested in the power of organizations inside the economic market sphere, but rather outside it. For him, this power is expressed by a conditioning of society that he considers detrimental. Guerreiro Ramos' work is not about conspiracy thinking or an analysis of the methods of mass communication used by companies. Instead, his analysis is quite different. Through a rigorous semantic analysis and with precision and finesse, he endeavors to demonstrate the existence of a slow, indirect, often nonconscious and deeply powerful conditioning process.

The angle of entry in his thinking is the question of rationality. The whole theory of organizations is centered on this basic question, with two key moments in the history of thought. Before Simon (1955), rationality was the object of absolute knowledge. It is carried by individuals arbitrating on markets, making choices, and taking decisions. At each stage, rationality guides their steps. It makes them economic actors. In return, all of these rational acts make it possible to guarantee the equilibrium of markets, the possibilities of adjustment, and economic regulation. After Simon, this rationality of human actors becomes limited. It can no longer be carried or embodied by isolated individuals. From this point on, perfect knowledge is not within their reach. If rationality has not disappeared, it has nevertheless shifted. It appears indeed that men can no longer carry the torch of reason alone. The complexity of the decisions to be taken (Luhmann, 2018) is confronted with the inherent limits of their cognitive capacities. The collective organization will therefore replace them and make up for their deficiency. For Simon, the computerization of organizations thus offers the possibility of moving toward perfect knowledge. The rise in power of computer architectures argues for the possibility of unlimited data processing. This shift in the burden of rationality from man to machine is very interesting to note for it implies a continuum between man and machine, but it also underlines the computational character of rationality.

According to Guerreiro Ramos, herein lies a fault in thought. Its origin is ancient, since Guerreiro Ramos traces it back to Hobbes, whom he criticizes for having been the initiator of this devaluation of reason. By reducing man to a being who calculates, one denies his capacity to distinguish vice from virtue. This eviction of the ethical dimension proper to rationality is characteristic of the dominant organizational thinking. The irruption of computer science into the debate is illustrative since the purpose of an economic algorithm is to calculate and not to ask moral questions. No higher value can alter or disrupt its sequence of logical operations. This is why formal organizations are characterized above all by the optimization of means over ends. For them, rationality is subordinated to the objective necessities inherent in the production processes deployed. For Guerreiro Ramos, this is the source of conditioning.

To demonstrate this, he endeavors to give semantic translations. Thus, the question of work is generally reduced to the notion of employment. Having a job means having a salary, a contract, training, and a framework within a formal organization. The job therefore has a virtue in itself. It introduces the employee to the life of organizations and provides him with a fixed income in return. Thanks to this, he can become a consumer and buy goods and services produced by these same organizations. Smith, before Ford, had anticipated this chain of events when in *The Wealth of Nations* he wrote that the division of labor leads everyone to become a merchant (Smith, 2013). In reference to Montesquieu's gentle commerce, for Smith this is a virtuous chain that transforms society into a market society. But, for Guerreiro Ramos, the substitution of the notion of employment for that of work has a counterpart. It makes invisible all the work done outside of employment. Everything that cannot be considered a resource or a production is thus rejected in the noneconomic space. Gone are the activities carried out within the family, cooking, cleaning, sports, gardening, time spent with friends, caring for one's family, civic engagement, and volunteer activities. Everything that has to do with personal development or reproduction is thus placed outside the economic field. So, what is there outside of employment? Guerreiro Ramos shows that the market society has created a concept to designate what is outside employment: leisure. This is synonymous with idleness and relaxation, that is, inactivity. The market offers the services associated with this inactivity through a leisure economy. It is as if the market could not really think of a space outside itself. Guerreiro Ramos is amused to recall that the meaning of idleness in ancient Greece was a state where leisure in its modern version was not possible. For the ancient Greeks, idleness (*Otium*) was indeed a state of inner calm, detachment, and studiousness far from the frivolous indolence of a leisure economy.

3.2.2 The Behavioral Syndrome Induced by the Formal Organization

Behind this semantic shift, Guerreiro Ramos hypothesizes the existence of a behavioral syndrome. Individuals are not insensitive to organizational prescriptions and to the economic doxa disseminated within formal organizations. A long process of unconscious internalization would follow until it becomes second nature. The individual would then be ready to become what Guerreiro Ramos calls a "fluid creature," that is, a being subjected to the permanent flow of injunctions and utilitarian criteria put forward by companies. According to Guerreiro Ramos, companies proceed to a reduction of meaning by being able to consider situations only from a functional point of view. Faced with this, the individuals employed in companies are faced with a dilemma: to fully adhere to the demands of the organization or to simulate adherence. In the first case, there is potentially disorientation, anomy, and a loss of values. In the second case, one must be able to manage multiple identities with different behaviors in one's professional and personal life. This can lead to Machiavellianism or stressful disarray.

For Guerreiro Ramos, there are therefore political and psychological consequences because of the hold that instrumental rationality has on modern societies. According to him, the individual subjectivity is prisoner of the instrumental rationality. He believes that capitalism limits the possibility of free and authentic communication between individuals. Formal organizations consciously or unconsciously use a "distorted language, with the intention of pushing people to interpret reality in terms that are profitable to the direct or indirect agents of this distortion." (Guerreiro Ramos, 1981, p. 76). That is why Guerreiro Ramos is very critical of the school of human resources. He accuses its theorists of legitimizing the expansion of formal organizations by talking about trust, authenticity, openness and practicing a "misplaced and misunderstood humanism" (Ibid, p. 84). For him, companies organized around the pursuit of profit cannot be the place for the authentic expression of individuals or for a possible coincidence between the goals of organizations and the individuals they employ. We cannot therefore fight alienation, which is a feeling of powerlessness, of loss of meaning that causes isolation and marginalization, simply by changing the type of technology used. We cannot fight against anomie by trying to rehumanize companies. For Guerreiro Ramos, there is an irreducible incompatibility in this attempt because "personal development and solitude are inseparable" (Ibid, p. 98).

One of the risks that weighs on the psychological balance of individuals is overorganization. This overorganization comes from the pressure of market logic on personal life time. Overorganization thus has a significant impact on the depersonalization of the individual. Guerreiro Ramos points out that education does not escape this pressure and tends more and more to lead to students gaining employment in the market system. Human needs are multiple, and the market system responds to them in a limited way. For the market, it is a question of standardizing needs to make them fit into its reference grid. To do this, the conditioning of individuals is necessary. Its purpose is, among other things, to flatten space, to linearize time, and to transform reason into calculation.

3.2.3 The Instrumental Reason of Formal Organizations

With this semantic analysis and the description of the behavioral syndrome, Guerreiro Ramos can launch into a frontal critique. Organization theory, as we know it, "is naive because it presupposes an instrumental rationality inherent in Western social science" (Ibid, p. 3). This criticism is mainly directed at authors who have tried to "legitimize modern society solely on utilitarian grounds" (Ibid, p. 5). According to Guerreiro Ramos, the concept of rationality is central in the analysis because it conditions the whole approach to social issues. He objects to the idea that the concept of reason can be aligned with the normative framework of modern society. For Guerreiro Ramos, rationality disappears in a world in which means and ends become the only references for human action.

At the same time, he defends rationality against what he calls an "ill-defined anti-rationality" understood as "one of the theses of those who define themselves as humanists" (Ibid, p. 5), yet who do not abandon their normative framework.

Guerreiro Ramos reproaches the tradition of the Enlightenment for its confidence in progress. He similarly criticizes Marx for having placed his confidence in the development of the means of production in order to ensure emancipation and freedom. He rejects the Hegelian idea (taken up by Marx, 1992) of a historical evolution that would allow pure reason to conform to practical reason. With Horkheimer, he maintains that "the denunciation of what is now called reason is the greatest service that reason can render" (Horkheimer, 1947, p. 187). For Guerreiro Ramos, the modern individual is indeed mainly occupied with expressing intentions and no longer knows how to use language for the transmission of meaning. Moreover, the reason that Guerreiro Ramos defends cannot be grasped easily. There is in reason an inherent impulse that conditions the possibility of this same reason.

He thus shares Voegelin's thesis according to which modernity is the bearer of a violent political attempt to summon paradise on Earth through the affirmation of a doxa concerning the form that this paradise must take. The violence is twofold insofar as the imposition of paradise goes hand in hand with the will to maintain it against all odds. For Voegelin, the corruption of such a proposal is intrinsic and cannot pretend to escape the cyclical law of decline and fall. To leave this gnostic vision, Voegelin refers to the Ancients. He shows that the Aristotelian notion of a good society is by no means univocal nor reduced to a single occurrence. It is the object of an adaptation that takes into account the circumstances and the context and of a choice that arbitrates between several possible scenarios. In this idea, Guerreiro Ramos finds arguments for a multicentered vision of the organization.

Guerreiro Ramos then retains a second argument of Voegelin's. The opposition between paradise and the here below appears as an irreducible existential tension. Reason cannot therefore be thought without the awareness of this tension. By envisaging the possibility of a paradise on Earth, modern reason not only proceeds from a distorted experience of reality but also disqualifies itself. By neglecting this tension inherent to the human condition, modern reason loses its own impetus and, for Voegelin, its ability and its creative force. If he takes up these criticisms of modern reason, Guerreiro Ramos reproaches Voegelin for not giving us any indication of the operational implications of these philosophical propositions with regard to contemporary society.

3.2.4 In Praise of Substantive Rationality

In order to go further than the sole criticism of market rationality, Guerreiro Ramos needs to propose an alternative. He looks for it in Weber. The latter provides him with arguments to defend a rationality different from modern instrumental rationality. Guerreiro Ramos underlines how Weber is conditioned by his time and envisages the bureaucracy as performing rational functions in the particular context of a market capitalist society. However, he retains from Weber the distinction between formal and material rationality. While, as we have seen, the former can be expressed through numerical or accounting reasoning, the latter takes into account other requirements from the point of view of values or purposes (Max Weber, 2019). Guerreiro Ramos retains the latter as a basis for his work. It seems to him coherent with the ideas defended by Voegelin. He describes material rationality as substantive rationality.

To support the soundness of the substantive rationality he defends, Guerreiro Ramos turns to Habermas. He is interested in what allows a society to continue to produce cohesion and meaning and how this is a matter of symbolic interaction. Habermas thus proposes a distinction between applied rational action (instrumental in nature) and communicative action (situated in symbolic interaction). The first refers to technical rules and can be true or false. The second is based on interpersonal relations free of external constraints and is founded on intersubjectivity and mutual understanding. Therefore, the stranglehold of instrumental rationality on modern societies can only be understood by the existence of a distorted communication. The superiority of the capitalist world over the modes that preceded it was imposed by two main means: an economic mechanism based on permanent expansion and the legitimization of this expansion in the political field in order to transform its requirements. This idea refers to the process of rationalization described by Weber. But for Guerreiro Ramos, Habermas does not approach moral values like Weber. By placing rationality in the space of communication, Guerreiro Ramos believes that Habermas implements an integrated critical social theory that opens up both a better understanding of the mechanisms of coercion and the possibility of considering emancipation. With this proposal for a concept of substantive rationality based on the thinking of the Frankfurt School, Guerreiro Ramos can envisage an extension of his thinking.

3.2.5 The Concept of Para-economy

Guerreiro Ramos puts forward the concept of para-economics to decentralize the analysis. He seeks to show that organizational dynamics cannot be reduced to market mechanisms and logics alone. Para-economics thus helps its author to take a step aside and show that the market is only one social enclave among others. What Guerreiro Ramos seeks through the concept of para-economy is to build a substantive political theory to qualitatively improve the social life of individuals. For him, "every citizen who seeks to promote alternative scenarios to market-centered systems is therefore a para-economist" (França Filho & de Freitas Boullosa, 2015, p. 213). Behind these alternative scenarios, Guerreiro Ramos' desire is to promote the development and recognition of isonomies and phenonomies as indispensable institutional arrangements for a more viable and sustainable society. For Guerreiro Ramos, any extensive organizational theory necessarily presupposes a social science of the same epistemological nature. If the equivalent of mainstream organizational theory is formal social science, what he calls the new science of organizations is substantive social science (Guerreiro Ramos, 1981).

For this, Guerreiro Ramos distinguishes two axes. In the first axis, he moves from anomie to prescription. Anomie is a concept put forward by Durkheim. Guerreiro Ramos uses it to designate individuals without norms who have no sense of relationship to others. The anomic individual is thus a person unable to create a social environment that allows him to subsist. Anomie, as a principle of inorganization, is opposed to the economy, which specifically values the work of normalization around the production of goods and services. The anomic individual is unable to create a social environment that can respond to the prescriptions of the market. For Guerreiro Ramos, the anomic individual must be assisted, protected, and even controlled by *ad hoc* organizations (associations, educational centers, care centers, prisons, etc.). In this context, anomie also calls for an organizational reflection that must be taken into account in the para-economic framework.

The second axis intersects the first at its center. It opposes a personal orientation and a community orientation. It allows its author to consider two paths in which he does not want to resolve himself: the individualism of the market and the collectivism of Marxism. This general framework of para-economics on two axes allows us to relativize the organizational model of the market and to open onto a possible emancipatory vision of the theories of organization. It also makes it possible to revisit organizational forms that have been delegitimized or marginalized by the market. Finally, it allows for a redefinition of the usual categories that the market economy has trivialized (Fig. 3.1).

3.2.6 Phenonomy

The personal organization translates into the existence of phenonomies that offer individuals maximum freedom of personal choice while guaranteeing minimum subordination to operational constraints. For Guerreiro Ramos, it is a "new environment, temporary or more or less stable, initiated and directed by an individual or a small group. It offers its members a maximum of personal choice and a minimum of subordination to operational prescriptions" (Guerreiro Ramos, 1981, p. 132). This environment allows for a great deal of creativity and allows its members to engage only in self-selected work. This can be a personal passion maintained in a space of one's own, such as the room in the house that is reserved for DIY or the creative workshop. Everything is done so that individuals can express their creativity and autonomy. The members of a phenonomy are creative and autonomous people who generally have an inner strength that drives them to act. They are therefore quite capable of

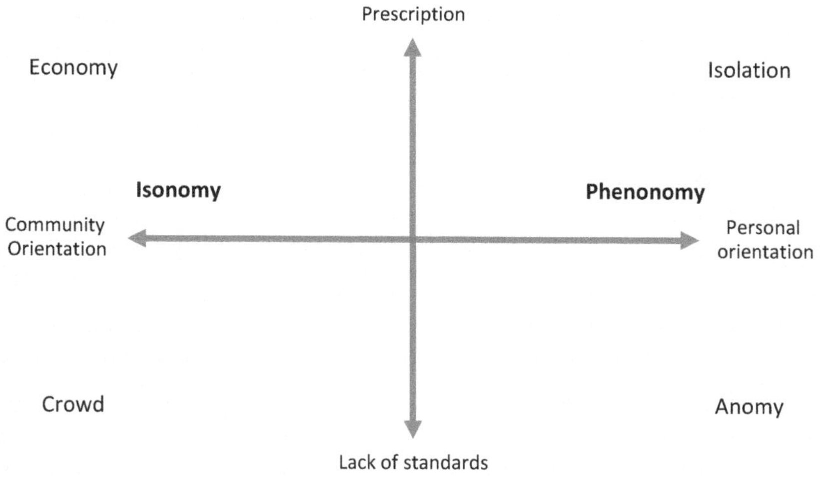

Fig. 3.1 The para-economic paradigm

carrying out their projects and following their vocation in a personal and isolated trajectory. However, the environment offered to them by a phenonomy is both protective and favorable. Each member of a phenonomy can thus share material and immaterial resources and benefit from the creative dynamics of the collective.

Guerreiro Ramos places four conditions on the implementation of a phenonomy. The first is to have an environment that is conducive to the expression of creativity in chosen forms. In such an environment, creation can take place either individually or in small groups. Secondly, members of a phenonomy only engage in self-selected work. This means that they are able to build their own agenda and define their own priorities. Since the tasks are freely chosen, it is up to the person who defines them to be able to assume the operating rules and the specifications. Thirdly, if the result of the activities undertaken within a phenonomy is put on the market, economic criteria remain secondary for its members. Phenonomies are social environments that protect themselves from the incursions of the market. One can even say that a phenonomy has the ambition to confront and take over the market system. Therefore, members of a phenonomy do not count their time. Fourth and last, the member of a phenonomy has a social sensitivity which does not betray his desire for original creation. He does not wish to withdraw from society but rather to make others aware of experiences that they could share and appreciate.

3.2.7 Isonomy

Guerreiro Ramos calls isonomy an association of equals constituted to provide a good life (in the sense of Aristotle, i.e., a happy life). Guerreiro Ramos establishes five principles for isonomies. The first principle of an isonomy is to allow the development of its members without imposed prescriptions. Members freely associate to accomplish rewarding actions. Prescriptions are minimal and, when unavoidable, established by consensus. Secondly, involvement in an isonomy is highly gratifying in that it leads to the free association of individuals around projects that they themselves consider worthy of interest. The power of isonomies lies in the creation of strong interpersonal relationships between members. The life of the group is thus reinforced by convivial links. One does not come to an isonomy with the intention of earning a living, but to participate in a generous reciprocity and to express a vocation. Thirdly, the reward comes from the outcome of the project and not from the monetary activity that one can get from it. The approach is therefore not utilitarian and individuals do not seek to maximize any utility function. Fourth, an isonomy is a community organization that assumes a strictly egalitarian decision-making system where authority is continuously passed from person to person according to the nature of the projects and the skills of the members. There are no divisions or established differences between members. Isonomy is thought of and lived as a community in which authority is based on common deliberation. Because there is no immutable and exclusive governing agency, Guerreiro Ramos refuses to think of isonomy as a representative democracy. This leads him to think of a fifth principle according to which, when the size of an isonomy grows, it systematically turns into an oligarchy or a bureaucracy. In this, he is in line with the iron law stated by Michels (2016). The isonomy is indeed dependent on the strength of the interpersonal relations which exist between its members.

3.2.8 Towards a Multicentric Society

From the scheme given by the para-economic framework and according to the characterization of the isonomic and phenonomic forms, Guerreiro Ramos comes to formulate the possibility of a multicentric society and one that he calls for. For Guerreiro Ramos, the proposal of a para-economic paradigm is above all a response to the emergence of the postindustrial society and its needs. The multicentric society that he associates with this paradigm implies the redefinition of the notion and role of the state. The latter must be able to distinguish in its actions what is market-based and what is not. This requires the implementation of specific allocation policies that support "social environments that are conducive to personal development, convivial relationships and the activities of citizen groups" (Guerreiro Ramos, 1981, p. 152). Guerreiro Ramos proposes to guide this public action by what he presents as a new law of organizations and refers to as the "law of necessary adequacy" (Ibid, p. 135). This law poses the principle that any society responsible for the development of its members must preserve the variety of these social systems and guarantee the independence of their specific forms of organization.

He states that no society has ever been in the same situation as ours. He warns that our "socialization process is subject to a cognitive politics exercised by large private interests beyond any control" (Ibid, p. 163). For Guerreiro Ramos, the implementation of a "multicentric society" (França Filho & de Freitas Boullosa, 2015) therefore assumes a resistance in relation to the hegemony of a market society that has invaded the living space of individuals. For him, as for Polanyi, it is not a matter of suppressing the market but of relativizing it. To do this, he needs to return to the usual categories that the market has the effect of reducing to functional visions. According to him, this is the case for technology, size, cognition, space, and time. The multicentric society indeed implies revisiting these usual notions (França Filho & de Freitas Boullosa, 2015, p. 209).

Technology plays a determining role in human societies. It is therefore particularly important to understand its logic. It is particularly important to be able to harmonize technological development with the balance of our social systems. This observation is in line with work on social innovation, which denounces the hold on our societies of technological innovations and the market that carries them (Klein et al., 2014). Guerreiro Ramos seeks to understand how technological development can free itself from market purposes to serve "local populations whose precise intention is not to respond to market demands" (França Filho & de Freitas Boullosa, 2015, p. 211). We cannot fail to make the connection here with free software and in particular the FLOK (Free, Libre, Open Knowledge) experiment in Ecuador. This was initiated in 2011 by a group of Spanish activists in collaboration with an Ecuadorian government minister. The idea was to deploy the free digital culture in a citizen and democratic framework with the minimum of natural resources. FLOK is the first project to have had such an ambition on the scale of an entire country. During the project, local communities exchanged with the hacker groups to develop a common culture and knowledge.

For Guerreiro Ramos, size refers to the number of people needed to implement a social scenario. For him, increasing the size is not a prerequisite. Finding the right size depends on the social system to be considered and its ambitions. However, he notes that the market (as well as the state) tends to favor the scale effect in favor of size growth, while isonomies are forced to maintain a small size in order not to disappear.

Cognition is important for Guerreiro Ramos in that it refers to the link that he considers crucial between the diversity of knowledge and that of social systems. The prevalence of cognitive schemes stemming from market logics impoverishes individuals and weakens their capacity to unleash their own creativity (in phenonomies) or to cooperate on an equal level (in isonomies). In order to break down hierarchies, which are also hierarchies of knowledge, Guerreiro Ramos' approach is similar to that of the popular education approaches developed in South America in the twentieth century (Freire, 1994).

The space was transformed for Guerreiro Ramos by the logics of market. For him, the proof of this is the urban development that was realized according to the needs of the market. Guerreiro Ramos underlines the link between the space thus transformed and the people's perception of it. He notes that space can help us, or hinder us, to release our tensions and also create stress in us (Guerreiro Ramos, 1981). Guerreiro Ramos believes that specific spatial requirements are inherent in each type of social environment. For him, the proper use of space in each of the social systems is a tool for better psychological balance. Thus, concerns such as "solitude, privacy, reserve, intimacy, anonymity and personal territory" (Ibid, p. 145) can be managed through a proper consideration of space. Guerreiro Ramos believes in the contribution of anthropologists and psychologists in order to realize sociopetal spaces, that is to say, spaces that are able to place society and the social at the heart of the organization. By definition, isonomies and phenonomies are sociopetal spaces. As such, they have the power to "resocialize anomic individuals" (Ibid, p. 146). In contrast, most market enterprises are sociofugal spaces that reject the social dimension and place it outside the organizational field.

Time is invoked by Guerreiro Ramos as a factor to be privileged in order to guarantee the possibility of a multicentric society. He mobilizes the theory of the multiplicity of social times put forward by Gurvitch (1968) to relativize sequential time as the only reference of the market and to find the times linked to the individual, that is to say those that favor personal creativity, those that are not quantifiable. The time of conviviality, for example, is cathartic and favors trust and sincere expression. Because it favors interpersonal relationships, isonomy goes hand in hand with conviviality. The experience of time is not reduced to a quantitative measure. Guerreiro Ramos thus refuses "the one-dimensionality of time that victimizes most people living in a market system" (Guerreiro Ramos, 1981, p. 150) with the increase of stress and psychic alteration. He proposes "para-economic policies" to reverse the current primacy and make market time align with social temporality.

3.2.9 Toward a New Science of Organizations

Guerreiro Ramos' urgency to found a new science of organizations stems from the realization that our world is sensitive to negative externalities, whether environmental or psychological, produced by unregulated market activities. According to him, the obsession with employment as the only criterion for assessing economic health is a fundamental error made by governments and their economists. For him, the economy is not only market activity. It is also made up of all the nonmarket activities that contribute to the quality of life and help improve it. In this para-economic field, “resources are infinite and production has no limit” (Ibid, p. 156). Nourished by reciprocity, examples of these para-economic productions can be found in the activities of associations, communities, and families. These activities generally seek to respond to needs that are not met (or are only partially met) by the state and the market. Some needs may also be voluntarily (or involuntarily) forgotten. The contribution of these activities is above all approached within the framework of a contribution on the scale of the whole of society. Guerreiro Ramos shows that a classic accounting evaluation is not relevant because it cannot account for all the value produced. In this respect, it is preferable to free oneself from the logic of the market, and he believes that for these activities, a subsidy is the required and appropriate mode of financing.

Hence, Guerreiro Ramos proposes a multidimensional model for the analysis and design of social systems, in which the market is seen as “a social enclave, legitimate and necessary, yet limited and controlled” (Ibid, p. 158). Indeed, the market can only mask and overwhelm the multiple dimensions of personal life and the variety of social interactions. For Guerreiro Ramos, it seems difficult to reconcile personal fulfillment and utilitarianism in the formal economic sense. If we want to guarantee both at the same time (because we consider them as imperatives of social life), then we have to define enclaves, where everyone can function in a satisfactory way. Guerreiro Ramos thinks of the construction of social systems as a multidimensional science and advances the idea that “living in accordance with the para-economic paradigm is a multidimensional art” (Ibid, p. 123).

He deduces a multidimensional framework for decision-making in which the market logic has no relevance outside its own perimeter. To avoid it overflowing, it is necessary to control its confinement. Guerreiro Ramos thus intends to preserve the possibility of a human blooming which, for him, is inversely proportional to the time spent in the universe of the consumption of goods. In the productive activities that encourage citizen engagement and collective feeling, Guerreiro Ramos sees the true vectors of the quality of life of a nation. Therefore, the challenge of human development is to ensure that these activities and the organizational forms that promote them have the necessary conditions for their existence, sustainability, and autonomy. To define such public policies, it is important to preserve the diversity of decision-making frameworks and associated rationalities. Thus, it is clear to Guerreiro Ramos that the formal logic of the market has no validity for judging or evaluating nonmarket activities. It is even counterproductive. Defending a multicentric society, therefore, means defending a multidimensional model that legitimizes substantive approaches and rationality. In this respect, the boundaries must be watertight between what he calls enclaves. For example, an association cannot be judged on the basis of profitability or productivity, nor should it be required to be financially independent. Clearly, the development of the market must be politically regulated so as not to undermine the basis of isonomic and phenonomic enclaves.

3.3 Organizing Solidarity Through the Search for Pluralism

The symbolic interaction that Guerreiro Ramos promotes assumes that social reality is made intelligible through experiences freed from the constraints and logics of the market. The latter in fact block authentic exchanges and proximity between people by maintaining an artificiality in social relations. These experiences outside the market are all the more necessary as each individual "participates in the making of the social reality" (Ibid, p. 111). By bringing to light isonomies and phenonomies, the substantive approach to organizations that he proposes thus engages in a desire to preserve pluralism.

Guerreiro Ramos' critique of modern reason is not intended to be abrupt. Guerreiro Ramos does not reject reason as a whole. For him, it remains the basic concept of any science of society and organizations. However, he intends to widen its framework of analysis to extend it to personal and social life. His ambition is in fact to open the way to the development of a new science of organizations in order to overcome a functional rationality (at the service of Western populations) which seeks to dominate nature and to increase production capacities. In this, he denounces both Western-centrism and the reductionism of utilitarian thinking, in order to promote awareness and open up the new intellectual perspectives that he calls for.

For Guerreiro Ramos, substantive rationality is at the heart of the human psyche. He therefore proposes that this psyche be considered as the reference in the organization of social life. His approach is a "preliminary statement to the new science of organizations." However, he is aware that "much remains to be done to transform the new science into a tool for social reconstruction" (Ibid, p. 169). As a Brazilian author, Guerreiro Ramos denounces the Western-centricity of organizational theory and social sciences in general. He points out that these sciences do not like to recognize the intrinsic viability of non-Western societies and tend to consider the Westernization of these societies as a guarantee of quality. He further notes that the process of institutionalizing "a multicentric society is underway, in a disorderly way and in multiple forms" (Ibid, p. 155). However, it needs to be sustained. For Guerreiro Ramos, "only a global organizational revolution will be able to stop the destruction of the planet and change the conditions of life" (Ibid, p. 164).

We have seen in this chapter the importance of the Polanyian grid for thinking about an economy compatible with the organization of solidarity. The framework offered by the substantive economy allows us to link two fields that the orthodox vision of the market economy has continually separated: the political and the economic. It also allows us to relativize the importance of the market by bringing to light what it invisibilizes or combats: redistribution, reciprocity, and domestic sharing. Guerreiro Ramos shares with Polanyi the need for a substantive approach. He confirms both the Polanyian observation of the historical exceptionality of market domination and the need to eliminate the negative externalities it produces. For both authors, the observation is serious, and the substantive approach is necessary to consider a return to the sustainability of our economic models. The interest of Ramos' thought is that, beyond the common observation, it extends the Polanyian approach into the organizational field.

3.3.1 The Convergence of the Conceptual Frameworks of Polanyi and Guerreiro Ramos

Thus, added to/in conjunction with the Polanyian intuition of an economy not based on scarcity, Guerreiro Ramos creates a substantive rationality that he seeks in Weber. This rationality in value allows him to make the link with Polanyi's substantive economy and to focus the analysis on the specificity of the decision-making modes of nonmarket organizations. With his concept of para-economy, he identifies three organizational forms outside the market enclave. These are isonomy, which favors equality in a community approach; phenonomy, which favors individual or collective creation; and anomie, which affects individuals who have been excluded from the market and who require care and support in dedicated organizations. With these three organizational forms, Guerreiro Ramos provides the conditions for the emancipation of individuals from the market and opening the path toward the diversity of a multicentric society. The pluralism that his theoretical proposal allows is particularly relevant when considering the demarketing of what Polanyi calls fictitious goods: work, money, nature. While for Guerreiro Ramos the market reduces work to employment, the enclaves of the para-economy (isonomy and phenonomy) reverse the proposition. They replace employment under sufferance by chosen work and give the actors back their autonomy. Similarly, economic activity within para-economy organizations does not aim to be valued and exchanged on the market. It does not imply the use of classical money. Because they are animated and guided by a substantive rationality, these enclaves of the para-economy protect nature. However, these enclaves are fragile. For lack of means, phenonomies sometimes take refuge in the domestic universe of families. As for the isonomies, they are often obliged to rely solely on voluntary work. From then on, the role of the state and of redistribution policies is of major importance. According to Guerreiro Ramos, the state must adopt a pluralist vision with regard to the different enclaves of the para-economy. It must not give in to the temptation to judge them according to market criteria. This is probably the greatest danger that Guerreiro Ramos points out and one of his greatest theoretical contributions.

Polanyi and Guerreiro Ramos share the idea that time and space (as understood in the formal logic of the market) cannot account for all the richness of human creation. They therefore both argue for a different approach to these questions. Polanyi shows that the market thinks of exchange in the present in a way that dissolves the social and condemns the long-term of socialization. For Guerreiro Ramos, time should not be thought in a linear mode. The organizations of the para-economy work in the time of conviviality and authentic exchange. As such, time cannot be reduced to a simple quantitative measure.

3.3.2 The Research Perspectives Offered by This Convergence

As we have just seen, the two authors complement each other in terms of their theoretical contributions in order to outline the contours of a pluralist society in which the market would be sufficiently controlled to be potentially thought of as an enclave among others. According to Guerreiro Ramos, it is a matter of protecting the enclaves outside the market from the pressure of the latter. Otherwise successful cooperatives can be emptied of their most dynamic cooperators by the financial attraction of the market. They may be tempted to resign or sell. By being too close to the market, the self-managed organization will be "undermined from within by the ambition of the most dynamic or greedy and by the inertia of the others" (Coutrot, 2002).

The central issue of both authors is to oppose a mortifying ideological process that consists in reducing the economy to the market and society to the market society. By showing the impact of this reductionism on the human psyche, Polanyi and Guerreiro Ramos highlight the violence at work in formal organizations. The strength of the two authors is found in the persistent topicality of their conceptual proposals. Indeed, one cannot fail to make the connection between isonomies and associations or solidarity economy organizations and between phenonomies and makers' movements (Lallement, 2015), professional amateurs (Callon et al.,

2001), or liberated enterprises (Gilbert et al., 2017). At the center on the axis linking isonomies and phenonomies, we can find the actors of what Stiegler (2010) calls the contribution economy, namely the free software movements and more generally the commons as we will see later. Finally, we can see an extension of Guerreiro Ramos' reflection on time in the work on slow management (Vitari, 2013).

References

Birchfield, V. (2014). La contestation de l'idéologie de marché : articuler Polanyi et Gramsci. In I. Hillenkamp & J. L. Laville (Eds.), *Socioéconomie et Démocracie : L'actualité de Karl Polanyi* (pp. 65–88). Eres Editions.

Burawoy, M. (2013). La sociologie publique face au marché. In I. Hillenkamp & J. L. Laville (Eds.), *Socioeconomie et démocracie : L'actualité de Karl Polanyi*. Eres.

Caillé, A. (2005). *Dé-penser l'économique : contre le fatalisme*. La découverte, Mauss. 307 pages.

Callon, M., Lascoumes, P., & Barthe, Y. (2001). *Agir dans un monde incertain : essai sur la démocratie technique*. Editions Seuil.

Coutrot, T. (2002). *Critique de l'organisation du travail*. La Découverte.

França Filho, G. C., & de Freitas Boullosa, R. (2015). Gouvernance démocratique, social management et para-économie. In Eynaud (Ed.), *La gouvernance entre diversité et normalisation* (pp. 205–215).

Freire, P. (1994). *Pedagogia do oprimido*. Paz e Terra.

Gilbert, P., Teglborg, A. C., & Raulet-Croset, N. (2017). L'entreprise libérée, innovation radicale ou simple avatar du management participatif? *Annales des Mines - Gérer et comprendre, 127*, 38–49.

Granovetter, M. (2000). *Le marché autrement, Sociologie économique*. Desclée de Brouwer. 239 pages.

Guerreiro Ramos, A. (1981). *The new science of organizations: A reconceptualization of the wealth of nations*. University of Toronto Press. 210 pages.

Gurvitch G. (1968). La multiplicité des temps sociaux. In Sorbonne, *dans La vocation actuelle de la sociologie* (pp. 325–430). Paris, Puf.

Hart, K., Laville, J. L., & Cattani, A. (2010). *The human economy: A citizen's guide*. Polity Press.

Hillenkamp, I., & Laville, J. L. (2014). *Socio-économie et démocracie: L'actualité de Karl Polanyi*. Eres Editions.

Horkheimer, M. (1947). *Eclipse of reason*. Oxford University Press.
Klein, J. L., Laville, J. L., & Moulaert, F. (2014). *Innovation sociale*. Eres Edition. 246 pages.
Lallement, M. (2015). *L'âge du faire. Hacking, travail, anarchie*. Editions Le Seuil. 448 pages.
Luhmann, N. (2018). *Organization and decision*. Cambridge University Press. 418 pages.
Marx, K. (1992). *Capital: Volume 1: A critique of political economy*. Penguin Classics. reprint, 1152 pages.
Maucourant, G. (2005). *Avez-vous lu Polanyi ?* Champs Essais. 262 pages.
Menger, C. (2002). In O. Meuwly (Ed.), *Grandsätze der Volkwirtschaftslehre*. Liberté et société. Original edition 1923. 264 pages.
Michels, R. (2016). *Political parties: A sociological study of the oligarchial tendencies of modern democracy*. Martino Fine Books. 380 pages.
Polanyi, K. (1977). In H. W. Pearson (Ed.), *The livelihood of man*. Academic Press.
Polanyi, K. (1983). *The great transformation, the political and economic origins of our time*. Gallimard. (original ed. 1944).
Polanyi, K. (1986, June). La fallace économiste. *Le Bulletin du Mauss, 18*. translation in French of an extract from "The Livelihood of Man".
Postel, N., & Sobel, R. (2010). Le concept de marchandise fictive, pierre angulaire de l'institutionnalisme de Karl Polanyi ? *Revue de philosophie économique, 2*, 3–35.
Simon, H. (1955). A behavioral model of rational choice. *The Quarterly Journal of Economics, 69*, 129–138.
Smith, A. (2013). *The wealth of nations*. CreateSpace Independent Publishing Platform. 426 pages.
Stiegler, B. (2010). *Economie de l'incurie et économie de la contribution*. Editions Galilée.
Supiot, A. (2012). *The spirit of Philadelphia: Social justice vs. the total market* (1st ed.). Verso. 160 pages.
Viard, B., & Vaillancourt, Y. (2000). *Pierre Leroux : socialiste associatif, Actualités de 1848*. Thierry Quinqueton Editeur.
Vitari, C. (2013). *Slow management: Undertaking the transition*. Pearson.
Weber, M. (2019). *Economy and society: A new translation*. Harvard University Press. 520 pages.

4

(Re)Solidarizing Organizations

We saw in the previous chapter that the organization of solidarity was possible by denouncing the economist fallacy and adopting a framework of reference extended to the substantive economy. From then on, the logics essential for solidarity as reciprocity, redistribution, and domestic sharing are made visible in the economic field. We have also seen that this change of framework leads to questions around rationality in value and the need to pay attention to the question of fictitious goods and their reintegration. With these lessons in mind, we can now ask ourselves what conditions are required to (re)solidarize organizations. To do this, we will analyze the different forms of democratic governance likely to activate such processes at the heart of organizations. We will then show that this (re)solidarization of organizations favors the possibility of a reconciliation between the economic and the social. We will conclude this chapter with examples of reconciliation resulting from the organizational reintegration of fictitious goods and the social innovation that ensues.

P. Eynaud, G. Carvalho de França Filho, *Solidarity and Organization*,
https://doi.org/10.1007/978-3-031-27568-5_4

4.1 Through the Search for Democratic Governance

(Re)solidarizing organizations cannot be decreed. Solidarity cannot be introduced into organizations simply by using particular management techniques or instruments (even if these cannot be neglected). Solidarity cannot be understood from a functionalist perspective because it presupposes an intersubjectivity in action. As Tocqueville points out, feelings and ideas are only renewed, the heart is only enlarged, and the human mind is only developed by the reciprocal action of men on one another (Tocqueville, 2002). Association is at the heart of the reciprocity evoked by Tocqueville and of the solidarity it expresses. It is situated at an intermediate level between primary and secondary socialities (Tönnies, 2021). It translates this possible link between the interests of each person and the common space of citizenship. By this particular positioning, the associative fact is inseparable from democracy (Laville, 2018, 2023). In this respect, the association constitutes a model for solidarity-based organization. Indeed, if we consider the solidarity economy as the project to democratize the economy (Laville & Salmon, 2016), solidarity management is defined analogously as the project to democratize management. Consequently, the relevant perspective for considering the strengthening of solidarity in organizations is that of democratic governance (Laville et al., 2015).

4.1.1 The Governance of Nonprofit Organizations and Associations

The associative initiative builds in a double movement of internalization and externalization. The nonprofit organizations and associations internalize societal issues and externalize its action with the aim of social transformation (Bucolo et al., 2015). This particular positioning induces "an associative dynamic deliberately inscribed in public action" (Ibid.) and places associations in a relationship of cooperation and confrontation with public authorities and their institutional coherence is strengthened. If we define governance as the alignment of the organization and its management with the association's project (Laville & Hoarau, 2013), then governance is the condition for this institutional coherence. Any intervention in public action presupposes an updating and exchange of information on the association's project and a critical analysis of the organization. This analysis is often difficult to carry out because it can be guided by external rationalization constraints. These, by their considerable significance, can weaken the legitimacy of the field, patiently built up over the long term.

The pressure from funders can be strong in encouraging the adoption of "good practices," that is, the standardization of associative practices. There is therefore a danger that associative governance will gradually be transformed under their pressure into a model similar to that of companies. As a reminder, corporate governance is a response to the asymmetry of information between managers and shareholders and to the need expressed by liberal theorists to reestablish checks and balances in favor of shareholders. According to orthodox economics, there is indeed an asymmetry of information between the manager who is an employee (present in the company on a daily basis) and the shareholder (present once a year at the general meeting). According to Chandler, the emergence of the concept of governance thus translates into the passage from the entrepreneurial company to the managerial company (Chandler, 1992). Through its culture of numbers, the managerial company authorizes the control of actions that have already been executed. It is interesting to note that corporate governance translates *de facto* into a minimal form of transparency. From then on, we can say with Perez that governance is born with the management of management (Pérez, 2009), that is, with the control of the manager by another manager (himself working on behalf of the shareholders): the auditor. Governance then becomes a market in itself for firms specializing in auditing who push for managerial professionalization, which is the condition of their activity, and punish the producer when he goes beyond good practices. But what can an audit of an association mean under these conditions? How can qualitative elements relating to the social purpose and solidarity be translated into figures? How can we prevent governance from functioning for the benefit of the strongest actor (often the financier in the case of an association) and endangering the collective project? What does the concept of performance mean in relation to an association? We agree with Naro's observation that it is essential to deconstruct management concepts from the commercial world. This work must be carried out in distinct ways, in each of the specific contexts in which it is to be deployed, if we want to "give meaning to the words of management in order to cure the ills of society" (Naro, 2015, p. 175).

It is therefore clear that the challenge of associative governance is to prevent the risk of such a normative confinement. The danger is that the associative project will be reduced to organizational constraints from the market (Eynaud, 2015). Faced with these challenges, the search for democratic governance is a means of preserving the inventiveness of the collective and its capacity to be a vector of social innovation. Democratic governance must explore alternative models based on the needs of a substantive economy. It is therefore possible to reflect on governance bodies other than the board of directors, the executive committee, or the committees. It opens up the possibility of new modes of organization (Laloux, 2014) such as sociocracy and holacracy. According to a term used by Comte, sociocracy designates a self-organized mode, without centralized power and with distributed decision-making modalities (Endenburg, 1988). Holacracy, on the other hand, can be approached as a form of sociocracy that functions in a/as a circle with a fractal mode of organization.

In this context extended to the field of the substantive economy, democratic governance can be a vector of emancipation if it translates into:

- Spaces for collective reflexivity and debate in order to be able to judge the coherence of the organizational choices made in relation to the associative project (Laville & Sainsaulieu, 1997);
- The co-construction of activity monitoring indicators between the various stakeholders in order to be able to collectively judge the results obtained. This requires a critical attitude toward the production of data and an awareness that can lead to the production of substantive indicators in Polanyi's sense. Such work, initiated at a global level in economics, must now be pursued at the level of organizations in order to develop a different approach to wealth (Viveret, 2004);

- Spaces of conviviality to learn to debate, to deliberate, and to manage conflicts between actors who do not share the same references nor the same interests. Thus, "conviviality, friendships, relationships with one's neighbors and sharing appear to be important assets and central values of life. However, these riches are not counted anywhere and therefore they do not count or count too little" (Renault, 2011, p. 167);
- The co-production of new rules and new tools for regulating collective action. Without this invention, there is a risk of being trapped in the arsenal of preexisting procedures and techniques and thus in an organizational isomorphism.

However, these emancipation criteria are themselves conditioned by two working perspectives that open up a set of questions. The first perspective relates to the conditions for opening up the perimeter of the actors concerned by the project and the organizational modalities of this opening up in order to organize a multi-stakeholder governance. Who are the relevant actors for the project? How can they be involved? How do we motivate them? How can we manage the growing number of actors involved and their heterogeneity? How can we produce forms of co-construction in pluralistic environments?

The second perspective concerns the difficult question of the social divide and the proposal for inclusive governance. Are there prerequisites for governance? Do we have to possess minimum competences to participate in governance? If so, what are they? How can members be trained while maintaining a diversity of views and perspectives? On the contrary, should we adapt governance structures to enhance the primary skills of the actors? How can we ensure that the question of competence is not a pretext for excluding certain actors? How can we integrate people who have little contact with public action? How can we overcome the aporias of participation practices?

4.1.2 Multi-stakeholder Governance

Ensuring the plurality of a collective appears to be an essential issue for an organization that wants to be part of public action (Laville & Salmon,

2015). Arendt noted this when she observed that the Earth is not inhabited by one man, but by men (Arendt, 1970). Plurality in the political field opens up forms of collective action that are particularly interesting because it refers to the logics of broadening and opening up the decision-making process.

Multi-stakeholder organizations are particular in that they bring together very different actors around the same project: employees, volunteers, beneficiaries, users, funders, supporters, and so forth. From a neo-institutional point of view, these organizations are able to minimize the costs related to information asymmetries. Indeed, the collaboration of all the actors concerned within the same governance bodies limits the gray areas and increases the capacity to understand and solve problems. The multiplicity of cross-views is an undeniable contribution to the quality of management, as it allows for the sharing of a great deal of information, for mutual control of actors, and for easier innovation (Borzaga & Depedri, 2009). Moreover, actors can be called upon to intervene on several levels "as consumers of public services (citizen-users), as co-deliverers, as controllers, as workers" (Bacqué et al., 2005). This accentuates their involvement and encourages a plurality of perspectives.

From a broader point of view, these organizations are of major interest in that they have a good propensity to respond to unmet needs and are able to bring together numerous resources, whether market, nonmarket, or nonmonetary (Borzaga & Depedri, 2015). They are able to produce social capital (Putnam, 1993) that can potentially be shared with the most marginalized people. The evolution of organizational forms in recent years testifies to the desire to take into account the contribution of this type of multi-stakeholder organization. The creation of cooperative societies of collective interest (SCIC) was the translation of this in France. These are legal structures designed to operate with a group of actors that are not limited to employees and beneficiaries. They include in their operation all citizens interested in the action undertaken.

However, multi-stakeholder organizations face a number of challenges. Bringing together a large number of stakeholders with different interests around a single project is not easy to manage (Valéau et al., 2018). Information sharing and communication between members is a complex process and misunderstandings can be a source of tension and can make it difficult to maintain the cohesion of the collective. The presence of users and beneficiaries in the decision-making process can lead to a drift toward consumerism (Chauvière & Godbout, 1992). The democratic sharing of decisions presupposes a formalism and procedures that may appear burdensome (or even counterproductive) for some actors.

The problem of vigilance in terms of solidarity is that of "the connection of the different circles of solidarity. This interaction/interdependency is necessary so that local solidarities do not degenerate into so many forms of categorical egoism and so that, conversely, the State does not attempt to dictate its conception of civil solidarities" (Supiot, 2015, p. 17). Indeed, solidarity always assumes a "perimeter of mutual aid that includes those it unites, but excludes or combats others" (Supiot, 2015, p. 14). An open-action solidarity therefore presupposes, as Supiot points out, the expression of collective solidarities capable of combining with an evolving vision of social justice. Indeed, the principle of solidarity is in part difficult to defend because it tends to "put the collective interest ahead of the individual interest and the interest of group members ahead of that of outsiders to the group" (Supiot, 2015, p. 15). It is true that solidarity is not the same depending on the size of the group (cf. Tonnies). The question of size hinges on the ability to maintain group cohesion. Solidarity can close the group in on itself if the social logic of the scapegoat or our propensity to victimize is allowed to operate (Girard, 1979, 1987). On the other hand, solidarity can open the group to the outside world if the general interest is taken into account. The choice between the two options can be conditioned by a possible deficit in social justice, inducing violence in organizations (Herreros, 2012).

4.1.3 Inclusive Governance

The multi-stakeholder perspective we have just mentioned is not necessarily favorable to those who have little contact with public action. Such persons may be put off by the possible complexities in the functioning of these groups. Inclusiveness implies considering solidarity as a "means of equalizing conditions" (Supiot, 2015, p. 13). It is then distinguished from charity in that it does not divide the world between "those who give without receiving and those who receive without giving anything" (Supiot, 2015, p. 12). By inviting each citizen to contribute according to their means and to receive according to their needs, solidarity is expressed in a reciprocal way with an egalitarian vocation. The problem is then to be able to "move from this somewhat natural social solidarity to an organized and effective solidarity, without losing the essence of the initial impetus" (Laborde, 2015, p. 112) in order to maintain democratic solidarity.

Therefore, the question of skills is central. It is at the heart of the issue of inclusiveness. To participate in decision-making, one must share knowledge, exchange with other members of the collective, and make choices. All this is not easy when one seeks to involve socially marginalized actors. Inclusiveness must therefore be built through patient work on empowerment, accompaniment, and mediation. We must ask ourselves, as Zask invites us to do, about the possibility of three important moments: taking part, benefiting, and contributing (Zask, 2011). Conviviality is undoubtedly a key word for enabling these different moments. Indeed, the basic principle of conviviality consists in "the affirmation of the common humanity and common sociality of all human beings" (Caillé et al., 2011, p. 21). But, it is not enough to answer the question about competence and the expertise that underlies it. The debate between Dewey and Lippman gives us the keys to the problem (Dewey, 2016). Lippmann thought the presence and mediation of the expert indispensable to making problems visible to citizens and giving them the elements of understanding. Without the expert, the problem can neither be understood nor solved. Dewey thinks that the expert is on the contrary to be banished. He is the bearer of private categorical interests that prevent him from fully serving the public interest. Moreover, Dewey refuses the observation of the citizen's incompetence, and he proposes to build and to expand the experience of each one by a collective device that he names the social investigation (Dewey, 2008). For Dewey, only an approach of radical democracy is able to answer the questions about the skills of socially marginalized people.

Such collective animation inquiry approaches can be played out in local public spaces (Gardin & Laville, 2017). The challenge is to know how to organize these devices since this implies a critical and reflexive approach to management arrangements. It is a question of being able to detect and prevent their potentially excluding effects and to favor those that proceed from a "technical democracy" in the sense of Callon et al. (2001), that is,, a dialogical democracy in which the technique is used to resolve oppositions.

The question of inclusiveness then pushes governance to reform itself and to improve its capacity to welcome and mobilize the actors concerned by the project. In particular, it is about analyzing the degree of openness of the bodies and of seeing how the actors benefiting from the action can be involved in the organization of the services intended for them. Two models of *bottom-up* action are available (Bacqué et al., 2005). The first is based on an empowerment approach for popular groups and minorities. It seeks community consensus in order to establish decision-making power. The collective has a high degree of autonomy to set rules for itself, the scope of which is at the micro-local level. In this case, the aim is not to broaden the scope of the actors but rather to improve the inclusion of the members already present. In a way, this work of inclusion is favored by a small membership. The second aspect of participatory democracy is the sharing of the decision with local public officials (Blondiaux, 2008). The procedure put in place aims to resolve the conflict by organizing a collective discussion around the general interest. The rules produced are co-decided and co-managed with the local authorities. There is a strong political dimension in this second model, and it is very close to democratic governance.

4.1.4 Democratic Governance

Democratic governance can be thought of as being at the intersection of the two perspectives we have just described in order to open up a new field of research (Steen-Johnsen et al., 2011). In a process of openness, it builds a heterogeneous and civic collective to explore all the dimensions of a project with the different actors concerned and give it meaning. This openness begins the registration of a public action process. In an inclusive approach, it raises the question of how to welcome these actors, how to recognize and value their skills, and how to involve them in

Table 4.1 Typology of governance modes

	Tightened solidarity of the members of the collective	Registered citizen solidarity in the public space
Job-focused competences	**Professional governance**	**Multi-stakeholder governance**
Competences open to the experience of the actors	**Inclusive governance**	**Democratic governance**

decision-making. Democratic governance thus intends to go beyond the close-knit solidarity that is the strength of a local collective and becomes part of a citizen's solidarity approach and broadens the field of accepted skills beyond professional competences in a convivial approach (Table 4.1).

At the intersection, it is therefore a question of simultaneously strengthening "representative democracy by developing participatory democracy (deepening) and democratizing the economic sphere (broadening)" (Dacheux & Goujon, 2016, p. 204). In the context of these different forms of governance, one can explore different ways of giving account or placing oneself in an accountability process. This term has two meanings. It refers both to the act of rendering an account and to the responsibility associated with it. It means that associations must be accountable to their funders and that this accountability commits them. Thus, communicating to a private donor the percentage of their donation that goes to the beneficiary is both useful information in itself and a public commitment. Indeed, if this percentage decreases, the association will have to explain and justify the change. Thus, Ostrower and Stone (2015) distinguished three forms of accountability (bottom-up, external, and internal). The bottom-up form corresponds to the needs of professional governance. The accounts are constructed and presented to public authorities and the donors who request them. These accounts are technical and are not intended to be discussed with the members of the association. The internal form consists of reports to employees and volunteers, and it corresponds more to inclusive governance. It is about associating more closely with the governance of those who are engaged and integrated workwise in the management of the collective. The external form is a reporting to the beneficiaries, users, networks, professional associations, and accreditation bodies, and in this case, the number of actors is large and the profiles very varied. This external form is similar to multi-stakeholder governance in the number of actors involved. The American researchers did not identify a fourth form, but we can deduce from their analysis that democratic governance combines all the forms in order to cross-reference them and put them into perspective. In democratic governance, transparency prevails, and data is shared among all members.

4.2 Networking on the Territory

If democratic governance can be used to re-solidarize organizations, its action can be completed and reinforced by the networking of solidarity actors on the area where they intervene. The democratic practices within the organizations can thus be enriched and developed by being crossed with those coming from other solidarity organizations. In other words, intraorganizational solidarity can be coupled with interorganizational solidarity. In a context of increasing commodification and competition between local actors, alliances and groupings between solidarity actors and organizations can appear to be good ways of responding to the multidimensional challenges of solidarity and of opening the way to a territorial development of solidarity that is a vector of another economy.

4.2.1 Alliances and Groupings

In France, social and solidarity economy organizations have experienced major changes in their environment over the past few decades. One of the most important is the increase in public bids and competitive calls for projects, which has had the effect of increasing competition between social economy organizations. This change has required actors to develop new skills such as project design, analytical monitoring, and indicator management (in order to enter into the evaluation processes required by funders). The size and technical nature of the projects proposed favored the larger players who were better able to respond. So, a large restructuring movement was undertaken, resulting in a large number of mergers between SSE actors (Eynaud & Gérome, 2014). The effect has been to enable SSE organizations to respond to new challenges and in particular to the new competition from market enterprises intruding on the social field, thanks to the benefits of institutional changes. The increase in the size of the actors implied a change in their management mode, which has become more professional and therefore closer to the methods used by market organizations. Professionalization, once synonymous with competence in the field of action, has evolved in its meaning to increasingly refer to the acquisition of managerial competence. In this domino effect, the smallest and financially weakest actors have been absorbed into larger structures, and their jobs were perpetuated. This has not been without consequences for the management methods of these organizations, but also for the projects, image, and legitimacy of these organizations (Marival et al., 2015). A restructuring can also result in a questioning of the psychological contract that binds the stakeholders and can provoke a feeling of injustice (Eynaud & Schmidt, 2012). Finally, it can call into question the ability to detect new needs and to innovate. We must recognize that one of the most common organizational ills, when faced with a problem, is to seek "to solve it from above through a higher-level organization" (Rey, 2014, p. 207). To combat this drift, a number of actors have sought to preserve their projects and protect themselves from the threat of mergers by cooperating and pooling their resources and means (Eynaud & Guibert, 2012).

Pooling can take many forms: sharing a building, a fixed asset, material resources, skills, practices, know-how, information, and so forth. It can be legally structured or not. Much sharing is done informally within the framework of reciprocity. Others are organized in a more structured way. Among these, the territorial pole of economic cooperation (PTCE), constituted by a group of actors (local authorities, associations, companies, research/training actors) ready to cooperate on the same territory, is a particularly interesting innovation because it aims to implement a common and continuous strategy of cooperation and mutualization in the service of innovative economic projects of sustainable local development. This innovation was born from reflections initiated during the SSE general assembly for a proposal for national valorization to be carried out in

2012 and leading to a recognition in the law on SSE in 2014 (Article 9, paragraph 1). In the charter of the PTCE, perspectives for networks are given: "Create, consolidate and develop activities, sustainable and quality jobs, for the benefit of its territory and its inhabitants; Work on the territorial anchoring of economic activities, in a space characterized by cooperation between stakeholders; Adopt a democratic governance based on principles of equity, reciprocity, on the voluntary commitment of people and involving all stakeholders; Involve in its territory citizens, actors and institutions of all sizes; Invest in social innovation and the search for social utility, in response to social or societal needs. The common values are the following: It respects, mobilizes and values its local heritage, the resources of its territory (human, natural, material, cultural, and financial) and relies on the commitment of its actors. It relies on mutual respect, recognized diversity, trust and conviviality, values in action of living together and acting together; It recognizes co-construction, training and knowledge as levers of development; It practices solidarity in action at the local and global levels; It places at the service of its development the search for social innovations; It promotes and demonstrates creativity at all stages of its evolution and the implementation of its activities; It seeks quality in exchanges in the communication and transmission of information."[1]

Behind these alliances, groupings, and their modalities, another vision and another understanding of the world are emerging. Against the widespread idea of associating "the small number with the primitive," one can argue that "the highest degree of civilization can be accommodated by modest size" (Rey, 2014, p. 87). As Guerreiros Ramos has shown with the para-economy, it is a question of preserving the fragile logics based on social links such as they are expressed in the isonomies and the phenonomies. From then on, it is not so much a question of making the apology for the small as it is of seeking in all things "the most appropriate size for the blossoming and the fecundity of existences" (Rey, 2014, p. 102).

[1] Extract from the charter of the PTCE network.

4.2.2 Solidarity-Based Territorial Development and Related Public Policies

As we have seen, democratic governance necessarily unfolds in a tense dialectic between the internal and the external. It presupposes a double dimension of sociopolitical action. On the one hand, it is a matter of impelling and maintaining locally a daily dynamic of self-organization, and, on the other hand, it is a matter of being part of a public action with a broader vocation. Democracy is strengthened by this double perspective. It makes the local dimension the fundamental place for its exercise. The territory thus appears as the ideal mediation space to link and translate the two perspectives. Consequently, the process of organizing solidarity linked to the affirmation of another economy is an exercise in territorial development. In other words, another economy (like the practices of the solidarity economy) cannot be conceived independently of the idea of territoriality. This leads us to a dual observation: (a) on the analytical level, the territory (and its development) is an inseparable element of the understanding of another economy; (b) on the practical level, another economy is a strategic element for the formulation of a renewed agenda in terms of territorial development. We will therefore develop our proposal in two stages. First, we will ask ourselves how to think about a territorial development strategy based on an economy of solidarity approach. Nevertheless, the answer to this question presupposes the consideration of another question of a more theoretical nature: How to redefine the role and the meaning of the economy in a renewed agenda of territorial development? This distinction is meant to be pedagogical, as these two elements are strongly intertwined.

Thinking Differently to Conceive a Solidarity Management of Territorial Development

In a conventional economic approach, the two questions we have just mentioned are irrelevant. Indeed, the territory has no real interest in itself. It is only approached and considered in its relation to the economy. The territory is supposed to be at the service of the company, but the latter is not linked to the territory. According to the economic principles of the self-regulating market, a company has the liberty to move around freely according to its strategic and financial interests. From this point of view, the territorial dynamic is guided by the economic activity without any real counterpart in the way the territory is managed. In other words, the territory is seen as a vector of attractiveness and an adjustment variable likely to attract the so-called productive investments. In general, the development of productive market forces guides the logic of territorial development. In this case, exogenous principles prevail over endogenous principles. By emphasizing the attractiveness of the territory, capital and foreign investment become the main drivers of territorial development. Three combined effects appear as common consequences of the development of the market logic in territories: (a) Accentuation of inequalities in the medium and long term, even if in the short term there is a certain degree of redistributive economic effect in the supply chain; (b) Dependence of local or territorial economies on productive activity that originates in investment; and (c) Risks of disinvestment due to the freedom given to companies. Disinvestment is generally followed by a significant social and environmental impact. These observations reveal the inability of traditional means to respond in the long term to the needs of territorial development. In such a context, it is imperative to look for alternatives.

If this search for alternatives is conducive to a shift in the relationship between the economy and the territory and to a re-embedding of the economy in the territory, the questions relating to territorial development strategies cannot move forward without a fundamental questioning of the economy. However, there is a general lack of critical reflection on the nature of the economy in relation to territorial development. Two reasons can be given to explain this absence:

(a) Marxist-inspired thought criticizes the market economy head-on on a national level but does not envisage any particular alternative at the level of smaller geographical divisions. Its analysis scheme remains global, and it remains trapped in a market rationality which it needs to deploy in the end;

(b) Economic anthropology studies are still insufficiently known or used in studies on territorial development. Without them, it is difficult to get to the heart of the reflection on the profound nature of the economy.

How to Redefine the Role and Meaning of the Economy in Territorial Management?

The redefinition of the meaning of the economy by changing the way we look at it is part of a tradition in economic anthropology studies. It is a matter of reversing the perspective of territorial development studies, of understanding how the economy is dependent on the territory, and of thinking about a redefinition of the relation between economy and territory. This means changing the register. It is not a matter of considering the economy as an end in itself but as a means to achieve other objectives. The economic anthropology developed by Polanyi is particularly relevant in this respect. Polanyi distinguishes the formal economy from the substantive economy, where the formal economy makes a logical link between means and ends and poses the principle of scarcity as a prerequisite. Thus, it can be thought of through the so-called maximizing behavior on the part of actors guided by a rational choice. In contrast, substantive economics escapes the abstract vision of market logic. It questions in a pragmatic way the deep dependence of man on nature and on other men. It is interested in the subsistence economy and the means necessary to cover natural needs. For this, Polanyi makes a detour through economic history. Over the long term, he shows the plurality of forms of economic activity, the diversity of modes of regulation, and their evolution. His analysis brings out principles that the market tends to make invisible (such as redistribution, reciprocity, and domestic sharing).

The strength of the substantive economic approach is that it brings out the question of reproduction. While the market economy remains focused on production, the anthropological view broadens our vision of the world. It allows us to reflect on the means by which societies construct the reproduction of their material conditions of existence and of social life. According to Weber, economic action can be considered as a type of social action. From then on, economic analysis cannot avoid the question of the reproduction of social life. Here, the approach is not abstract. It is constructed historically in relation to a given territory. In practice, it is a matter of understanding how the economy builds its relations with the social, cultural, political, and environmental spheres locally. Several lessons can be drawn from this. First, the broader understanding of the economy made possible by economic anthropology opens the way to the exploration of another economy. Second, the vision of the economy is transformed by its inclusion in the spheres of life in society. Then, the institutional dimension and the local dimension direct the studies on territorial development toward the solidarity approach. Finally, the other economy that the anthropological viewpoint outlines includes a diversity of interacting forms of economy that can be approached through the notion of plural economy.

Territorial Management and Plural Economy

The notion of a plural economy contains two ideas. First, it is intrinsically suited to the possibility of a social and ecological transition because of the pluralism it presupposes. Secondly, it aims to guarantee a balance between the different components that make it up. In particular, the hegemonic character of the market dimension must be contained in order to leave space for the other components. The verb "to contain" itself refers to two ideas. If the plural economy is to contain the logic of the market, it is necessary to be able to define this content precisely, that is, a perimeter within which the market is possible. It is then necessary to reflect on the means of preventing a possible predatory extension in order to contain possible negative externalities. The two meanings of the verb "to contain" thus participate in a horizon of socioeconomic regulation. This is where democratic governance can play its role in regulating economic activity, promoting cooperation, and encouraging nonmarket economic logics. The enrichment of democracy on the territory is the condition of this regulation.

A renewed territorial development strategy (based on a different economy) requires an agenda that is itself part of a public policy. For this to happen, a reflection on regulation must be undertaken with the local public authorities. The first step is to reanalyze the mediation or negotiation relationship with external actors and investors. Possible external contributions must be filtered according to criteria that favor the whole of local society. Regulation is then envisaged as a system of protection capable of blocking the negative externalities of future investments. It is also a question of opening up a time for institutional reconstruction, that is, for the endogenous dimension of analysis, design, and territorial action. These two stages of conception/action allow us to propose a draft public policy for territorial development based on the idea of a plural economy.

Draft Policy of Solidarity Management of the Territories

The main lines of such a policy are outlined according to two strategic levels (institutional regulation and institutional reconstruction) and four lines of intervention. The first three represent the principles of public action in institutional reconstruction: (1) the re-signified market principle, (2) the redistributive principle, and (3) the reciprocal principle. The fourth axis concerns the relationship with external investors and expresses a modality of institutional regulation. These four areas of intervention should not be conceived as isolated practices. Their distinction brings out the specific nature of each economic principle in an analytical manner, but their complementarity should be emphasized and enhanced in practice. The translation of the concept of plural economy allows us not only to model specific forms of economic actions but also to invent forms of action combining (or merging) the diversity of economic principles. The implementation of these axes does not obey any particular order a priori, nor any hierarchy. The greater or lesser importance given to each of them is defined by the demand and the characteristics of the local context (Table 4.2).

The first line of action consists in revaluing the market principle in the sense of re-signifying these practices. To do this, it is necessary to introduce mechanisms of cooperation and solidarity between economic agents in local production activities, service provision, marketing, consumption, and financial services. This axis emphasizes the need to support the

Table 4.2 The lines of development of a territorial solidarity management

Areas of institutional reconstruction	1. Re-signed contract 2. Redistribution 3. Reciprocity
Institutional regulation area	4. Search for solidarity investors

creation and/or consolidation of social and solidarity economy organizations. It leads public policies to support cooperatives, associations, foundations, and social and solidarity enterprises in their actions. The vocation of these public policies must be broad and should include private for-profit agents that adopt economic models that are favorable to sharing and better distribution of wealth. Their objective is to support the actors who innovate by re-signifying market activities. The examples are numerous and particularly promising. We can mention fair trade, which was one of the first to innovate in this sense. Fair trade organizations place themselves in the market space to modify the rules from within. With fair trade products, they break the free play of markets to invent a framework at the source of market exchanges according to social and ecological rules. Thus, fair trade works with small producers to whom it guarantees a fixed price on which they can reasonably plan their domestic economy. The purchase price is thus removed by self-produced rules from the mechanisms of free market fixing. Another example can be found in the short circuits through the associations that maintain small local agriculture (AMAP). These associations bring together family farms with groups of consumers in their neighborhood. It is a question of agreeing on the sale of the production under reasonable conditions for the producer, who can then better plan their activity and escape the dictates imposed by the distributors. It also authorizes exchanges of free services between consumers and producers. Finally, we can point out other examples such as solidarity-based finance, local currencies, and also community banks which participate in the development of financial activities organized under the democratic control of local collectives. The common ambition of all these very diverse initiatives is to re-embed fictitious goods and to re-signify the market according to principles of citizen solidarity.

The second line of action concerns the best use of the transformative potential of the redistributive principle through its capacity to generate a nonmarket economy logic. At this level, public policies take on the task of financing activities that have a strong potential for transfer, reallocation, or social impact. These are activities that cannot generate all the resources they need but that have a strong socializing power. They contribute to fostering social ties, increasing the level of knowledge and training of people well removed from public action, and facilitating the necessary work of recognition and identity of marginalized groups and individuals. The public policy effort is therefore situated in the blind spot of market activities and of classic analyses of territorial development. This type of public support is part of a long-term strategy to rehabilitate the territory, even in its most remote areas, and to support the population, including those who are the most difficult to access. The priority activities in this type of public policy are social welfare, sports, art, and culture.

The third level of action refers to the reciprocal principle, including a logic of a nonmonetary economy and opening up a space for a disinterested monetary circulation following the example of various forms of mutualization of financial resources. The challenge for public policy is to find out how to help structure productive activities that escape monetary circulation or else through mechanisms of democratic appropriation of financial resources. These are activities that involve selfless giving, mutual aid, pooling of resources, and volunteering. They are mostly self-organized collective actions that allow for social innovation by solving everyday problems. These actions can be classical activities such as LETS (free or local exchange system) or forms linked to new digital tools. New technologies can thus help develop creative solutions in terms of reciprocity. In this field, we can mention cooperative platforms and sharing applications (such as carpooling and house sharing). These initiatives help to strengthen social ties and enrich individual life through the discovery/acquaintance of other people.

The fourth line of action concerns negotiations with potential external investors. Public actors are called upon to review the elements for appreciating and measuring expected contributions linked to external investments as part of a strategy to establish territories of solidarity. It is important to consider not only the positive points linked to the arrival of new capital but also all the possible negative counterparts on the social, cultural, or environmental level. Such a policy is by nature preventive and aims at zero negative externalities. It favors investors who come to settle in the area in a sustainable way and who commit themselves accordingly. It favors local reinvestment solutions with redistribution objectives. The intention in this case may be to align the demands on external investors along the lines of the previously mentioned other levels in order to reinforce them. Actors such as "*Terres de Liens,*"[2] which propose to buy up local farms in order to keep small farmers on the land and avoid real estate speculation, or "*Habitat et Humanisme,*" a recognized[3] player in social project management, are part of this fourth axis.

It appears that the work of re-solidarization of organizations can largely benefit from the public policy strategies that we have just mentioned. Combined, they allow us to envisage completely original and creative policies for the solidarity-based development of territories (Eynaud, 2018). In connection with the plural economy approaches, they have medium- and long-term effects that are cumulative and reinforcing. In this respect, it is particularly interesting to exploit the experience accumulated in the many countries that practice solidarity-based public policies.

4.3 By Reconciling the Economic and the Social

In this chapter, we have discussed the way in which the (re)solidarization of organizations defines the contours of substantive management. We have seen that a first important characteristic of this substantive management is the search for democratic governance. A second characteristic lies in the wish to include management in a territorial development dynamic. We will now explore a third characteristic through

[2] *Terre de Liens* is an associative network started in 2003, associated with an SSE company and a foundation. This network is at the junction of several fields such as popular education, organic and biodynamic agriculture, ethical finance, solidarity economy, and rural development. The network mobilizes for the preservation of arable land and access to land for young farmers. https://terredeliens.org/.

[3] *Habitat et Humanisme* is a social project management organization that builds, purchases, and renovates housing for people in difficulty. https://www.habitat-humanisme.org.

processes of re-solidarization aimed at reconciling the economic and the social. This reconciliation denotes the complex character of contemporary organizational and/or managerial practices which (for some of them) are no longer limited to a single purpose but seek to combine the economic and the social. What then is a reconciliation between the economic and the social? How can it be defined? With what analytical framework can it be analyzed? What are the challenges to be met in order to move toward reconciliation?

4.3.1 Reconciling the Economic and the Social: A Polanyian Interpretation

The field of economic sociology has always emphasized the interweaving of the economic and the social. Granovetter has shown that the behavior of economic agents—and therefore their rationality—cannot be understood independently of the social structure of these same actors (Granovetter, 2007). This author inaugurates a fresh look at the dynamics of markets (Granovetter, 2000), opening up the theme of networks in the sociological analysis of market organizations. His analysis highlights the way in which social aspects influence the economic behavior of market actors. However, it does not focus on the link between economic and social objectives in organizational dynamics. The analytical effort required in this sense requires going beyond an economic sociology of markets (Lévesque, 2009; Swedberg, 2009). More recently, a number of works have sought to analyze the relationship between economic and social dynamics within organizations whose ambition is not reduced to the market. Among these references, we should first recall the seminal text by Laville and Sainsaulieu (1997) proposing a sociology of the association. From this work, reflections could be extended to the politics of the association (Laville, 2010), its management (Bernet et al., 2016), and its governance (Eynaud, 2015; Laville & Hoarau, 2013). A more precise understanding of the relationship between the economic and the social can be greatly informed by the Polanyian perspective. Beyond the sociology of markets and the sociology of the associative fact, it proposes an anthropology of the economic fact in life in society (Polanyi, 1986;

Polanyi, 1977). For Polanyi, economic analysis questions the meaning of action and its institutionalization in society. He thus proposes an expanded vision of economic interactions that goes beyond the strict perimeter of the activity of market organizations. Economic anthropology and in particular the Polanyian perspective, as we showed in the third chapter, offer us a variety of economic logics such as market, redistribution, reciprocity, and domestic sharing (Hillenkamp, 2013). The Polanyian approach feeds into three analytical perspectives: (a) the first is to recognize the diversity of rationalities of economic behavior and understand their specificities, (b) the second involves understanding how these different rationalities can be linked and how they interact under different forms of organizations or institutional systems, and (c) the third focuses on how each of these rationalities can be re-signified through these interactions.

From the Polanyian analysis on the institutional forms of the economic (Polanyi, 1986), we can deduce that the inseparability between the economic and the social has been the rule historically. Before the development of self-regulating markets, premodern societies did not dissociate the economy from social life (Polanyi, 1977). Two phenomena made this dissociation possible. First, the great transformation that Polanyi speaks of was the disembedding of the market from social life. Second, it has been a long ideological undertaking to reduce the economy to the market economy (Polanyi, 1986). By dissociating life in society from the economic, the social has become a category of the organization of society. From then on, the social is strongly exposed to the rules and rationality of the principles of self-regulating markets. As Polanyi tells us, the advent of modernity coincides with the autonomization of the economic sphere of the market and its separation from other spheres of social life. However, Polanyi also tells us that this movement is not irreversible and that there is a constant dialectical tension between two opposite and opposing movements: embedding and disembedding. This dialectic allows us to distinguish between the idea of a conciliation (defined as an attempt to juxtapose the economic and the social) and a reconciliation (conceived as a dynamic interaction between the two terms). It is this line of work/research that we will now follow.

4.3.2 Proposal of an Analytical Grid

The problem of reconciliation thus posed highlights the need for reflection in terms of the rationality of organizational practices. To answer this question, we propose a twofold analysis. The first is to describe the purpose chosen for the guidance of management. The second defines the chosen management mode. With this proposal, the intention is not limited to understanding the relationship between two juxtaposed economic and social logics but to understand the synergies of their dynamic interaction. The management purpose criterion is defined in accordance with the principles, guidelines, and norms that guide the conduct or behavior of the initiative under analysis. Through this criterion, two other subcriteria are approached: social utility and financial viability. Social utility is defined here by the conduct of the initiative according to social, cultural, environmental, and/or political objectives (by definition nonmarket). The means for making resources viable is not limited to self-financing under market conditions. Financial viability refers to conduct that is primarily guided by self-financing under market conditions (and therefore not very sensitive to nonmarket dimensions). Choosing a management mode implies defining the organizational process, the organizational dynamics, the decision-making, the principles, and the standards to be retained. The choice of management mode is therefore strongly linked to a type of governance. To illustrate our analysis, we will use two contextual criteria: democratic governance on the one hand and technocratic governance on the other. As we saw earlier, by democratic governance we mean all management practices that are oriented toward collective dynamics and based on principles of cooperation and sharing. Democratic governance establishes that all decisions and choices regarding norms, rules, and procedures are subject to political deliberation by the collective. Technocratic governance, on the other hand, is defined by management practices that are not subject to collective deliberation but are mainly guided by technical and financial directives.

In the analytical grid (Fig. 4.1), we have on the X-axis the criterion of the purpose of management and on the Y-axis the criterion relating to the management method. The objective is to try to understand the

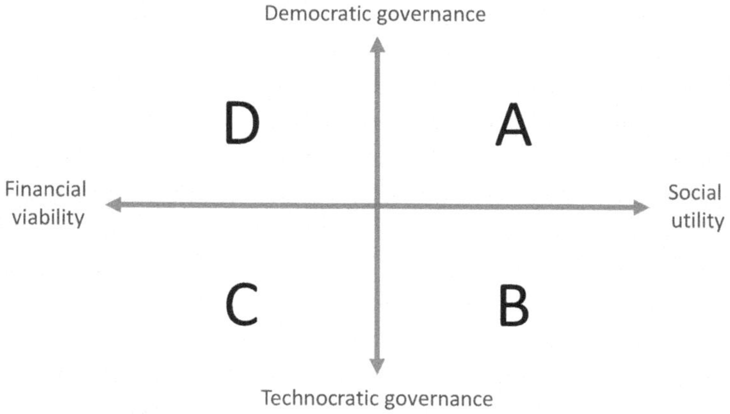

Fig. 4.1 Analytical grid of the relationship between the economic and the social

conditions under which a reconciliation between the economic and the social is possible. In quadrant A, the organizations have a democratic management style, and their actions are guided by social utility objectives. In quadrant B, the management mode is technocratically regulated despite a desire to respond to a social utility objective. In quadrant C, financial viability prevails and the management style is technocratic. In quadrant D, organizations emphasize financial viability, even though they seek democratic decision-making mechanisms.

Given the above approach, the question is to know how the different socioeconomic practices draw or trace the relationship between the economic and the social. We have seen through the previous discussion that reconciliation between the economic and the social requires a reflection on the conditions of the dissociation of the two terms in the practice of the organizations concerned and on the possibility of an embedding of the economic in the social (in Polanyian terms). Reconciliation thus lends itself to a logic of reversal of the dynamic in order to give the social its primacy over the economic. We consider that the existence (or absence) of reconciliation in the socioeconomic practices in question can be identified by the purpose of management and its mode of operation. The grid suggests that reconciliation between the economic and the social is possible under the following cumulative conditions: (1) the purpose of social utility subordinates the imperatives of market mobilization of resources (financial viability) in the organizational dynamic, and (2) the form of democratic governance takes precedence and imposes its practices in the face of the demands of the technical-administrative structure. Therefore, quadrant A in Fig. 4.1 shows the field of possible reconciliation between the economic and the social. It is now a question of knowing what types of organizational experiences are related to this field. What characterizes it? What kinds of challenges does it face? How do we characterize the other quadrants that do not emerge from a reconciliation of economic and social? The literature offers a wide range of definitions covering the universe of socioeconomic practices. Among these, some concepts are particularly relevant to cover all these practices: social business, the third sector, the social economy, and the solidarity economy. We suggest going through the analysis grid with reference to these concepts.

4.3.3 The Relationship Between the Economy and the Social in Social Business

The concept of social business has gained popularity with the work of Yunus (2008, 2010). It enters into dialogue with the notion of social entrepreneurship (Tiscoski et al., 2013) and social enterprise (Borzaga & Defourny, 2001; Oliveira & Vaasconcelos, 2011). The concept of social business goes hand in hand with the notions of social responsibility, inclusive business, and, more recently, social impact enterprises (Limeira, 2015). Social business is to be approached according to the following characteristics: (a) its mission is to meet the demands of vulnerable and low-income segments of the population, (b) it develops and markets products and services tailored to these social demands, (c) it generates sufficient revenues to cover its own expenses, (d) it reinvests part of the economic surplus in the expansion of the business, while the other part constitutes a reserve to cover unforeseen expenses, and (e) some investors do not receive dividends but can recover their investment after a period to be defined (Limeira, 2015). In short, for Yunus (2010), a social business must have a vocation to solve a social problem. According to him, a business can generate sufficient surpluses to cover its own needs and social ambitions. In this sense, Yunus' notion of social enterprise differs from the Anglo-Saxon tradition in that it emphasizes demand "from the bottom of the pyramid." Thus, Gattes and Kiviat (2008) point out that social business initiatives seek to integrate people who are far from the market offer.

In Brazil, autonomy and profitability are fundamental aspects of the social business approach. According to Comini (2011; cited in Limeira, 2015), social enterprise, inclusive enterprise, and social business are terms used to identify organizations that aim to solve social problems with efficiency and financial sustainability through market mechanisms. Naigeborim (2011; cited in Limeira, 2015) also emphasizes market mechanisms by stating that these enterprises should not—and cannot—escape the law of supply and demand. For this author, these initiatives are planned in order to generate sufficient resources to cover all its activities and contribute to their growth. However, in this kind of business, "profit is not an end in itself, but a means to develop solutions that help reduce poverty, social inequality and environmental degradation." On the same line of argumentation, Oliveira and Vaasconcelos (2011, p. 7) consider social and inclusive business to be profitable entrepreneurial models although generating social impact. For these authors, social mission and profitability are concomitantly possible.

All of these approaches assume that these social business initiatives are economically viable. However, the literature lacks empirical demonstration. There are hardly any accounting studies to support this feasibility. In practice, there are two cases:

1. *the social qualification of the enterprise is given by the chosen business niche*. The social aspect is considered a strategic choice and the marketing is oriented toward a customer niche. An example is a Brazilian company that offers housing repair services to favela dwellers;
2. *the initiative of admitting a certain degree of transfer of resources to an audience considered as "social."* An example of this is a luxury clothing store that donates a percentage of its overall sales to the needy through agreements with charitable organizations.

It is surprising to realize that economic initiatives by civil society in connection with sociopolitical movements are sometimes cited as belonging to social business even though they do not fit into this category. We can give the example of the Palmas community bank in Brazil which defines itself as an actor of the solidarity economy. We can therefore ask ourselves if their classification as social business is appropriate since the Palmas bank does not have the objective of financial viability. This is a contradiction that can be explained by the desire of the supporters of social business to position themselves as a response to the new context of civil society organizations hit by the tightening of public funding.

4.3.4 The Relationship Between the Economy and the Social in the Third Sector

The term "third sector" comes from North America and reflects a proximity to the idea of philanthropy. In a context where there is no tradition of a social state, the term essentially groups together organizations from the nonprofit sector. Although the third sector does not claim to have a particular socioeconomic approach, one can infer from its definition the primacy of noneconomic objectives and the need (in the absence of public support) to mobilize resources to achieve these objectives. Salomon and Anheier (1992) show that these organizations have five essential characteristics. They are formal, private, independent, do not distribute profits and involve a minimum of voluntary participation. Two other characteristics are exclusionary: organizations must not be political or faith-based. Thus, political parties and religious organizations are not part of the third sector. The classification of the third sector known as the International Classification of Non-Profit Organizations (ICNPO) has been maintained by the Johns Hopkins Foundation since the early 1990s. This classification serves as the basis for international research on the third sector, and it brings together many countries to produce statistics. This classification does not include informality in its approach. As a result, a wide range of initiatives that play an essential role for a large part of the population in Latin American countries are ignored. As a result, the concept is criticized by many civil society organizations involved in social movements.

While the export of the term "third sector" from the countries of the North to those of the South does not seem particularly relevant, the generalization of its use (including in the South) testifies to a relationship of domination. According to the dominant interpretation in Anglo-Saxon literature, the existence of the third sector is linked to certain market imperfections (notably information asymmetries) and to the need to satisfy the demands of minority groups (not covered by the state). From the point of view of organizational practice, the notion of the third sector implicitly emphasizes the achievement of social objectives. Many non-profit organizations have adopted techno-bureaucratic standards and formal management procedures. In fact, we are currently witnessing a conceptual rapprochement between third sector actors and social business actors. In short, the idea implicit in the notion of the third sector is the establishment of a specific equation combining a social utility objective and technocratic governance.

4.3.5 The Relationship Between the Economy and the Social in the Social Economy

Unlike the notion of the third sector (typically North American), the notion of social economy refers to the context and history of the European continent. The tradition of the social state allows us to envisage a social economy "in constant historical interaction with the public authorities" (Laville, 2000). In the first half of the nineteenth century, Europe saw the emergence of a large number of experiments in mutual aid and relief within the working populations, as we have seen in the introductory chapter of the book. These experiences were formalized around three types of organizations: mutuals, cooperatives, and associations. These innovations were the result of workers' experiences that aimed at autonomy and social transformation on the margins of the Marxist doctrine that aimed at state centralization. As we have seen, the term "utopian socialism" was proposed by Engels to characterize these experiences. This would discredit them by opposing utopian socialism to scientific socialism. At that time, large sections of the population in Europe were living in conditions of great poverty. The popular initiatives of mutuality were born in very difficult conditions because they had no legal character. The law even tried to prevent the constitution of such experiences of sharing and cooperation within the working class.

However, their role and their contribution eventually imposed themselves, and these social innovations gradually gained the recognition of the public authorities. Specific legal statutes were gradually consolidated during the second half of the nineteenth century and the beginning of the twentieth century. This late standardization allowed the actors of the social economy to integrate into the dominant economic system. Cooperatives would then participate in the market economy by occupying "areas of activity where capital intensity had remained low" (Laville, 2000, p. 532). The mutuals were to become stronger and more commonplace. The first militant managers of these organizations were gradually replaced by professionals with a strong technocratic culture. The technical or functional dimension of these organizations ended up taking precedence over the initial political project. Thus, the development of the social economy was accompanied by its institutionalization throughout the twentieth century. The organizations of the social economy became commonplace, and a large number of them adopted operations very similar to those of commercial enterprises, with which they were in competition.

4.3.6 The Relationship Between the Economy and the Social in the Solidarity Economy

The concept of solidarity economy has been built around a wide range of self-managed initiatives from civil society and working-class communities. For the actors of the solidarity economy, it is a question of returning to the original ambition of the actors of the associationist movement (Chanial, 2010): to democratize the economy (Laville & Salmon, 2016). Such a project does not necessarily fall under specific statutes. In connection with social movements, these initiatives proclaim a strong political dimension (Laville, 2010). Strongly marked by self-management experiences, the solidarity economy is built around the desire to include experiences from the popular economy in Brazil (França Filho, 2006). It is therefore a question of grouping together collectives under a common name that may be formal, informal, or in the process of being formalized, depending on the different contexts. These organizations are at different stages of maturity in terms of management practices. In the best of cases, we observe advanced practices in terms of deliberation, shared decision-making, managerial transparency, and the rotation in positions of responsibility. The diversity of experiences makes it difficult to strictly define the field. The collective dimension of the work with its socialization space and the productive dimension of the activity (regardless of its level of performance) can be retained as criteria for defining the experiences.

To illustrate our point, we will take two examples. The first initiative (IA) is located in a small town. It is an association of housewives. They meet in the evenings for the same activity—embroidery—and they form a very close-knit group and enjoy meeting regularly. They do not necessarily try to sell their production, and their turnover is very modest. When they do sell products, they decide together on the price and the distribution of the income. Their decision-making is democratic. At first sight, it seems that the social dimension of the association is strongly marked. A second initiative (IB) is an association dealing with the treatment and recycling of waste. Each member of the association works alone. The group's sales activity is very strong, and the members share the general costs of marketing. For this purpose, they meet regularly and discuss decisions on an equal basis. We can think that IA is marked by a strong collective dimension of work and a weak productive activity. Conversely, IB has a weak collective dimension in work but a strong productive activity. However, a more detailed analysis shows that the two initiatives are similar. The women actually perform a double workday. Their life time is divided between time devoted to the family, to household tasks, and to the craft activity. The handicrafts constitute the accumulation of a sales potential. In this way, they complement the family income. The waste recycling association has a collective activity that generates more income, but the pooling of marketing costs is a choice of solidarity between members. Despite their differences, both initiatives are part of the solidarity economy in that they share a democratic governance and build social links. The relationships established between the members of both organizations are rewarding. In the exchange around democratic practices, both organizations affirm the centrality of the social utility dimension in their purpose.

4.3.7 The Conditions for Reconciliation

Social business initiatives are characterized by a management purpose built around financial viability and a management mode inscribed in a technocratic governance. The social aspect is not primary. It is thought of as an induced or collateral effect of the economic activity, and its feasibility depends on the nature of the market activity and its monetary potential. Thus, the financial logic remains primary. It guarantees access to the only resource on which the organization can rely. The strategy is commercial. It is first of all a question of identifying potentially exploitable commercial niches in order to then bring philanthropic approaches into play. Democratic governance is not essential. What is important is the efficiency and speed of the decision-making process. Although it announces its social vocation, the social business type of organization legitimizes the radical separation between the economic and the social. It makes the economic the condition of the social. According to the proposed grid, the initiatives of a social business type translate a non (re)conciliation between the economic and the social.

Third sector initiatives are distinguished by a social utility purpose characteristic of nonprofit organizations and by the strong need to mobilize monetary resources. The professionalization of resource collection methods leads the vast majority of nonprofit organizations to adopt the classic format of technocratic management. The literature on the third sector does not consider organizational democracy as a central element of their analysis, and there is currently a significant rapprochement with private sector actors and corporate foundations. This brings some third sector organizations closer to the social business model. However, this rapprochement is not systematic. Some third sector organizations base their management on rigid rules, but at the same time they admit the need for a certain democratic openness. This is particularly true of certain historical NGOs. According to the proposed grid, third sector initiatives reconcile the economic and the social.

Social economy organizations, on the other hand, in practice combine a strong quest for economic results with the valorization of democratic governance mechanisms. However, this first observation needs to be clarified. In some cooperatives, we observe a low intensity in the quest for financial viability with an emphasis on the importance of community development. In this type of situation, the purpose of management is closer to the social utility quadrant. In contrast, other cooperatives are characterized by a low intensity of democratic governance and a strong technocratic practice. In this case, financial viability takes precedence as a management objective. This is common in cooperatives with a strong market isomorphism. According to the proposed grid, social economy-type initiatives reconcile the economic and the social.

Solidarity economy initiatives are characterized by a management purpose guided by social utility and a management mode included in a democratic governance. The meaning of the economic activity is nourished by the history of the people who run it. The democratic governance process is never taken for granted but is subject to continuous questioning and learning. Solidarity economy initiatives participate in a reconciliation between the economic and the social in that the economic nature of the initiative becomes inseparable from its social, political, cultural, or environmental practices. Two characteristics of the economic dynamic shape the organizational practice that can lead to reconciliation: (a) a greater appeal to principles of economic solidarity such as redistribution and reciprocity, and (b) the re-signification of market practice in the initiative's dynamic. The introduction of logics of cooperation and solidarity within commercial mechanisms and relations (through charters, labels, and pacts) is part of this re-signification work. From a conceptual point of view, reconciliation finds its translation in the principles of the substantive economy.

The quadrants in Fig. 4.2 indicate a horizon of possibilities for each context of the reality of socioeconomic initiatives. This makes it possible to draw a panorama of the modes of relationship between the economic and the social. However, this panorama is not fixed. Trajectories can be observed within each quadrant. The relationship to purpose and

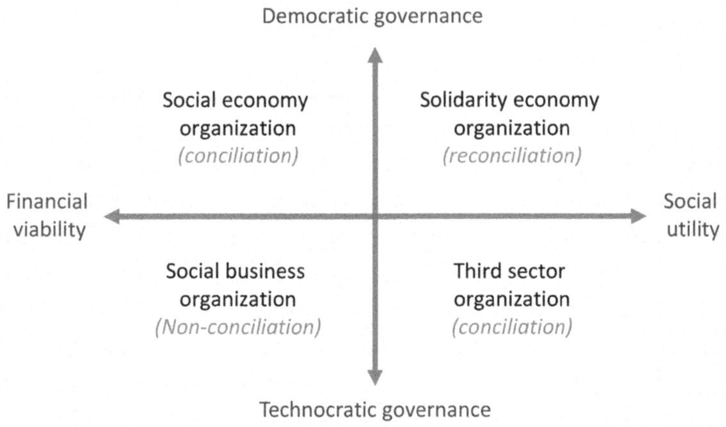

Fig. 4.2 Typology of the relationship between the economic and the social

management mode must also be understood in terms of the intensity expressed on the two axes: the intensity of democratic governance or technocratic governance, and the intensity of social utility or financial viability. It is in these respective intensities that non-conciliation, conciliation, or reconciliation will be expressed with more or less force. The analytical grid is therefore an aid in situating each initiative in relation to its own challenges and ambitions. We can deduce from this analytical grid that reconciliation can only be expressed through the reintegration of the economic into the social. However, this is impossible in a market economy. Another economy is therefore a necessary condition for reconciliation. It requires the expression of a democratic governance and the affirmation of social utility as an end.

It is useful to specify that reconciliation is played out in a dynamic of learning and sharing that is not without a certain number of challenges in terms of the sustainability of initiatives. The challenge is then to know how the process of reintegrating the economic into the social is carried out and how sustainability is defined. As this reintegration is the condition of a substantive approach to the economy (in theory), the problem of the demarketing of fictitious goods refers to the practical construction of the other economy. This engages a reflection around the organization of a process of decommodification of work, money, and nature.

4.4 Reentering the Fictitious Goods

After the end of World War II, the Declaration of Philadelphia recognized the need for a new economic model that gave priority to social development. The economy was thus seen as a means in the service of the social. In the wake of this declaration, Keynesian economic policies accompanied a long cycle of growth known as "*Les Trente Glorieuses*" (the Thirty Glorious Years of economic growth after World War II). In France, this period was accompanied by the development of a social state that allowed the generalization of social protection and health insurance systems in many countries. During this period, the organizations of the social economy (management associations, cooperatives, mutual societies) were consolidated but were not able to have any political scope. These organizations were trivialized and to a large extent faced competition from capitalist enterprises. This resulted in the obligation to follow the same precautionary rules and adopt the same standards as those capitalist enterprises. This extension of the market economy beyond its original boundaries was built around the promotion of the commodity and the society of spectacle (Debord, 2002). The transformation of a market economy into a market society has made it difficult, if not impossible, for a self-conscious society to affirm itself (Jappe, 2017). As a result, these years of strong economic growth came at the price of the adoption of pesticides in agriculture, the deployment of the nuclear industry, and the abuse of the planet's natural resources. This period of thirty years was also devastating (Pessis et al., 2015) because they were energy-intensive years, initiated the age of waste, and developed the productivist ideology while invisibilizing the victims of various industrial pollutions. Generally speaking, it did not eliminate inequalities between countries nor did it allow for the generalization of democracies.

However, as a corollary to the liberation movements in the countries of the South, there has been the rise of new social movements in the North: feminism, insubordination, ecology. Thus, new ways of thinking emerged which favored the birth of new economic proposals aiming at transforming the system from the inside. Through the search for a fair price and the support of producers' and consumers' networks, relevant initiatives such as fair trade, short circuits (such as associations for the maintenance of small-scale agriculture), and social currencies have been born. We will now detail how these initiatives have produced modes of organization likely to respond to the management issues raised by the commodification of the world and also to initiate a process of reintegration of the fictitious commodities identified by Polanyi, namely labor, money, and nature.

4.4.1 Cooperative Activity and Demarketing of Work

For Weber, to put work at the service of a rational organization which provides humanity with its material goods has always appeared, unquestionably, to the representatives of the spirit of capitalism, as one of the goals of their task (Weber, 2002). From then on, Taylor's scientific management fulfills an eminently primordial task. It is not just one method among others. It is the management way of thinking (Coutrot, 2018). Drucker is not mistaken. He states without hesitation that scientific management is much more than a philosophy of work. According to him, it is the most important contribution made by America to the West after the contribution of the Founding Fathers (Drucker, 1954). While the idea may be laughable, the economic forces behind such a position cannot be overlooked. We must therefore agree with Drucker that the stakes are high and that it is necessary to engage in a critical analysis of the scientific dimension of the approach.

As Braverman points out, scientific management of work is less interested in work than in its unlimited adaptation to the needs of capital (Braverman, 1998). Scientific management thus makes it its essential mission to ensure that "the worker adapts to his work" (Bouquin, 2010, p. 164) without ever considering the opposite solution. Thus, workers are subjected to "perpetual instability, to permanent modulation" (Allard-Poesi & Loilier, 2009, p. 7). For Taylor, as Postone (1996) shows, it is a question of controlling the performance of workers with the help of a chronometer in order to make the performance of work objectively measurable. The challenge is in fact to substitute "living labor with dead labor (…) if not with more docile categories of labor" (Bouquin, 2010, p. 177).

By dead labor we mean the work of machines or of men transformed into machines (as brilliantly shown in Chaplin's 1936 film *Modern Times*). Thus, technocratic thinking "has transformed social problems into technical problems" (Chanlat, 2013, p. 8). More fundamentally, scientific management is at fault when it leaves the decision-making power to the worker (Braverman, 1998). Braverman thus points out that while economists admit that objects are made by humans, they forget that these same humans are themselves "made" (Bouquin, 2010). In other words, economists (and scientific managers with them) neglect social constructions. The market—with the help of the competition it promotes—is responsible for destroying solidarities by pitting employees against each other (Allard-Poesi & Loilier, 2009). There is a collusion between the two types of scientific management promoted by Taylor and Mayo. The first is responsible for the performance of the production of goods and services, and the second deals with the damage caused by the first (Braverman, 1998). The first responds to the needs of economic warfare, the second seeks to heal the wounded.

Thus, Taylorism is not dead. It is constantly being reborn from its ashes, with new precariousness as a result. Uberization is a contemporary example of this. For Feher (2017), this case testifies to a shift in the social question. The significant growth in the number of people with self-employed status is representative of this shift. Through the outsourcing of activities, it consists in transforming jobs with the protected status of employee into activities assumed by independent entrepreneurs (Abdelnour & Lambert, 2014). As Gorz notes, the individual must become a business himself (Gorz, 2010). The large digital commodity platforms play an important role in this casualization. Their particularity is that they require more than the simple provision of labor power. In fact, for those who engage in them, they require the double provision of a capital of resources and a reputational capital. If we take the case of Uber, the drivers must make available to the platform a smartphone, a configured application, and a car. The monitoring carried out by the application will then determine and build the reputational capital that is essential for the continuation of the activity. According to Feher, this inaugurates a form of securitization of human relationships (Feher, 2017) with a connection between investors and investees. Management becomes disembodied (Dujarier, 2014). Uber drivers do not work for the platform. The platform invests in them and so it is up to them to be attractive for investment. Faced with this, the usual protections fall away or are circumvented. In a context where the uberization of labor "combines with the hegemony of finance capital, governments primarily determined to keep the confidence of their creditors will hardly be able to include the emancipation of all workers in their specifications" (Feher, 2017, p. 149).

Postone (1996) notes that in order to get out of domination, it is necessary to stop considering labor as a transhistorical category and to consider it as a category specific to capitalism (Harribey, 2009). From then on, it is a matter of describing it in its specificity and contemporaneity. First of all, it is a system that undermines its own foundations. As in the Greek myth of Erysichthon,[4] capitalism is self-destructing (Jappe, 2017) since it exhausts the very forces on which it relies. It must be noted that the system generates ill-being for workers by promoting self-exploitation. It reinforces the domination in place and in particular its patriarchal dimension (Jappe, 2017). Capitalism thus promotes production (under the control of men), to the detriment of so-called reproductive activities (often invisibilized) which take place "above all in the domestic sphere and are generally devolved to women" (Jappe, 2017, p. 234). Thus, the study of representations of the economy "from gender social relations highlights a hierarchy that valorizes market production to the detriment of reproduction largely confined to the non-market and non-monetary categories" (Laville, 2015). Sauvy[5] observed ironically that when a bourgeois man marries his housekeeper, he decreases the GDP. Indeed, the wife continues to do the housework but no longer receives a wage for this service. In this situation, service production remains unchanged before and after marriage, but the market sphere no longer recognizes it after marriage (since it no longer has a monetary translation). Housework is in fact only one of the typical expressions of a vast shadow economy, a ghost economy, which has developed in all industrial societies as a complement if not a source of the expansion of paid work (Gorz, 2010). The

[4] Erysichthon is a character from Greek mythology whose insatiable hunger led him to devour himself.

[5] Alfred Sauvy (1898–1990) was a French demographer, anthropologist, and historian of the French economy.

development fostered by the market economy implies the monopoly of paid work over all other forms of work and a reorganization of the environment such that space, time, resources, and projects are oriented toward production and consumption, while use-value-creating activities, which directly satisfy needs, stagnate or disappear (Gorz, 2010). It is clear that "inequalities of access to and control of the so-called productive and reproductive spheres are at the heart of gender inequalities" and that women's marginalization "has been fueled by their exclusion from or difficulty in accessing these forms of wealth, be it employment, property or finance" (Guérin et al., 2011, p. 15). To get out of this aporia and the invisibilization of activities that are indispensable to our societies, Polanyi's framework of substantive economics appears particularly appropriate. By including reciprocity, the domestic economy, and redistribution in the framework of analysis, it contributes to the emancipation of actors. It also allows us to think about the reintegration of work. As a conclusion to this part, we would like to give two examples relating to work that testify to the organization's ability to place itself at the service of the demarketing of fictitious goods. The first concerns cooperatives of activity and work, and the second concerns platform cooperatives.

The first French "*Coopérative d'Activité et d'Emploi*"[6] (CAE) was created in the 1990s. The initial objective of this proposal was to encourage the unemployed to create their own business. The initial idea may have seemed similar to an incubator or a business incubator. Very quickly, however, this CAE pragmatically explored the idea of a mutual work association, that is, "a collective enterprise in which people protect each other, over time, in their professional careers" (Delvolvé & Veyer, 2009, p. 2). The principle of a CAE thus consists in paying the members of the cooperative, who are all individual entrepreneurs. To do this, the CAE assumes the legal responsibility for the collective and pools the cash flow of all its members. The salary paid by the CAE depends on the level of activity of each entrepreneur. The strength of the proposal is that each entrepreneur remains independent and in control of his own decisions, while enjoying the protection of being an employee. As soon as they start trading, "each project leader signs an open-ended employment contract

[6] Business and employment cooperative.

with the CAE and becomes an *employee-entrepreneur*" (Sangiorgio & Veyer, 2009). He is integrated into the cooperative "without presuming the future success of his activity and is accompanied by the structure to specify and launch his project" (Sangiorgio & Veyer, 2009). The presence of an entrepreneur in a CAE can be temporary or long term. This depends on the entrepreneur's personal choice and the evolution of his activity. The logic of a CAE is distinct from that of a wage portage organization. Indeed, the project holder in the CAE is not placed in a relationship of client to service provider. In a CAE, "the accompanying and the accompanied are associated with the same project" (Stervinou & Noël-Lemaître, 2008, p. 70). The management adopted by the CAE generally allows for the avoidance of imposed preliminary exercises such as market research, business forecasts, and/or prospective criteria of economic profitability (Sangiorgio & Veyer, 2009, p. 55). The mentor/mentee relationship is established on a parity basis. The help provided to the project leader is "neither assistance nor management advice, but rather a sympathetic ear and peer support" (Sangiorgio & Veyer, 2009, p. 55). Moreover, the collective framework of the cooperative means it can "break the isolation of the project leader and organize a collective support work, through practice exchange workshops for example" (Sangiorgio & Veyer, 2009, p. 55). The CAEs claim a political approach by refusing to take for granted "the atomization of the relationship to work" (Delvolvé & Veyer, 2009, p. 2). They intend to fight against the perverse effects of the generalized development of self-employment as well as against the consequences of "the deregulation of work as much as the flexibilization of economic relations" (Ibid.). They do so not only by securing the creation of individual enterprises but by building "an alternative to them, via a collective entrepreneurship project" (Sangiorgio & Veyer, 2009, p. 56). They thus aim to reverse the displacement of the social question that Feher talks about. By developing the mutualization of resources, any CAE can build up a sufficient financial base to consider developing "its own investment fund, its own mutual aid fund, its own mechanisms for covering operating losses" (Sangiorgio & Veyer, 2009, p. 57). Two important dimensions can be seen here. The first is that CAEs are intended to link the social and professional dimensions by bringing together individual actors with entrepreneurial and professional projects in the same space of solidarity.

Similar to places such as co-working spaces, hackerspaces, or fablabs, a CAE like Coopaname offers "a common physical space for professionals of very diverse specialties, thus favoring unexpected encounters and associations and, consequently, innovation and the emergence of collective projects" (Bureau & Corsani, 2015, p. 225). The second is that the will of the CAEs is expressed in the context of a broad response to social protection issues by offering cooperators the possibility of a status, paid remuneration, and a relationship not based on the mechanisms of the market economy. Thus, the wealth of CAEs "exceeds the market value of the activities they house" (Bureau & Corsani, 2015, p. 228). By refusing to consider work as a commodity, CAEs have an emancipatory ambition toward their members and are de facto part of public action.

Another example of substantive management regarding work can be found in platform cooperatives that seek to respond to the new challenges posed by the digital and its commodification. In their report, Barbezieux and Herody show that the great potential of the collaborative economy should not make us forget the need for reflection on transparency, social protection, taxation, and the sustainability of digital platforms (Barbezieux & Herody, 2016). The collaborative economy is indeed generating major upheavals that are likely to call into question work in its traditional form. New forms of work are appearing, grouped under the term digital labor. They do not have the taste, appearance, or smell of work (Scholz, 2013). Thus, when an Internet user uses an online service, he provides feedback on the functioning of the processing algorithm of the service provider platform through the management of his personal data. This activity can be considered as unpaid work carried out for the benefit of the commercial platform, since the production of value is carried out in the absence of a contractual framework (Casilli, 2015). There are many studies on digital labor, and they refer to the valorization of Internet users' personal data and their use, as well as to the exploitation of content produced by amateurs or to the casualization of certain professions (Broca, 2017). Taking into account these reflections on digital labor and the changes brought about by the transition to an economy of the immaterial (Gorz, 2010), the platform cooperative movement proposes an alternative to commercial platforms. The idea behind this cooperative revival is the production of digital platforms that are from the outset transparent, democratic, fair, and sustainable. Platform cooperativism thus consists in articulating the historical experience of the cooperative movement with the social needs of Internet usage (Scholz & Schneider, 2016). It is thus defined as the search for democratic models of collective ownership adapted to the Internet and is thought of in three stages (Scholz, 2016). First, it is about cloning the technology at the heart of platforms such as Uber, Task Rabbit, Airbnb, or UpWork. Second, it is about managing this technology in a solidarity framework with collective ownership protected by nonmarket organizations (unions, cities, associations, foundations, citizen collectives). Finally, it is a question of defining principles of action in order to prevent any commodification. These include collective ownership, respect for workers, decent wages, transparency of processes, data portability, involvement of the community of users in decisions, a regulatory framework to define and protect the rights of everyone, and so on. The strength of the platform cooperative movement is that it can open up synergies between solidarity economy actors and communities associated with free software (Conaty & Bollier, 2014). According to Bauwens and Kostakis (2017), this intersection opens up five types of meaningful engagement. First, open cooperatives commit to refusing to organize scarcity for commercial purposes. They recognize all contributions from the community by practicing open accounting. They are inspired by open-source public licensing models to ensure[7] a fair distribution and value sharing system with "CopyFair" licenses. They adopt open design tools that can offer a guarantee against programmed obsolescence strategies. They coordinate with each other using open logistics systems to promote the circular economy and reduce waste production.

The reflections around platform cooperatives are expressed in the question of the protection of social data. Historically, modernity has been accompanied by a dual movement in which work leaves the private sphere and enters the public space and in which social control over individuals diminishes in favor of the development of a space for privacy (Gorz, 2004). What we have observed in recent years with the hegemony of

[7] CopyFair licenses are modeled after open-source licenses and encourage commercial activity based on reciprocity. CopyFair requires commercial users to provide a demonstrated form of reciprocity within the sharing community. This contribution to the commons is eventually financial.

commercial platforms is the reversal of the previous order. The confidentiality of private data is no longer guaranteed, and privacy is increasingly exposed in the public space. This loss of privacy is the result of a lack of regulation on the part of public actors. Thus, as Maurel and Aufrère (2018) point out, it is the market that increasingly regulates the use of personal data. This regulation comes through contractual negotiation and agreement between the parties. However, the asymmetry is so great between the platform and an isolated individual that negotiation cannot exist in practice. This is a space that must be regulated by social law. In this context, user associations and advocacy collectives have a decisive role to play in making it happen. For Casilli, associations and collectives are able to bring about a model of "privacy as a negotiation" where privacy has ceased to be an individual right and has become a collective negotiation (Casilli, 2013). Maurel and Aufrère suggest a three-step framework for organizing this model and preventing abuses. They propose to:

- promote class *actions* to allow individuals to defend their individual rights against platforms in court through representatives such as associations;
- Strengthen the protection of users in the general conditions of use of platforms on the model of collective agreements (so that they can be subject to legal recourse);
- move from individual portability to citizen portability, that is, allow users of an online service to retrieve the data they have entrusted to an operator to transfer to a competitor or use for their own purposes.

Employment and activity cooperatives, like platform cooperatives, are organizational forms that participate in the same intention to re-embed work in order to free it from market logics. These two initiatives show that it is now possible to resolidify the organization on the question of work. However, it is the responsibility of public policies aiming at sustainability and the protection of individual data to promote such experiments in the struggle for the demarketing of work. As Gorz reminds us, the civilized or barbaric form of the exit from capitalism depends on how this struggle turns out (Gorz, 2018).

4.4.2 Social Money and Demarketing of Money

Under the name of social, local, or complementary currencies, a growing number of experiments in various countries testify to the search for new forms of appropriation of money. These initiatives are conceived from different perspectives than those of market currencies (Zelizer, 2005). In the early twentieth century, discussions of money in the economy began to focus on the issue of neutrality. In orthodox theory, money is seen as a medium of exchange incapable of affecting the relationships between things and people involved in exchange. This idea of monetary neutrality is expressed mainly through the universality of accounts and measures. However, sociology and economic anthropology have largely highlighted the inherently social and institutional nature of money (Lietaer & Kennedy, 2010; Zelizer, 2005). Lietaer and Kennedy (2010) criticize the neutrality of money based on a study of exchange systems founded on complementary currencies in Germany. They show that people in need accept help from their friends in social money and refuse the same service if it is offered in official money. For economic anthropology, money is not unique, uniform, and generalized. It exists in multiple forms. Various studies show the historical variety of uses and currencies. In certain ancient societies, a complex social system was constructed with a hierarchy between the different types of money (money for marriages, money to settle disputes), and depending on their use in daily life, currencies were assigned meanings (Zelizer, 2005). Thus, there was no abstract currency, but many currencies related to the agent who used them and the context in which they operated. Focusing on the study of market money would therefore leave out nonfungible, nonportable, subjective, and therefore qualitatively heterogeneous currencies (Blanc, 1998; Zelizer, 2005). In short, money would thus be the most irreplaceable of personal objects (Zelizer, 2005).

Back to the Anthropological Approach to Money

Orthodox economists tell the story of the birth of money as follows. There would have been a golden age—that of primitive societies marked by an original communism—where all wealth was distributed among the members. The exchange between communities was regulated by barter. However, the growth of exchanges finally made it necessary to find a means of exchange. The currency then imposed itself as a mechanism of expression of the value of things and a tool of reserve. The end of the story. Anthropologists know that this story is a farce (Caillé, 1994). Economic anthropology shows that money is linked to systems of reciprocal exchange that have been present from the outset in ancestral and premodern societies. In ancient Greece, values depended on a complex system of mutual recognition around objects, status of people, and categories of use values (Aglietta & Orléan, 1982). Money thus appears as an entanglement of debts and credits that form and construct society and is a link that unifies social life through debt systems. It is an active representation of society as a whole "since it participates in its construction from the beginning" (Théret, 2008, p. 3). From this point of view, money operates as a symbol linked to other symbols. Meanings are shared, exchanged, and have meaning. In an intermediate conception between the purely symbolic and the purely economic, money is seen as an institutional form linking people and things (Théret, 2008).

Ethnographic research has contributed greatly to our understanding of money. It contrasts with the explanations and interpretations of economists. Rospabé (1995) shows that the precious objects used by archaic communities to purchase goods or services must also be understood as symbols, guarantees, and compensations. Among other things, Rospabé (1995) studies the "purchase" of a woman. The author shows the relationships that are formed between donor groups (the woman's family) and recipient groups (her husband's family). Monetary payment does not free the payer. It does not absolve one of future obligations. On the contrary, the payment maintains a debt. Thus, "far from definitively acquiring a wife and her children, the 'payers' of women become indebted to those who are 'donors' of their daughters" (Rospabé, 1995, p. 41). If the anthropology of money as a field of knowledge indicates the diversity of uses and functions of money in different societies and cultures in the course of history, the different manifestations of the use of money today reaffirm the need for this broader vision.

A Plurality of Currencies: Parallel, Complementary, Local, Social

According to Blanc (1998), parallel currencies constitute a broad set of monetary instruments. The term "parallel" is given to these currencies because they coexist with the national currency. Lietaer and Kennedy (2010) refer to them as complementary currencies, and these sometimes emerge as a result of a crisis, as was the case in Argentina in July 2001 (Colliac, 2005). Complementary provincial currencies in Argentina have been widely accepted, including by the federal state. Among these, the *patacón*, a parallel currency in Buenos Aires, was used to pay public debts. In addition, other institutions, including banks, adapted to this reality by beginning to accept and open accounts in the other currency (Colliac, 2005). There are countless examples of alternative currencies, each with its own specificities and context. In general, such currencies, contrary to what one might think, do not compete with the national currency (Blanc, 1998; Lietaer & Kennedy, 2010). In Brazil, the case of Curitiba can also be highlighted, with respect to the use of complementary currencies. In 1971, the city's mayor created a complementary currency in the form of transport vouchers to solve the problem of waste. Each bag of garbage deposited in the recycling bins earned a voucher. From then on, what began as a public health project turned into a transportation and unemployment management program (Lietaer & Kennedy, 2010).

It is worth mentioning another example of complementary currency that does not necessarily use paper money but only hours of work contributed by members. One of the best-known systems is the Time Dollar in the United States. The exchange of services (or hours of service) is done between neighbors or members of a local network. When a service hour is received, the recipient is charged for one hour and the service provider is credited with one hour. The time unit is always 60 minutes. There is no interest or inflation. According to Soares (2009, p. 255), social money is a form of parallel currency set up and administered by its own users. Local currency systems originating from noncommercial groups of people are organized "on the basis of a social debt maintained indefinitely" (Blanc, 1998, p. 85), like LETS (Local Exchange Trading Systems) in

Anglo-Saxon countries and SEL (*Systèmes d'Echanges locaux*) in France. In Brazil, these systems are often called social currencies (Búrigo, 2002; Menezes & Crocco, 2009; Soares, 2006, 2009). According to França Filho and Silva Jr (2009), the term "social" refers to the communities that create and implement it to address their social and economic problems.

What Is the Relationship Between Social, Parallel, Complementary, and Local Currencies?

The social or democratic control of the currency is the criterion most mentioned to define a social currency in Brazil and more widely in Latin America. It was with a view to reinventing the economy that the first social currency of the community development banks (BCD), called Palmas, was created in 2000. Its creation can be seen as an evolution of its exchange club (*clube de trocas*). This social or democratic character is expressed in the framework of associative collectives. We can also mention REGIO, a network of regional currency associations in Germany, Austria, and Switzerland. Parallel currencies, for their part, can sometimes constitute an economic circuit parallel to the official money circuit. The complementary nature of social money appears when it interacts with the official currency through a convertibility mechanism. In this case, the social currency acts as a medium for the local economy with a parity relationship with the official currency. This requires a prior agreement between social actors and institutions in a given territorial context. However, the vast majority of complementary currencies are not social currencies simply because they are not issued by democratic institutions or do not circulate according to democratic criteria or principles. Social currencies are necessarily parallel, sometimes complementary, necessarily local. The local character of the currency potentially reinforces the democratic control of the currency in a local development perspective. Recent innovations have broadened the perspective of use of social currencies, and, among these, the use of electronic social currencies offers the possibility of networking social currencies. The Brazilian experience of community development banks points to new ways in this direction. In short, social currencies have a cumulative character.

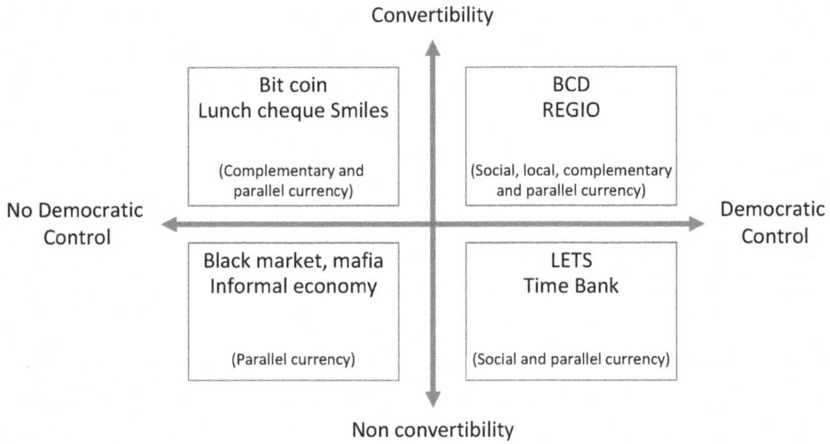

Fig. 4.3 Overview of parallel currencies

Figure 4.3 attempts to summarize the four characteristics of currencies. This exercise does not lend itself to proposing a typology of currencies already done in a seminal work by Blanc (2011). In particular, Blanc has shown how the typical ideals of community, complementary, and local currencies combine to offer a great diversity to the concrete forms of social currencies. For our part, as a distinctive feature of the analysis, we highlight the importance of democratic control in defining social currencies.

When convertibility is combined with democratic control in the management of money, social money is everything at once: local, complementary, parallel. Its democratic control is precisely the condition for the demarketing of social money.

Social Currencies and BCD in Brazil

Reaffirming the centrality of the democratic dimension, social currencies can appear in various forms, such as time banks, mutual credit systems, complementary currencies, or local social currencies (Primavera, 2003). Typically, social currencies are created to address money scarcity, to distribute wealth, to generate awareness, and to support popular economies.

For this reason, many authors recognize that social currencies go beyond an economic role to reveal themselves as political, social, and cultural instruments (Albuquerque, 2003; Melo Neto & Magalhães, 2005; Menezes & Crocco, 2009). Analyzing social money from the point of view of time banks, Soares (2009) states that they are "the reflection of a quest to put the economy back at the service of social objectives and the reintegration of its values to the socio-cultural sphere. Under these conditions, social money must be seen as an openly normative institution, which is associated with people who share the same values" (Soares, 2009, p. 255). The author also states that social currencies are used in practices of reinventing the economy (Soares, 2009). With social currency, BCDs encourage residents to buy locally, and they promote the circulation of money locally by preventing the exit of wealth from the territory (Rigo, 2014; Rigo & França Filho, 2017). In this sense, they are considered the main instrument of BCDs in promoting development. Social currencies promote purchasing within the locality; they value local trade and encourage the creation of new jobs in the community (Melo Neto & Magalhães, 2005; Menezes & Crocco, 2009; Passos, 2008). With them, the territory becomes a large exchange club with benefits that go beyond the economic. Social currencies can thus contribute to the training/education of people and the empowerment of communities (Melo Neto & Magalhães, 2005; Passos, 2008).

The main characteristics of these social currencies are as follows: (a) they are designed to complement the national currency without the intention of replacing it; (b) they are made with security components; (c) they circulate freely in local commerce, usually offering discounts to those who use them; and (d) they can be exchanged for the official currency only when merchants need to buy goods outside the community (Melo Neto & Magalhães, 2006). In addition, there is no interest charged for their use in order to discourage their accumulation and improve their circulation. Finally, they are based on social control (Albuquerque, 2003; Menezes & Crocco, 2009). Access to money is voluntary. It is accessed through loan applications directly to the BCD, through the receipt of a payment in social currency, through direct exchange at the BCD, or through a local business (Melo Neto & Magalhães, 2006). The objective of social currencies is to circulate as much as possible in the territory, since their mission is "to promote the exchanges necessary for the sustainability and development of a group, a community and/or a society" (Albuquerque, 2003, p. 200). In order for social money to circulate and promote the development of the territory, it is necessary that all stakeholders (BCD, merchants, and residents) act in a concerted manner. According to Melo Neto and Magalhães (2006), the level of organization of each BCD, the history of the community, and the sociopolitical context of the locality are the main factors to be taken into consideration. A negative impact can be expressed (a) when merchants or residents do not want to accept the currency (out of fear, ignorance, or simply because they do not want to join the system), (b) when the BCD has no control over the circulation and the amount saved, and (c) when there are no incentives for its use (Melo Neto & Magalhães, 2006).

The Territorial Embedding of BCDs

The BCDs can be thought of as solidarity finance practices that benefit popular economies located in territories with a low human development index (França Filho & Silva Jr, 2009). Structured on the basis of local associative dynamics, the BCDs rely on a series of tools to generate and increase income in the territory. To this end, central lines of action can work together in an intervention process: solidarity credit funds, local currency, local producers' fairs, and training in solidarity economy. Unlike classic microcredit practices oriented toward an individual organization, the BCDs are part of a territory. This can be a popular urban neighborhood, a rural community, or a small municipality. In this sense, the BCDs seek to invest simultaneously in the production, service generation, and consumption capacities of the territory. To this end, they finance and guide the construction of socio-productive initiatives, the offer of local services and local consumption. In addition to the dissemination of microcredits with multiple purposes according to the defined lines of credit, the objective of the BCDs is to build local networks of solidarity economy by coordinating local producers, service providers, and consumers. These are also called networks of prosumers. A prosumer is an individual who both consumes and produces. It is a question of associating producers, local consumers, and all the actors of the territory interested in the implementation of short circuits. This implies a break with the classic production/consumption dichotomy characteristic of the classic market logic. These networks seek to concretize the expression of another economy on their territory. Their objective is to strengthen local economies and to reorganize them in order to promote solidarity-based territorial development. The BCDs are asserting themselves as actors of a solidarity economy movement. They do so through regional and national forums and through the Brazilian network of community banks (França Filho, 2013; Rigo & França Filho, 2017).

The creation of a BCD presupposes the expression of a collective desire and the strong mobilization of the actors in the territory. At the beginning, the BCD must build up a basic financial capital for its credit fund and have sufficient financial resources to meet its operating costs. It must form an association and have qualified people to manage the credit and provide advice, assistance, and mediation with the community. An important aspect of the functioning of a BCD is the security provided by the existence of a control based on relations of proximity and mutual trust. When registering a credit application, the BCD manager can rely on the knowledge of the neighborhood network to complete his analysis. This same network is an additional guarantee for the repayment of loans. Four principles characterize the BCDs: (a) the coordination of the initiative and the management of resources are community-based; (b) the granting of microcredit is guided by the desire to serve the community in a fair manner; (c) the management of loans is served by proximity relationships and a control that is more social than economic; (d) the creation of instruments to encourage local consumption (such as the social currency) is perceived positively by local producers, traders, and consumers.

From Social Currencies to Electronic Social Currencies

There are currently about 100 BCDs throughout Brazil, all of which are part of the same national network. The most important recent innovation is the creation of an electronic social currency. While the social currencies of each BCD are unique and valid locally, they can now be extended through a common electronic social currency. This allows for use within and outside the local territory. The use of an electronic social currency by the DCBs has been made possible by the development of an independent platform/software. Thanks to this platform, the members, inhabitants, or traders can carry out different types of financial operations (transfers, purchases, payments, telephone credit recharging, credit requests, extracts, etc.) online (Internet, cell phone). These functionalities allow for a better circulation and dissemination of the social currency at the local level. The platform is managed by the network of BCDs at the national level. It has its own legal structure and is endowed with democratic governance. The development of the platform was possible, thanks to the framework law (number 12.865) instituted by the Brazilian government in 2013 to regulate the circulation of all electronic currencies in the country. The main novelty of this law is to allow some institutions not belonging to the financial system (such as some civil society organizations dedicated to microcredit) to be able to manage a certain number of financial transactions up to a maximum amount of 500 million reais (about 100 million euros).

With the electronic platform for managing social currencies, the BCDs are opening up a new horizon not only for those involved in solidarity finance, but also for all those involved in the solidarity economy. First of all, this experiment allows for a level of growth never before imagined. Indeed, this system allows resources from the market economy to be redirected to the solidarity economy through simple online operations by users. This is an opportunity for the BCDs to build up significant equity and to have the power to reinvest in their territories. This horizon of possibility is not without some significant challenges. First of all, the national network platform of the BCDs has to face competition from large financial players and also from a multitude of small FinTech players. The latter see the e-currency field as a new market. They are making numerous service offers and especially offers which are accessible on cell phones.

What remains for the BCDs is the strength of their political project based on a different economy. This supposes the active participation of the inhabitants in each territory to which the BCDs belong. It is these inhabitants who, as associates and users of the platform, constitute the strength of the national network. The strategy of the BCDs now aims at reinforcing their inclusion in a solidarity economy while meeting the legal requirements of their field of activity. This is above all a challenge regarding their legitimacy for solidarity finance practices.

4.4.3 Solidarity Incubator and Demarketing of Nature

We have seen that the use of social money in Brazil has a collective dimension. The practices of the BCDs only make sense insofar as they promote a network of actors and institutions in a territory and are thus distinguished by their strong capacity to mobilize territorial actors. The vocation of the BCDs is community-based and the social currency appears to be the privileged element of a solidarity-based ambition. The territory that supports this solidarity has its own character. It symbolizes attachment, roots, and nature and constitutes the local ecosystem to be defended. In this respect, an obvious link can be made between the attachment to the territory as a space to be protected and the implementation of solidarity economy incubators.

Solidarity economy incubators differ significantly from the business incubators that appeared in Brazil in the early 1980s and were linked to research centers and science parks as part of the decentralization of policies. According to the definition of ANPROTEC (*Associação Nacional de Entidades Promotoras de Empreendimentos Inovadores)*, business incubators are premises specially created to host companies by providing a structure to stimulate, accelerate, or facilitate the transfer of research results to productive activities. To this end, it is expected that the company will be ready to face the reality of the market by relying on its own resources (ANPROTEC, 2008). Often, incubators physically house these companies at an early stage with a support service.

Incubation in the solidarity economy has a very different objective. Known as Technological Incubators of Popular Cooperatives (ITCPs), these experiences are distinguished by the support they provide to popular initiatives. They support these initiatives in the form of cooperatives and associations. The first experience began in 1995 at the Federal University of Rio de Janeiro as part of a graduate program in engineering

(COPPE/UFRJ). In the following decade, the number of these incubators increased considerably in Brazil in an institutional political context favorable to the support of the solidarity economy. Currently, there are more than 100 such incubators organized in two national networks. The origin of this kind of experience seems to have opened up in the Brazilian University a preoccupation concerning the conduct of the development of technological research toward work or society, reversing the traditional logic of the investment made in the market. This incubation work in the solidarity economy seems to reflect a new moment in the history of support for popular organizations in Brazil. Indeed, these are strongly linked to some NGOs and progressive church institutions. To some extent, incubation in the solidarity economy revisits a number of practices of support for social movements. In particular, it reemphasizes the importance of management support for these organizations (França Filho & Cunha, 2010).

Fundamental Differences: From the Object to the Incubation Method

In operational terms, there are differences between "solidarity economy incubation" (SEI) and business incubation. SEI is generally aimed at a low-income public, organized in most cases in small cooperatives. Moreover, the incubated initiatives are not housed (except in some cases of public incubators), and they implement self-management processes (França Filho & Cunha, 2010). The priority audiences for solidarity economy incubation are territories characterized by a high degree of socioeconomic exclusion. In these territories, traditional actors seek to implement restorative social actions. SEI is different in that its primary objective is not to repair but to revive a dynamic of solidarity-based activity through innovation.

Solidarity economic initiatives (*empreendimentos econômicos solidários*) are in most cases managed by people with low incomes, few diplomas, and low qualifications in the labor market. These people combine multi-activity (often informal) with precariousness. They are vulnerable in socioeconomic and socio-professional terms and are often excluded from productive investment policies, even though they are part of the active population. Their territories suffer from a lack of public investment. They are rural areas with traditional communities (riverside and living from fishing and shellfish), favelas, or peripheral districts of large urban centers. From the point of view of method, the SEI breaks radically with the classic practices of business incubation (which play on technology transfer, hierarchy, and specialization of knowledge). Indeed, SEI does not promote technological solutions unless they have a socially affirmed dimension. Instead of the classic technology transfer, SEI prefers the co-construction of solutions combining academic knowledge and popular knowledge. The objective is to promote the emancipation processes of individuals, groups, and their respective territories. In this sense, an ecology of knowledge is mobilized combining hard sciences (engineering) and humanities (human sciences and popular knowledge). Through its collective dimension and its transformative aim, popular education plays a major role in SEI.

From the Incubation of Initiatives to the Incubation of Territories

The SEI strategy has broadened from strengthening popular cooperatives and self-managed enterprises to strengthening their territory and institutional context. The territorial incubation perspective attempts to go beyond the incubation of cooperatives. In doing so, the SEI moves from a socioeconomic concern to a sociopolitical approach and from a socio-productive concern to a socio-organizational approach. In all cases, the aim is to strengthen the capacity for self-organization at the local level. This implies two levels of intervention. The first is local and aims to promote the various mechanisms of public action in the territory. The second is outward-looking and seeks to involve supra-local organizations and entities in the territory. On the sociopolitical level, the SEI favors the establishment of spaces for public debate in order to engage in dialogue on the common problems encountered by the populations of the territory. The idea is to facilitate public discussion practices. To this end, the SEI has a policy of supporting local associations likely to maintain such local public spaces (Laville, 1994). Encouraging the associative dynamic at the local level is a springboard for the development of solidarity-based logics on the territory. Solidarity on the territory can be approached by the sustainability of local solidarity economy enterprises and/or initiatives and by the degree of autonomy which the territory has with respect to its own development (França Filho & Cunha, 2010; Mance, 2003).

A solidarity economy network can be trans-territorial, territorial, and mixed (França Filho & Cunha, 2010). At the trans-territorial level, the network involves a combination of solidarity enterprises or initiatives intervening in the production chain of a given product or service. Such a network implies bilateral (or multilateral) agreements and contracts between organizations in different fields or at different levels of action. Fair trade is a good example of this type of solidarity network. At the territorial level, a solidarity economy network requires the contribution of different fields of activity such as ethical consumption, solidarity finance, free technologies, self-managed production, and local services. In this sense, this type of network implies a linkage between initiatives of very different natures: socioeconomic, sociopolitical, sociocultural, and socio-environmental. Finally, the third type is mixed because it implies a territorial dimension with trans-territorial interactions. In practice, local solidarity economy networks are often mixed. It is indeed rare to find experiences limited to a single geographical area (Mance, 2000, 2002). The very logic of these networks leads them to establish contacts outside their local territory. Moreover, we observe that the stronger the local presence, the greater the capacity to connect to other territories (Dowbor, 2007; França Filho & Cunha, 2010; Mance, 2000, 2002).

Thus, solidarity economy networks participate in complex cooperation strategies that are favorable to local development (França Filho & Cunha, 2010). By engendering their own marketing and production channels, these networks inaugurate new modes of socioeconomic regulation that replace the principle of competition with that of local democratic solidarity (França Filho, 2007; Laville, 1994). For this to happen, it is necessary to establish principles, values, and rules that frame the imperatives of economic profitability of the activity. These principles include citizenship criteria regarding access to rights, equitable distribution of resources, decent wages, environmental protection, commitment to the local context, fair practices, ethical and conscious consumption, and environmental education. It is also about institutionalizing new forms of relationships with public authorities, particularly in terms of public purchasing and negotiated contracts.

Solidarity economy networks invent new forms of institutional articulation between solidarity economy actors and public institutions. From the point of view of a development logic (Dowbor, 2007; Sachs, 2006), the bet made on the solidarity economy networks breaks strongly with the solutions generally known in the fight against unemployment. The idea is to replace the "insertional-competitive" concept with a "sustainable-solidarity" concept (França Filho, 2008). The activity of local solidarity economy networks is the practical translation of the principles of another economy. In the logic of a conventional economy, the market, suppliers, and demanders are independent agents. It is the responsibility of competition and the price setting mechanism to harmonize the relationship between these actors. In the logic of local networks in the solidarity economy, on the other hand, offers are organized and hierarchized within public spaces managed by citizens. In other words, there is a process of democratic control over supply and demand. Contrary to an ordinary market logic, where companies are free to act without having to worry about the impact of their activity on the territory, the solidarity economy perspective poses the principle of a democratic local diagnosis and the respect of ethical principles and values. Solidarity initiatives involve the inhabitants in both the management of the network and the provision of services. This contributes to reinforcing the short circuits on the territory.

Through daily discussion and deliberation within the associative spaces, a learning process takes place. The inhabitants build up a democratic political culture through their interactions. In this respect, local solidarity economy networks are not exclusively economic networks as they are able to combine socio-productive and socio-organizational perspectives as we have seen. The network is a kind of map that the community uses to guide its own development process.

In this context, community development banks play a prominent role in Brazil. The CDBs have a strong potential to endogenize income at the local level. They generate resources through micro-credit and stimulate the local circulation of these same resources through social currencies

(França Filho, 2013; Rigo & França Filho, 2017). On the other hand, the inhabitants are led to manage these resources in practice, thus authorizing the construction of real social pacts on the territory. Thus, when shopkeepers from a popular neighborhood or a traditional community take part in network meetings, an important step is taken in the concretization of an economic alternative. The presence of economic actors such as shopkeepers in the residents' collective is an essential step in building a relationship of trust at the local level and is a guarantee for the sustainability of the initiative.

An Emblematic Example: Matarandiba

Matarandiba is a small village of fishermen and gleaners located on the coastal part of Itaparica Island (facing the large bay forming part of the coast of the city of Salvador in Northeast Brazil). Itaparica Island includes two municipalities with low socioeconomic indicators. With slightly fewer than a thousand inhabitants, Matarandiba is about 40 km away from the Vera Cruz, which is its administrative headquarters. It is therefore understandable that its fate is of little concern to public actors and public policymakers. Its remoteness from the administrative center and its small size combine to serve it poorly. In order to fight against the lack of local resources, for more than ten years its inhabitants have undertaken a self-organized community development of an associative type. This has been possible, thanks to a partnership with the Technological Incubator of Solidarity Economy and Territorial Development Management of the School of Administration of the Federal University of Bahia (ITES/EAUFBA) and other institutional partnerships. The solidarity project started with a series of activities aimed at increasing the ownership of the territory by its inhabitants. The networked initiatives were gradually built up, reshaping the cultural and economic landscape of Matarandiba. The diversity of perspectives which were opened (socio-productive and socio-organizational, socioeconomic and sociopolitical, sociocultural, and socio-environmental) gives the scope of the action. Two associations have been formally constituted and are in charge of coordinating the multiple and diverse local initiatives. The Matarandiba Community Association

(Ascoma) supports projects such as the Ilhamar Community Bank and its social currency called concha. In addition to the Ilhamar BCD, Ascoma also supports a radio station, a small community newspaper, a community cinema initiative, a community infocenter, an agro-ecological food production activity, an oyster artisanal mariculture initiative, a community bakery, a local public transportation service, and a community-based tourism initiative that respects the principles of preservation of the village's environmental, historical, and cultural heritage. The Cultural Association of Matarandiba (Ascomat) carries out intense work in the management of local culture through various initiatives to rescue and preserve a diverse collection of traditional folk culture manifestations, as well as organizing activities such as local events and celebrations (dance and music), a community museum, management of a cultural and heritage center, a library, and tutoring. Responding to public tenders in the cultural field has been one of Ascomat's main strategies, and the association has thus been able to finance more than ten projects. With this wide range of local initiatives, the Matarandiba solidarity network is now considering the strengthening of its local economy through the preservation of its natural habitat and its living ecosystem. This requires the consolidation of its capacity for self-organization and leading a collective deliberation. An essential step for the preservation of the natural space is the strengthening of the collective memory of the place because culture and nature come together in the evocation of the village's past. The project is audacious considering the small number of inhabitants, but its strength lies in the fact that it has been built in an intergenerational perspective.

This example shows that incubation practices in the solidarity economy can enable inhabitants to reclaim their territory through a process of democratic learning and a process of demarketing nature. This virtuous dynamic on natural spaces could not have been set in motion without a parallel process of demarketing work and money. The Matarandiba community sought to give meaning to work by creating activities that could benefit the community, and the use of a social currency has allowed the local population to become aware of their power and their ability to meet their own needs. Innovation has been a constant. However, one may wonder about the nature of this innovation. It is tempting to make the link between the process of demarketing fictitious goods undertaken by the community and the need for it to innovate. From this link, we can surmise a renewed definition of social innovation.

4.5 Through Social Innovation

The practices of demarchandization of labor, land, and money are being invented in different parts of the world and are the result of the collective action of citizens who are committed to the management of their own resources. It is this process of research and organizational invention that we will now study. The fundamental question is how to define the nature of innovation in the processes of demarketing labor, money, and nature. To do this, we need to study the nature of the innovation at stake in these processes. Often reduced to the technological aspect, the conventional approach to innovation seems insufficient to grasp the practices associated with substantive management. It is therefore useful to redefine the concept of innovation within the academic debate on social innovation. This effort seems important to us in order to avoid the risks of trivializing the very idea of social innovation. It is a question of preserving the heuristic value of this concept.

4.5.1 Technological Innovation and Social Innovation: Genealogy of a Concept

If there is innovation in the practices of solidarity economy incubators, it is important to understand its nature. Innovation is not a uniform concept, for it is one that is subject to different interpretations. In Western societies, innovation is often invoked as the fundamental element for a possible exit from the crisis. Focusing on companies, this approach emphasizes changes in the organization of work, improvements in technical procedures, productivity gains linked to new technologies, and the invention of new products and services (Klein et al., 2014). A distinction is generally made between process innovation and product innovation. The former concerns the implementation or adoption of new production or distribution methods. Such changes may affect—separately or simultaneously—materials, human resources, or work methods (Oslo Manual, OECD, 1997). The second is the deployment or sale of a better performing product to provide the consumer with new or improved services (Oslo Manual, OECD, 1997). In all cases, the understanding of innovation is focused on the field of engineering, industry, and natural sciences. The implicit idea common to all these definitions is that innovation is a matter for specialists and technicians, and therefore, it can only be solved by investments in research and development. This type of predominantly technological innovation enjoys significant institutional support, and it impresses political leaders with the possibility of patentability and rapid diffusion to the public.

Generally, innovation thinking is opposed to a deterministic view of the evolution of society, that is, a view in which progress and the modernization of social practices are characterized by a form of irreversibility (Klein et al., 2014). The first major author to focus on innovation was Schumpeter. In his classic work *Theory of Economic Development* (Schumpeter, 1935), he analyzed the causes of the development process. He highlights two key factors that interact: innovation and entrepreneurship. Innovation is understood as a disruptive element that generates a disruption of the equilibrium and/or a rupture of the established order. As such, innovation produces changes that have a material or value impact. Schumpeter's vision is pragmatic. Economic activity is guided by those who make decisions, that is, entrepreneurs. Although they are rarely inventors, they are, on the other hand, facilitators. Entrepreneurs are the actors of change because they are able to produce and disseminate innovations. This is where Schumpeter's theory differs fundamentally from deterministic and macro-social perspectives. He sees innovation as a creative response to three main categories of obstacles: the uncertainty associated with risk, the difficulty of creating, and the resistance of the environment (Schumpeter, 1935). Schumpeter shows that it is not enough to produce satisfactory soap—one must also train people to wash themselves (Klein et al., 2014). This leads him to distinguish invention from innovation. He thus posits that innovation is the result of the diffusion and appropriation of an invention. In other words, innovation is a successful invention. Schumpeter's pioneering work laid the foundations for thinking about innovation. However, his analysis remains limited to the area of technical change and the perimeter of the firm. The perspective opened up by Schumpeter is completed by Perroux (1993). This author associates innovation with what he calls "growth poles." He states that innovation does not arise everywhere or simultaneously. It follows a complex trajectory because its dissemination is linked to a process of gradual adoption. For Perroux, innovation is important because it generates growth and cultural changes and allows the modernization of productive structures.

4.5.2 Understanding Innovation as Social Innovation

The emergence of the concept of innovation is undoubtedly linked to the increased complexity of the socio-environmental problems we have to face. The methods inherited from the past no longer seem to be adapted to the current context. Our societies have high expectations as regards new answers. For many years, creativity has been encouraged, and innovation has become a central theme in the debate. This centrality has allowed this concept to extend beyond the technological question to have a wider scope in the social field. Thus, very interesting work has been carried out by the *Centre de Recherche sur les Innovations Sociales* (Crises) at the University of Quebec in Canada. They have made it possible to establish an initial definition of social innovation. Thus, "any new approach, new practice or new intervention or any new product designed to improve a situation or solve a social problem that has found its destination, whether at the level of institutions, organizations or communities" (Bouchard, 1999) is a social innovation. In other words, social innovation can be understood as "a successful and reproducible social experiment" (Chambon et al., 1982). With this definition, social innovation is the object of a triple validation: by the market, by institutions, and by society itself. Social innovations can then be presented as organizational innovations, institutional innovations, new institutional arrangements, new rules of social and socioeconomic regulation, and/or new forms of resolution of social and socioeconomic problems. The interest of these approaches is to allow the inclusion of other relevant fields of analysis in the study of innovation. Researchers thus show that social innovations are not only present in the private and industrial sectors but that they can be observed in the public sector, in the social economy, and in civil society initiatives (Lévesque & Mendell, 1999; Lévesque & Ninacs, 2000). This extension of the scope is particularly interesting for us because it brings our fields of analysis up to date. Andion (2014) goes further. For him, social innovation emerges from the initiative of individuals or groups focused on the public interest (Novy & Leubolt, 2005). By emphasizing the public interest dimension, the definition proposed by Andion (2014) attempts to escape the risks of trivialization that affect the diffusion of the concept of social innovation and emphasizes its role as an engine of social transformation (Murray et al., 2010).

4.5.3 From the Trivialization of Social Innovation to Its Revival

As we have seen, the concept of social innovation arose from the need to extend thinking beyond its technological dimension. In doing so, this current of research has been interested in innovation practices in a variety of fields of activity and fields of action. However, if innovation is located in market and nonmarket activities, in public institutions, in civil society, and in popular circles, its definition becomes polysemous and loses some of its density. Social business actors can then position themselves to propose a private treatment of social innovation based on the rationality of the market. In order to avoid this trivialization, certain additional analysis criteria can be put forward: (a) the purpose of the innovation, (b) the mode of access to the innovation, (c) the mode of use or appropriation by the users of the innovation, and (d) the mode of generation of the innovation.

The first criterion, linked to the purpose of the innovation, helps us to distinguish between innovation as a response to a social need and innovation as a response to a market demand. In the first case, the response is not conditional on a specific form, whereas in the second case the innovation is the proposal of a good or service from a private operator. The confusion between the two is frequent, as many goods or services are available on the market. The social need then ends up being dissolved in the use of certain goods and services. These are identified by consumers as necessities, and the act of consumption comes to be claimed as a social need. The single criterion of purpose thus seems insufficient to avoid the trivialization of social innovation.

The second parameter is the mode of access to innovation. It can be done through the market, and then it supposes a purchasing relationship with a price and an act of consumption. In this case, economic selectivity characterizes access to innovation, since it is a purchasing relationship. Access can also be provided by the public service. In this case, individuals must meet certain access criteria defined by the public policy concerned (social criteria) and comply with the required formalism. Finally, access can be provided through services offered by civil society organizations and more broadly by the SSE (independently or in conjunction with the public authorities). In this case, the formalism may be less because the organization can more easily adapt to the needs of the actors or act as a facilitator of the relationship between the individual and the public institution. In the end, the question of access thus comes down to a consumer/client option (with resource conditions) and a citizen/user option (with rights conditions).

The third parameter concerns the mode of use or appropriation of the innovation by the target audience. This parameter indicates the degree of effectiveness of the innovation measured by its inclusion in the daily lives of individuals. A primary question is the power of replication of the innovation. If this power is high, appropriation will be facilitated. However, replicability in turn presupposes standardization and normalization of use. The logic that prevails in this case is technical. This tends to crowd out any form of social adaptation. The technical dimension of innovation inaugurates a movement of separation from the social, which it seeks to tame in order to better subordinate it. Standardization takes place to the detriment of local social and cultural contexts. In-depth observation of practices shows the importance of designing technical solutions in line with the way of life of the inhabitants and inscribed in their social relations and their culture. The diversity of the modes of use inherited from the different contexts of use opposes replicability. This diversity is a guarantee of social creativity for it allows the emergence or the enlargement of own solutions. It is a manifestation of the dormant richness of each culture and each territory. It is also a relevant perspective for considering the democratization of use or even for a democracy of users (Godbout, 1987).

The fourth parameter is related to the mode of generation of innovation. Questioning the conditions of the emergence of social innovation implies studying the movement of production of the innovation by distinguishing between the logics of diffusion (top-down and-bottom up) and the logics of origin (exogenous and endogenous). In our presentation, we will distinguish three cases.

In the first case, social innovations are conceived by agents outside the territory (outsiders). These innovations generally follow a top-down logic according to the precept of technology transfer. The presupposition here is that of a hierarchy of knowledge between the designers of the innovation and the users. The nature of the knowledge in this case is purely technical and does not cover sociocultural aspects. There is a power relationship between the knowledge holders and the others.

In the second case, social innovations are designed by the users themselves (endogenous logic). The possible technical dimension of the innovation is embedded in the culture of the community that produces it. The mode of emergence follows the logic of self-organized collective processes. In this way, social innovation expresses the creativity of the collective and invents forms that are natively compatible with the expectations and values of the actors who constitute it. The spirit of parity guides these self-organized collectives in peer-to-peer mode.

In a third case, we combine an endogenous and exogenous logic. Most of the time, these are alliances, partnerships, or links created between different institutional agents. This can be a relationship between a university and a community (as we have seen with the example of incubation in solidarity). Innovation is then defined as a co-construction between the members of the collective and the representatives of the university. This type of partnership emphasizes dialogue and listening. It requires empathy and humility on the part of the external actor (Table 4.3).

At this stage of our analysis, we can identify four characterizations of the criteria mentioned to support a definition of social innovation that escapes instrumentalization:

Table 4.3 The boundary between technological and social innovations

	Technological innovation	Innovation social
Purpose	Economic	Social
Access mode	Market services	Public, common, and/or re-signified market services
Mode of ownership	Technique	Social
Generation mode	Exogenous	Endogenous and/or endogenous—exogenous

- **The purpose** of social innovation is not the same as a market objective. If the innovation mobilizes economic resources, it re-signifies its economic activity. In this case, the economic criteria of the market are called upon to be democratically requalified on the basis of values of cooperation and reciprocity;
- **The logic of access to** social innovation does not take place through market mechanisms, criteria, and conditions (unless the market logic is re-signified through regulatory mechanisms originating from society itself, as witnessed by fair trade or solidarity finance practices). Access to social innovation takes place notably through public service or common services offered by the self-organization processes of society;
- **The mode of use or appropriation** of social innovation does not depend on standardized methods of use. It presupposes taking into account the uses of the inhabitants and their involvement. Innovation is socially appropriate and opens up the possibility of a democracy of uses;
- **The mode of generation** of social innovation is not conceived by subjects or institutions outside its context of use. Social innovation is generated either endogenously or in a relationship between endogeny and exogeny marked by the principles of cooperation and reciprocity.

4.5.4 On the Relationship Between Science, Technology, and Innovation

Rethinking the "science, technology and innovation" (STI) paradigm implies rethinking its respective terms. We will discuss them in turn. Science is marked in the first place by the opposition between exact sciences and human and social sciences (hard science vs soft science). This opposition reflects a balance of power. The exact sciences dominate the humanities and social sciences by a greater claim to scientificity. This balance of power is so strong that it extends to the heart of the social sciences. Thus, orthodox economics feeds on this claim. It opposes heterodox economics not so much by the strength of its theoretical arguments as by the use of mathematizable and mathematized approaches. In this, it satisfies a universal need for certainty that is philosophically problematic as Dewey (2015) shows. Technology, on the other hand, seeks to present itself in its procedural neutrality and also seeks to be outside the humanities and social sciences. Yet, sociotechnical approaches have perfectly demonstrated the strong link between technology and human and social sciences (Emery & Trist, 1960; Trist & Bamforth, 1951; Woodward, 1970). However, innovation is still marked by a technological vision based on the exact sciences. This strong anchoring explains the difficulty in thinking about a noninstrumentalized social innovation.

The STI paradigm is very well recognized by political and institutional circles. Its visibility essentially favors innovation that is compatible with market solutions. Thus, when a collective from a working-class neighborhood mobilizes in the search for innovative solutions to specific problems in its area, there is a good chance that the request will be considered as a social policy. Policymakers generally cannot imagine that such a demand would emerge from an ITS investment program. This means that large investments raised on innovation issues are unlikely to reach socially innovative terrain. There is thus an obvious paradox. Innovation is invoked as a response to the crisis, but the resources released to serve it can barely go where the crisis hits hardest.

More generally, the discrediting of the humanities and social sciences is detrimental. It is commonly accepted that the development of technologies is nourished by progress in the knowledge of natural sciences and engineering. However, it is less consensual to note that major advances in public services and public action can benefit from social science knowledge (Lévesque, 2009). Research on social innovation is undoubtedly an opportunity to change things. This will require a rethinking of the STI paradigm with the help of the humanities and social sciences. The latter can help us to better understand the technical changes underway. They can also promote a comprehensive approach in the formulation of public policies and contribute effectively through applied social science work (Lévesque, 2000, 2002). This renewal of reflection on innovation also invites us to think of another positioning for the exact sciences and engineering. In the field of social innovation, there is a possible and highly relevant space for interdisciplinary work combining exact sciences and human and social sciences. The production of such knowledge is particularly encouraging in order to imagine new connections between scholarly knowledge and popular knowledge. This is an unprecedented challenge of transformation.

4.5.5 Characteristics of Innovation in the Solidarity Economy

The preceding analyses show the variety and extent of solidarity economy practices as well as the possibility of constituting a field conducive to the development of social innovation that is not reduced to its market and technical dimensions. In our opinion, this field has some characteristic features. The first aspect concerns the collective nature of the initiatives. In this sense, these initiatives cannot be confused with commercial entrepreneurship, which is always experienced as an individual initiative. Social innovation is only able to respond in a sustainable way to social problems insofar as it respects this character of collective action and decision. The second characteristic aspect concerns the process of learning about democratic governance. Social innovation induces processes of change that can contribute to the construction of a democratic political culture. It is possible to think of innovation as a participatory process (Laurent et al., 2018). In this, it can be seen as a democratic space that fosters autonomy, freedom of expression, self-management, and self-organization. The third characteristic trait concerns territorial rootedness. Studies show that social innovation is never conceived independently of the characteristics (sociocultural, socioeconomic, or sociopolitical) of its local context of insertion. One of the objectives of the solidarity economy is therefore to develop the link between innovation and the population through a strong presence in the territory. This is achieved through networked cooperation strategies, the promotion of solidarity development, new forms of relationships between the actors of this development, and new institutional relationships. The fourth feature corresponds to the mobilization of local knowledge. From a solidarity economy prospect, social innovation draws on the knowledge of the territory in which it is deployed. This is precisely why it tends to be culturally "tempered." In most cases, this local knowledge interacts with scientific or technical knowledge provided by an external agent. It is in the transdisciplinary perspective that a synthesis concerned with respect and dialogue between distinct knowledge can be played out. From this point of view, the very idea of a technological transfer is rejected as inappropriate. Social innovation develops in the co-construction of local solutions and the ethical respect of the parties involved. The fifth characteristic trait accounts for the psychosocial dimension of the practice through the process of recognizing the subjects involved. In this way, the processes of personal transformation are linked to the institutional transformations mentioned. This dimension of intersubjective recognition shared between the subjects is the result of a dynamic of recognition (Honneth, 2000). This includes the recognition of the local context, its knowledge, and its culture. This dynamic implies the establishment of relationships guided by principles of autonomy and dialogue. In contexts characterized by great socioeconomic vulnerability, this question of recognition is of decisive importance since it is the basis for a strengthened social fabric and is the condition for relevant social innovation. This innovation combines a democratic anchoring with the objective of demarketing fictitious goods.

References

Abdelnour, S., & Lambert, A. (2014). L'entreprise de soi : un nouveau mode de gestion politique des classes politiques ? *Geneses, 95*(2), 27.

Aglietta, M., & Orléan, A. (1982). *La violence de la monnaie*. PUF. 324 pages.

Albuquerque, P. P. (2003). Moeda social 2. In Cattani (Ed.), *A outra economia*. Veraz Editores.

Allard-Poesi, F., & Loilier, T. (2009). Qu'est-ce que la critique en sciences du management ? Que pourrait-elle être ? *Economies et Societes*, 1975–1999.

Andion, C. (2014). Inovação Social. In R. F. Boullosa (Ed.), *Dicionário para a formação em gestão social* (pp. 98–102). Ciags/UFBA.

ANPROTEC. (2008). *Associação Nacional de Entidades Promotoras de Empreendimentos Imovadores*. Perguntas e respostas. http://www.anprotec.org.br/publicacao.php?idpublicacao=117

Arendt, H. (1970). *The human condition*. University of Chicago Press. 340 pages.

Bacqué, M. H., Rey, H., & Sintomer, Y. (2005). *Gestion de proximité et démocratie participative : une perspective comparative*. La découverte. 314 pages.

Barbezieux, P., & Herody, C. (2016, February). *Report to the Prime Minister on the collaborative economy*. 94 pages.

Bauwens, M., & Kostakis, V. (2017). *Cooperativism in the digital era, or how to form a global counter-economy*. Opendemocracy.net.

Bernet, J., Eynaud, P., Maurel, O., & Vercher, C. (2016). *La gestion des associations*. Eres édition.

Blanc, J. (1998). Les monnaies parallèles : évaluation du phénomène et enjeux théoriques. *Revue d'économie financière, 49*, 81–102.

Blanc, J. (2011). Classifying "CCs" – Community complementary and local currencies' types and generations. *International Journal of Community Currency Research, 15*, 4–10.

Blondiaux, L. (2008). *Le nouvel esprit de la démocratie. Actualité de la démocratie participative*. Seuil, coll. La république des idées. 109 pages.

Borzaga, C., & Defourny, J. (2001). *The emergence of social enterprise*. Routledge.

Borzaga, C., & Depedri, S. (2009). Working for social enterprises: Does it make a difference? In A. Amin (Ed.), *Social economy. International perspectives on economic solidarity* (pp. 82–114). Zed Press.

Borzaga, C., & Depedri, S. (2015). Multi-stakeholder governance in civil society organizations: Models and outcomes. In J. L. Laville, D. Young, & P. Eynaud (Eds.), *Civil society, the third sector and social enterprise: Governance and democracy* (pp. 109–121). Routledge.

Bouchard, M. J. (1999). *Recherche en sciences humaines et sociales et innovations sociales, Contribution à une politique de l'immatériel.* Conseil québécois de la recherche sociale (CQRS), Québec, les Publications du Québec.

Bouquin, S. (2010). Harry Braverman face à la sociologie du travail. *L'homme et la société, 4*(178), 159–179.

Braverman, H. (1998). *Labor and monopoly capital: The degradation of work in the twentieth century.* Review Monthly Press.

Broca, S. (2017). Le digital labor, extension infinie ou fin du travail ? Tracés. *Revue de sciences humaines, 32*, 133–144.

Bucolo, E., Eynaud, P., & Haeringer, J. (2015). La gouvernance des associations en pratiques. In P. Eynaud (Ed.), *Gouvernance entre diversité et normalisation.* Collection Hors Série Juris Association, Editeur Dalloz.

Bureau, M. C., & Corsani, A. (2015). Les coopératives d'activité et d'emploi : pratiques d'innovation institutionnelle. *Revue Française de Socio-Économie, 15*, 213–231.

Búrigo, F. L. (2002). *Moeda social e circulação de riquezas na economia solidária.* Disponível em: http://money.socioeco.org/documents/67pdf_Moeda.pdf. Acesso em ago 29, 2010.

Caillé, A. (1994). In Coll. Recherches, Série Bibliothèque du Mauss (Ed.), *Don, intérêt et intéressement : Bourdieu, Mauss, Platon et quelques autres.* La Découverte.

Caillé, A., Humbert, M., Latouche, S., & Viveret, P. (2011). Vers le convivialisme. In *De la convivialité : dialogues sur la société conviviale à venir* (pp. 15–24). La Découverte.

Callon, M., Lascoumes, P., & Barthe, Y. (2001). *Agir dans un monde incertain : essai sur la démocratie technique*. Editions Seuil.

Casilli, A. (2013). Contre l'hypothèse de la fin de la vie privée. *Revue française des sciences de l'information et de la communication, 3.*

Casilli, A. (2015). *Digital labor: Work, technologies and conflictualities.* https://halshs.archives-ouvertes.fr/halshs-01145718

Chambon, J. L., Davis, A., & Devevey, J. M. (1982). *Les innovations sociales.* PUF. Collection Que sais-je?

Chandler, A. D. (1992). Managerial enterprise and competitive capabilities. *Business History, 34*(1), 11–41.

Chanial, P. (2010, January 30). La délicate essence du socialisme. *Revue du MAUSS permanente.*
Chanlat, J. F. (2013). Les études critiques en management : Un rappel historique. *Communication, Information médias théories pratiques, 31*(1).
Chauvière, M., & Godbout, J. T. (1992). *Les usagers entre marché et citoyenneté.* L'Harmattan.
Colliac, S. (2005). Monnaies parallèles provinciales et fédéralisme budgétaire en Argentine. *Revue d'économie financière, 81*, 1–20.
Conaty, P., & Bollier, D. (2014, August 27–28). *Toward an open co-operativism: A new social economy based on open platforms, co-operative models and the commons.* Report on a commons strategies group workshop, Berlin, Germany.
Coutrot, T. (2018). *Libérer le travail : Pourquoi la gauche s'en moque et pourquoi cela doit changer.* Edition Seuil. 303 pages.
Dacheux, E., & Goujon, D. (2016). Les promesses théoriques des recherches sur les initiatives solidaires : L'exemple du délibéralisme. *Revue française de socio économie, 16*, 201–214.
Debord, G. (2002). *The society of the spectacle.* Black and Red Publisher. 132 pages.
Delvolvé, N., & Veyer, S. (2009). *De la coopérative d'activités et d'emploi à la mutuelle de travail : produire du droit pour accompagner un projet politique d'économie sociale.* Juin.
Dewey, J. (2008). *Logic – The theory of inquiry.* Saerchinger Press. 844 pages.
Dewey, J. (2015). *The quest for certainty: A study of the relation of knowledge and action.* Andesite Press. 332 pages.
Dewey, J. (2016). *The public and its problems: An essay in political inquiry.* Swallow Press. 304 pages.
Dowbor, L. (2007). *Democracia econômica: um passeio pelas teorias.* BNB.
Drucker, P. (1954). The practice of management. 280 pages.
Dujarier, M. A. (2014). *Le management désincarné.* La Découverte.
Emery, F. E., & Trist, E. L. (1960). In C. W. Churchman (Ed.), *Socio-technical systems, management sciences models and techniques.* Pergamon.
Endenburg, G. (1988). *Sociocracy as social design.* Eburon.
Eynaud, P. (2015). *Gouvernance entre diversité et normalisation.* Collection Hors Série Juris Association, Editeur Dalloz.
Eynaud, P. (2018). Quand développement territorial rime avec économie solidaire. *Revue Diagonal, 203*, 12–14.
Eynaud, P., & Gérome, F. (2014, Février 19). Faire face aux défis. *Juris Associations, 492.*

Eynaud, P., & Guibert, G. (2012, Novembre). La course à la taille dans le secteur associatif des musiques actuelles : de la crise de sens à la proposition alternative d'une plateforme collaborative. *Revue RECMA, 326.*

Eynaud, P., & Schmidt, G. (2012). Le monde associatif en mutation : Restructuration, Les singularités du secteur. *Juris Associations, 465*, 30–32.

Feher, M. (2017). *Le temps des investis: essai sur la nouvelle question sociale.* Editions la Découverte.

França Filho, G. C. (2006). Políticas públicas de economia solidária no Brasil. In França Filho, Laville, Medeiros, & Magnen (Eds.), *Ação Pública e economia solidária - uma perspectvia internacional* (pp. 259–267). EDUFBA/EDURGS.

França Filho, G. C. (2007). Teoria e prática em economia solidária: problemática, desafios e vocação. *Civitas-Revista de Ciências Sociais, 7*(1), 155–174.

França Filho, G. C. (2008). Definindo gestão social. In Silva Jr., Mâsih, Cançado, & Schommer (Eds.), *Gestão social: práticas em debate, teorias em construção* (pp. 26–37). Imprensa Universitária.

França Filho, G. C. (2013). *Bancos Comunitários de Desenvolvimento (BCD's) como expressão de Finanças Solidárias: por uma outra abordagem da inclusão financeira* (1st ed.). Arte Visual.

França Filho, G. C., & Cunha, E. V. (2010, Out./Dez). Incubação de redes locais de economia solidária: lições e aprendizados a partir da experiência do projeto Eco-Luzia e da metodologia da ITES/UFBA. *Revista Organizações & Sociedade (O&S-EAUFBA), 16*(51).

França Filho, G. C., & Silva, J., Jr. (2009). Bancos Comunitários de Desenvolvimento (BCD). In Cattani (Ed.), *Dicionário Internacional da Outra Economia* (pp. 31–37). Edições Almedina.

Gardin, L., & Laville, J. L. (2017). L'économie solidaire. In D. Nyssens (Ed.), *Economie sociale et solidaire : socio économie du 3ème secteur* (pp. 187–219). Editions Deboeck.

Gattes, B., & Kiviat, B. (2008, Jul 31). Making capitalism more creative. *TIME Magazine.* 4p. Disponível em: http://content.time.com/time/magazine/article/0,9171,1828417,00.html. Acesso em de novembro de 28, 2013.

Girard, R. (1979). *Violence and the sacred.* John Hopkins University Press. 352 pages.

Girard, R. (1987). *Things hidden since the foundation of the world.* Stanford University Press. 470 pages.

Godbout, J. T. (1987). *La démocratie des usagers.* Les Éditions du Boréal Express. 192 pages.

Gorz, A. (2004). *Critique of economic reason* (2nd ed.). Verso. 256 pages.

Gorz, A. (2010). *The immaterial*. Seagull Books.

Gorz, A. (2018). *Ecologica*. Seagull Books. 186 pages.

Granovetter, M. (2000). *Le marché autrement, Sociologie économique*. Desclée de Brouwer. 239 pages.

Granovetter, M. (2007). Ação econômica e estrutura social: o problema da imersão. *RAE eletrônica, 6*(1).

Guérin, I., Hersent, M., & Fraisse, L. (2011). *Femmes, économie et développement : de la résistance à la justice sociale*. Eres Editions.

Harribey, J. M. (2009). Ambivalence et dialectique du travail : Remarques sur le livre de Moishe Postone, Temps, travail et domination sociale. *Contretemps. Nouvelle série, 4*, 137–149.

Herreros, G. (2012). *La violence dans les organisations : plaidoyer pour des organisations réflexives*. Eres Editions.

Hillenkamp, I. (2013). Le principe de householding aujourd'hui. Discussion théorique et approche empirique par l'économie populaire. In I. Hillenkamp & J.-L. Laville (Eds.), *Socioéconomie et démocratie. L'actualité de Karl Polanyi*. Erès.

Honneth, A. (2000). *La lutte pour la reconnaissance*. du Cerf. (ed. or. Kampf um Anerkennung, 1992). 232 pages.

Jappe, A. (2017). *La société autophage : capitalisme, démesure et auto-destruction*. Editions la découverte.

Klein, J. L., Laville, J. L., & Moulaert, F. (2014). *Innovation sociale*. Eres Edition. 246 pages.

Laborde, J. P. (2015). La solidarité entre adhésion et affiliation. In A. Supiot (Ed.), *La solidarité : enquête sur un principe juridique* (pp. 109–123). Collège de France, Edition Odile Jacob.

Laloux, F. (2014). *Reinventing organizations: A guide to creating organizations inspired by the next stage in human consciousness*. Nelson Parker. 382 pages.

Laurent, B., Baker, M., Baudoin, V., & Raulet-Croset, N. (2018). *Innovation et participation: approches critiques*. PSL, Presses des Mines. 282 pages.

Laville, J. L. (1994). *L'économie solidaire : une perspective internationale*. Desclée de Brouwer.

Laville, J. L. (2000). *Qu'est-ce que le tiers secteur ? La Revue du MAUSS* (Vol. 16). La Découverte.

Laville, J. L. (2010). *Politique de l'association*. Seuil. 350 pages.

Laville, J. L. (2015). La théorie critique : de l'impasse au renouveau. In Frère (Ed.), *Le tournant de la théorie critique*. Desclée de Brouwer.

Laville, J. L. (2018). *L'association, sociologie et économie*. Fayard – Pluriel.

Laville, J. L. (2023). *The solidarity economy*. University of Minnesota Press.

Laville, J. L., & Hoarau, C. (2013). *La gouvernance des associations*. Editions Erès. 368 pages.

Laville, J. L., & Sainsaulieu, R. (1997). *Sociologie de l'association : Des organisations à l'épreuve du changement social*. Desclée de Brouwer, Collection Sociologie économique. 403 pages.

Laville, J. L., & Salmon, A. (2015). *Associations et Action Publique*. Desclée de Brouwer. 630 pages.

Laville, J. L., & Salmon, A. (2016). Les associations et leur contribution à la démocratie : un défi contemporain. In R. Lafore (Ed.), *Refonder les solidarités : les associations au cœur de la protection sociale* (pp. 147–162).

Laville, J. L., Young, D., & Eynaud, P. (2015). *Civil society, the third sector, social enterprise: Governance and democracy*. Routledge Publisher. April, paperback.

Lévesque, B. (2000). Innovation sociale et innovation technologique: l'apport de la recherche en science sociale et humaine. *Report to the Conseil de la Science et de la Technologie du Québec*. Bibliothèque Nationale du Québec, Bibliothèque Nationale du Canadá. www.cst.gouv.qc.ca

Lévesque, B. (2002). *Les entreprises de l'économie sociale, plus porteuses d'innovations sociales que les autres ?* Cahiers de l'ARUC-ÉS.

Lévesque, B. (2009). Contribuição da nova sociologia econômica para repensar a economia no sentido do desenvolvimento sustentável. In A. C. B. Martes (Ed.), *Redes e Sociologia Econômica* (pp. 107–127). Editora UFSCAR.

Lévesque, B., & Mendell, M. (1999). L'économie sociale au Québec : éléments théoriques et empiriques pour le débat sur la recherche. *Lien social et Politiques, 41*, 105–118.

Lévesque, B., & Ninacs, W. (2000). The social economy in Canada: The Quebec experience. In Shragge & Fontan (Eds.), *Social economy. International debates and perspectives* (pp. 112–129). Black Rose Book.

Lietaer, B., & Kennedy, M. (2010). *Monedas regionales: nuevos instrumentos para una prosperidad sustentable*. La Hidra de Lerna Ediciones.

Limeira, T. (2015, junho). *Empreendedorismo social no Brasil: estado da arte e desafios*.

Mance, E. (2000). *A revolução das redes*. Vozes.

Mance, E. (2002). *Redes de colaboração solidária*. Vozes.

Mance, E. (2003). *Como organizar redes solidárias*. DP&A, Fase, IFIL.

Marival, C., Petrella, F., & Richez-Battesti, N. (2015). Coopérer : entre économie d'échelle et reconquête du fait associatif ? In *XVes Rencontres du RIUESS - La créativité de l'économie sociale et solidaire est-elle soluble dans l'entrepreneuriat ?*

Maurel, L., & Aufrère, L. (2018). *Pour une protection sociale des données personnelles*. https://hal.archives-ouvertes.fr/hal-01903526
Melo Neto, J., & Magalhães, S. (2005). *O poder do circulante local: a moeda social no Conjunto Palmeiras*. Palmas.
Melo Neto, J., & Magalhães, S. (2006). *Bancos comunitários de desenvolvimento: uma rede sob controle da comunidade*. Instituto banco palmas de desenvolvimento e socioeconomia solidária.
Menezes, M., & Crocco, M. A. (2009). Sistemas de moedas locais: uma investigação sobre seus potenciais a partir do caso do Banco Bem, em Vitória/ES. *Economia e Sociedade, 18*(2), 36.
Murray, R., Caulier-Grice, J., & Mulgan, G. (2010). *The open book of social innovation*. ESTA/The Young Foundation.
Naro, G. (2015). Le new public management ou la gestion malade de la société. In Dietrich, Pigeyre, & Vercher-Chaptal (Eds.), *Dérives et perspectives de la gestion : échanges autour des travaux de Julienne Brabet*. Septentrion, Presses Universitaires. 180 pages.
Novy, A., & Leubolt, B. (2005). Participatory budgeting in Porto Alegre: Social innovation and the dialectical relationship of state and civil society. *Urban Studies, 42*(11), 2023–2036.
OECD. (1997). *Oslo manual.*
Oliveira, F. R., & Vaasconcelos, J. J. (2011). Os desafios da gestão nos negócios sociais e inclusivos: marco regulatório. In Instituto Walmart (Ed.), *Mapa de soluções inovadoras - tendências de empreendedores na construção de negócios sociais e inclusivos* (Vol. 4). Instituto Walmart/Ashoka. Gestão de negócios sociais e inclusivos, 24p.
Ostrower, F., & Stone, M. (2015). Governing boards and organizational environments: Growing complexities, shifting boundaries. In J.-L. Laville, D. Young, & P. Eynaud (Eds.), *Civil society, the third sector and social enterprise: Governance and democracy* (pp. 75–90). Routledge.
Passos, O. A. (2008). *Explorando novas práticas organizacionais em economia solidária: conceito e características dos bancos comunitários*. Anais do V Encontro Nacional de Estudos Organizacionais.
Pérez, R. (2009). *La gouvernance de l'entreprise*. La Découverte. 128 pages.
Perroux, F. (1993). *œuvres complètes* (6 volumes). Presses universitaires de Grenoble.
Pessis, C., Topçu, S., & Bonneuil, C. (2015). *Une autre histoire des trente glorieuses*. La Découverte. 309 pages.
Polanyi, K. (1977). In H. W. Pearson (Ed.), *The livelihood of man*. Academic Press.

Polanyi, K. (1986, June). La fallace économiste. *Le Bulletin du Mauss, 18*. translation in French of an extract from "The Livelihood of Man".
Postone, M. (1996). *Time, labor, and social domination: A reinterpretation of Marx's critical theory*. Cambridge University Press. 440 pages.
Primavera, H. (2003). Last Tango in Buenos Aires. Paris. *Revue du MAUSS, 21*, 113–118.
Putnam, R. D. (1993). *Making democracy work: Civic traditions in modern Italy*. Princeton University Press.
Renault, M. (2011). Elaborer des outils pour construire une société plus conviviale : d'une expérience de terrain à un raisonnement théorique. In Caillé, Humbert, Latouche, & Viveret (Eds.), *De la convivialité : dialogues sur la société conviviale à venir* (pp. 167–187). La Découverte.
Rey, O. (2014). *Une question de taille*. Les essais.
Rigo, A. S. (2014). *Moedas Sociais e Gestão de Territórios: Aplicações e Implicações Teóricas e Práticas*. Tese (Administração) - Universidade Federal da Bahia.
Rigo, A. S., & França Filho, G. C. (2017). *Bancos Comunitários e Moedas Sociais no Brasil - Reflexões a partir da noção de economia substantiva*. Edufba. Coleção E-Livro.
Rospabé, P. (1995). *La dette de la vie*. Éditions La découverte/Mauss.
Sachs, I. (2006). *Desenvolvimento includente, sustentável e sustentado*. Garamond.
Salomon, L., & Anheier, H. (1992). Search of nonprofit sector: The quest for definitions. *Voluntas: International Journal of Voluntary and Nonprofit Organizations, 3*(2), 267–311.
Sangiorgio, J., & Veyer, S. (2009). Les coopératives d'activités et d'emploi : un exemple de construction d'une innovation sociale. *Projectics/Proyéctica/Projectique, 1*(1), 51–61.
Scholz, T. (2013). *Digital labor: The internet as playground and factory*. Routledge.
Scholz, T. (2016). *Platform cooperativism: Challenging the corporate sharing economy*. Rosa Luxembourg Stiftung.
Scholz, T., & Schneider N. (Eds.). (2016, November). *Ours to hack and to own*. OR Books. 272 pages.
Schumpeter, J. (1935). *Theory of economic development*. Routledge. 234 pages.
Soares, C. (2006). *Moeda social: uma análise interdisciplinar das suas potencialidades no Brasil contemporâneo*. Tese (Doutorado) - Centro de Filosofia e Ciências Humanas, Universidade Federal de Santa Catarina.
Soares, C. (2009). Moeda social. In Cattani (Ed.), *Dicionário Internacional da Outra Economia* (pp. 255–259). Edições Almedina.

Steen-Johnsen, K., Eynaud, P., & Wijkström, F. (2011, September 1–11). On civil society governance: A new field of research. *Voluntas Journal.* Special thematic issue on Civil society organizations governance.

Stervinou, S., & Noël-Lemaître, C. (2008). Les coopératives d'activité et d'emploi (CAE) : un outil juridique au service d'un entrepreneuriat responsable. *Management & Avenir, 20*, 65–86.

Supiot, A. (2015). *La solidarité : enquête sur un principe juridique*. Collège de France, Edition Odile Jacob.

Swedberg, R. (2009). A Sociologia econômica do capitalismo: uma introdução e agenda de pesquisa. In A. C. B. Martes (Ed.), *Redes e Sociologia Econômica* (pp. 161–198). Editora UFSCAR.

Théret, B. (2008). Os três estados da moeda: abordagem interdisciplinar do fato monetário. *Economia e Sociedade, Campinas, 17*(1), 1–28.

Tiscoski, G., Rosolen, T., & Comini, G. (2013). Empreendedorismo Social e Negócios Sociais: Um Estudo Bibliométrico da Produção Nacional e Internacional. In *Encontro Nacional da ANPAD* (Vol. 27). Anais.

Tocqueville, A. D. (2002). *Democracy in America*. University of Chicago Press. 722 pages.

Tönnies, F. (2021). *Community and society* (1st ed.). Mockingbird Press. 320 pages.

Trist, E., & Bamforth, K. (1951). Some social and psychological consequences of longwall method of coalgetting. *Human Relations, 4*, 3–38.

Valéau, P., Eynaud, P., Chatelain-Ponroy, S., & Sponem, S. (2018). Toward a reassessment of the role of rank-and-file stakeholders in nonprofit organizations. *Nonprofit and Voluntary Sector Quarterly*, 1–27.

Viveret, P. (2004). *Reconsidérer la richesse*. Editions de l'aube, Poche essai.

Weber, M. (2002). *The protestant ethic and the spirit of capitalism*. Penguin Books. translated by Peter Baehr and Gordon C. Wells.

Woodward, J. (1970). Technology, material control and organizational behavior. In J. P. Schwitte & A. R. Negandhi (Eds.), *Organizational behaviour models* (p. 21). Kent State University, Comparative Administration Research Institute.

Yunus, M. (2008). *Um mundo sem pobreza: a empresa social e o futuro do capitalismo*. Ática.

Yunus, M. (2010). *Criando um negócio Social: como iniciativas economicamente viáveis podem solucionar os grandes problemas da sociedade*. Elsevier.

Zask, J. (2011). *Participer : essais sur les formes démocratiques de la participation*. Editions le bord de l'eau.

Zelizer, V. (2005). *La signification sociale de la monnaie*. Seuil.

5

In Search of Another Type of Management

This chapter is an opportunity to return to the double unsustainability mentioned in the introduction to this work. We propose to detail here the analysis of two proposals that are rich in terms of substantive management, that is, management based on solidarity and sustainability. The first is South American, and it arises from the Brazilian school of thought on *gestão social.* [1] This is driven by abundant, long-term discussion. It can be seen as a conceptual and practical response from a country long characterized by strong inequalities. The second is North American, and it concerns the management of the commons. This school of thought is in line with the work of Ostrom, and it initially began with the problems of preserving natural spaces, but is not limited to them. We will see how these two schools of thought differ and complement each other. The practical dimension of these two proposals will help us define the field that we propose to call "the Other Management."

[1] *Gestão social* can hardly be translated as "social management" because the scope of reflection of *gestão social* goes far beyond the framework of human resources management. It would be more accurate to call it "social and solidarity-based management." In order to remain as close as possible to the thinking of the Brazilian authors, we will keep the Portuguese qualifier.

P. Eynaud, G. Carvalho de França Filho, *Solidarity and Organization*,
https://doi.org/10.1007/978-3-031-27568-5_5

5.1 The Brazilian School of *Gestão Social*

The conceptualization around *gestão social* dates back to the 1990s (França Filho & de Freitas Boullosa, 2015). The *gestão social* has found its credentials in Latin America and more precisely in Brazil. It remains deeply European in its choice of academic references. Although it is contemporary with the work on social entrepreneurship and social business, it is rarely cited. We can wonder about this lack of renown. The language barrier is undoubtedly a first explanation. In fact, this research is presented in Portuguese and cannot benefit from the same dissemination as an English-language publication. But this does not explain everything. Its position, which is far removed from the orthodox vision of management, is also undoubtedly a factor. Historically, the beginning of the reflection took place in an international context around a training course given by South American professors in the framework of the Inter-American Development Bank. The training course initially sought to explore the possible content of a *gestão social* in a neoliberal perspective. This reflection was then extended in the Brazilian context well beyond the training context. It took a critical stance by initiating organizational thinking linked to the concepts of public space and public action. At the end of the 90s, three research subgroups were distinguished by their object: democracy, territory, and the third sector. As a result, the concept of *gestão social* began to gain a wider audience among management and administration teachers, students, and field actors. The popularity of the concept was based on the possibility of a management oriented toward democratic deliberation and to the interaction between the state and civil society. In 2007, the community of researchers and practitioners of *gestão social* decided to set up an annual national meeting. Since then, the community has continued to grow through the establishment of training and university degrees and the publication of specialized journals and books. Since then, the community of researchers has questioned the possibility of validating the existence of a field of knowledge associated with a discipline. The concept of *gestão social* is complex because it combines an analytical dimension with a practical dimension. It also meets a double expectation. Thus, it can respond both to the needs of organizations whose objective is not economic and to those of organizations that seek to develop a social response in their environment. This leads the analysis to explore different rationalities and institutional arrangements. The concept of *gestão social* also has a heuristic character in that it allows the economic and the social to be linked in practice. The position of *gestão social* is one of refusal in the face of the reduction of the organization to instrumentation, of the social to the economic, and of the economic to the market (França Filho, 2003). For this reason, *social management* aims to make visible the plurality of resources in a substantive economy.

5.1.1 The *Gestão Social* and the Public Space

Tenorio is a Brazilian researcher who has linked *gestão social* to Arendt's and Habermas' concept of public space. For him, *gestão social* takes up the idea that there must be spaces for deliberation to reconnect private people with public action (Tenorio, 1998). As such, *gestão social* cannot be a space for coercion. For this, particular attention must be paid to the intelligibility of the language, to the transparency of system of dialogue, and to the conditions of emancipation of the actors associated with the debates.

In this context, the contribution of Cançado et al. (2015) is to mobilize Tocqueville's concept of "self-interest" according to which, in a democratic society, the particular interest meets the general interest. Unlike the notion of the "invisible hand" attributed to Smith, Tocqueville's "self-interest" raises the question of the political subject. From then on, the *gestão social* is presented as the organization of a public space in which the actors can participate in their own emancipation while inventing new approaches to solve the problems that arise for them collectively. Thus, *gestão social* can also be approached through the co-production of public goods and services in democratic spaces that bring together local authorities and actors in civil society. It is a question of opposing New Public Management by establishing a virtuous circle between co-production and social innovation. *Gestão social* is thus seen as a mediator of relations between actors at the local level, with a view to enriching public space.

5.1.2 The *Gestão Social* and the Public Action

For the *gestão social*, public action can be carried out either by a public institution or by an association defending the general interest. Both options are possible. In practice, this makes it possible to renew the orientation of local public policies by involving associative actors and citizen groups. From a conceptual point of view, the *gestão social* thus opens up two perspectives of analysis. In the first, it is a matter of opting for a societal orientation. Management tends to be confused with a "public management of society" (França Filho & de Freitas Boullosa, 2015, p. 207). It is a matter of broadening and extending organizational analysis to give it a more sociopolitical dimension. "By opening up such a perspective, the concept of *gestão social* makes it possible to understand the role of civil society and the initiatives of popular organizations as self-organized systems directly related to the demands and services of society itself" (França Filho & de Freitas Boullosa, 2015, p. 207). The risk of project drift or instrumentalization of this type of project is always present and requires a number of precautions. In the second perspective, collective action and public action are superimposed in favor of a multi-actor public policy mechanism. We are close to Cefaï's proposal on collective action, defined as "any attempt to form a collective, more or less formalized and institutionalized, by individuals seeking to achieve a shared objective, in contexts of cooperation and competition with other collectives" (Cefaï, 2007, p. 8).[2] Collectives confront problems of public significance and seek to resolve them by deploying what Dewey calls a social inquiry (Dewey, 2008).

The two perspectives come together to define the contours of a *gestão social* that can enrich the range of local public policies from the perspective of sharing with the inhabitants. Its contribution is then linked to "a set of processes and dynamics that activate and shape (within the framework of public policies) a community of actors motivated by public interest, the resolution of important problems or the preservation of public goods" (França Filho & de Freitas Boullosa, 2015, p. 208).

[2] Quoted by Franca Filho, Boullosa, 2015, p. 208

5.1.3 The *Gestão Social* and the Governance

By combining the issues of public space and public action, we promote the enrichment of local democracy in a radical perspective. It is about offering individuals new forms of autonomy. In a radical democratic approach, *gestão social* develops practices where everyone can come and take part in the decisions that concern them. *Gestão social* thus intends to distance itself from the tutelage of experts who are called upon to enlighten the decision-making of groups of actors but not to decide in their place. We join here the debate begun between Dewey and Lippman on the status of the experts that we evoked previously. The *gestão social* is on the side of Dewey in hoping for governance modalities that allow for an emancipation of the actors and an autonomy in the decision-making process. The theoretical framework of *gestão social* has invested little in the field of governance. This differentiates it from the current of thought on the commons.

5.2 Management and Governance of the Commons

From the point of view of the relationship between solidarity and organization, the theory of the commons is particularly interesting because it is complementary to the *gestão social*. If we bring them together, we will be able to respond perfectly to the issues raised in the introduction to this book. While *gestão social* originates in the solidarity between humans, the starting point of Ostrom's thinking is the study of solidarity between humans and nature. Thus, the work of Ostrom and his team is initiated in the study of natural commons such as fisheries, irrigation systems, and forests. Ostrom seeks to analyze and understand how collectives self-organized around these natural resources can establish sustainable and durable management mechanisms (Ostrom, 2010a). The emergence of self-organization presupposes the free interaction of local actors, spaces for discussion, and forms of conflict resolution. Ostrom's approach is pragmatic. She goes out into the field and observes the nonhierarchical modes of governance implemented around locally exploited and managed natural resources. What Ostrom finds in these different fields of observation is a great diversity of forms of collective action and institutional arrangements (Ostrom, 2005). She hypothesizes, as Orsi notes, that if "group members are allowed to freely arrange their organization, they will be able to gradually construct an efficient and adaptive system" (Orsi, 2015). For Ostrom, the commons are characterized by a long process of adaptation, adjustment, and trial and error. This provides the necessary conditions for the explicitness of the general interest and its defense against particular interests. The self-organized forms of the commons are therefore superior to market logics for the preservation of resources. For her demonstration, Ostrom goes through successive conceptual stages that refer to theoretical issues raised by distinct but related fields of knowledge: the third sector, the social economy, and the solidarity economy (Laville & Eynaud, 2018).

5.2.1 Third Sector and Shared Resources

Standard economics makes the market the principle through which it is desirable to structure economic relations. However, this undeniable preference for the market does not deny the existence of other goods. Orthodox economics thus recognizes the presence and existence of public goods (such as national defense). To make her own proposal, Ostrom extends the list of exceptions to market logic. Ostrom and her husband propose a typology that extends the category of goods beyond private and public goods. They take McNutt's proposal in terms of club[3] goods as a starting point and thus draw a matrix that distinguishes goods by crossing two criteria: rivalry and excludability (Ostrom & Ostrom, 1977). This makes common goods (called common pool resources) appear logically as rivalrous and non-excludable goods alongside private goods (rivalrous and excludable), public goods (non-rivalrous and non-excludable), and club goods (excludable and non-rivalrous goods such as private cable channels) (Table 5.1).

[3] A club good is a collective good that is both non-rival and excludable, such as a program broadcast on a private cable television channel.

Table 5.1 Type of assets

Property	Excludable	Non-excludable
Rivals	Private property Food, clothing, cars, parking	Common goods Fisheries, forestry, coal
Non-rival	Club property Movie theaters, private parks, cable TV	Public goods Broadcasting, air, national defense

The non-excludability of access and rivalry means that actors compete for the resource and that free riders can come and take it at the expense of everyone else (Hess & Ruth, 2006). Thus, Hardin has developed the idea that there is a tragedy of the commons (Hardin, 1968). Ostrom takes issue with Hardin since all of his work will allow him to develop the opposite thesis. Ostrom shows that a specific form of governance (not reducible to the market) is able to preserve the commons against the tragedy of the market.

According to the same logic of adding categories, the third sector is built on the recognition of organizations that cannot be reduced to private and public organizations. These organizations are part of a third field (the third sector) that includes services with a strong relational dimension, such as childcare or home help. In this field of activity, the service provider benefits from a position of strength in relation to the consumer by virtue of information asymmetries that favor him. Thus, when parents entrust their baby to a childcare service, they can hardly know in the evening when they pick up the child whether the service has been of good quality (or not). The payer of the service (the parents) is not the beneficiary of the service, and the baby cannot accurately account for the course of its day. In this configuration, the provider may be tempted to offer a lower quality service for the same price. The asymmetry of information between the service provider and the payer blocks the regulatory mechanisms of the market. In such a configuration, the nonprofit association is welcome. It sends the signal expected by parents in these particular markets. If the organization is not guided by the profit motive, the opportunism of the provider will be reduced, and the service will be of better quality.

On the basis of these propositions, the commons and third sector organizations claim their existence alongside the market and the state. Both theoretical frameworks do so on the basis of criteria accepted by orthodox economics. This means that standard economics, far from being reduced to the discourse of the all-market, examines the conditions under which it is legitimate to find solutions through the commons and/or the third sector. This is not a renunciation of orthodox assumptions. Even if the commons and the third sector are recognized by standard economics, the market remains for it the relevant answer, and the hypothesis of maximizing individual rationality is not contested. If the organizational choices are diverse, they can all be explained by the search for personal interest. The logic is atomistic in the sense that interdependencies between actors are expressed through comparisons made by each of them, without communication or collective deliberation. As a result, institutions arise from cost-benefit calculations and are maintained only if they are effective in adapting to changing environments. The strategic and instrumental rationality that characterizes human action in this paradigm prevents the consideration of any political motivation. This utilitarianism is impervious to sociological data, and the history it promotes is marked by economic determinism. The classification of goods and services by their nature also suggests that there are intrinsic qualities that differentiate private, public, and common goods, in the same way that there are market, state, and third sector activities. Hence, common goods and third sector organizations are still viewed in their residual dimension.

5.2.2 Social Economy and Common Property Regime

Once the recognition of an additional category of common goods alongside private and public goods has been achieved, the challenge for Ostrom is to understand how these can be managed sustainably. To this end, a second level of her thinking focuses on the study of what she calls the bundle of rights. It is a question of knowing how to ascertain the rights of access to the resource, the rights of appropriation of the products of the resource, the rights of management of the resource, the right to determine who will have the rights of access and how they can be transferred.

The plurality of these rights determines the institutional plurality that she observes in the field. The analysis of the rights that a self-organized community gives itself to manage its shared resource allows Ostrom to open up the question of collective property (Nyssens & Petrella, 2015). In doing so, she distances herself from orthodox theory, finding that prevention against the threats of free riders increases with the community's ability to produce rules by itself and for itself (Ostrom, 2010a).

In this perspective, from Olson's analysis, Ostrom retains the need to rely on small collectives (Olson, 1965), the only ones capable of developing mechanisms for agreement and definition of rules as well as effective mechanisms for monitoring and control (Ostrom, 2010a). Ostrom notes that the small size of collectives facilitates deliberation, vigilance, and compliance with agreed-upon rules. There is an affirmation of the virtues of localism and a willingness to develop institutional analysis at the finest level (Orsi, 2015). According to Laville and Salmon, Ostrom thus moves "away from the neo-institutionalism of Williamson to the historical institutionalism of Commons and Veblen" (page 182 of Laville & Salmon, 2015b). This is reflected in her work by the recognition of the existence of actions not strictly guided by interest, the role of institutions in value making, and a genealogical and evolutionary approach to economics (Chanteau & Labrousse, 2013). Ostrom adopts an institutional problematic that details the modalities through which collectives give themselves practical rules, experiment with them, evaluate them, and modify them (Ostrom, 2010a). In concrete terms, she shows that these forms of self-organization are more relevant to the governance of common goods than to market or state procedures.

The social economy rejects the residual approach suggested by the concept of the third sector. It is the desire of organized actors to promote cooperation through mutual aid societies that explains the emergence of the social economy (Desroche, 1976; Vienney, 1994). The authors note that social protection systems were initiated by associative, cooperative, and mutualist actors before being taken up as achievements within the framework of the social state. The social economy was born with the will to create noncapitalist organizations. In parallel with the theory of the commons, the strong point of the social economy is to be a reflection of the internal rules of these organizations. Thus, the voting rule "one person—one vote" inscribes the democratic principle of their functioning in the statutes of social economy organizations. While social economy organizations have been able to resist market pressures over time, they have unfortunately not succeeded in transforming the economic landscape as a whole. It can even be said that the market economy has had the last word by containing their development and then transforming these organizations from within through standardization and professionalization. We can see how decisive the reflection on rules is, and in particular how important it is to think about the junction of internal rules with external rules. Ostrom has addressed this problem through her concept of polycentric governance (Ostrom, 2010b). This type of governance assumes that actions can come from different levels (local, national, international), each of which produces specific requirements, rules, and solutions. Polycentric governance refers to a process of regulation that respects the diversity of action processes and does not necessarily give precedence to the highest level.

5.2.3 Solidarity Economy and the New Commons

In a book co-authored with Hess, Ostrom also opens up the question of the information commons (Hess & Ostrom, 2006). The two authors specify under which conditions free software appear as commons. They note that, unlike the physical commons, the informational commons are built on non-rival goods. Consequently, the question of the size of the collectives is expressed differently. The informational commons require new protections. In 1989, a famous programmer, Richard Stallman, had the idea of working with a lawyer to produce a public license (the "General Public License" or GPL) whose purpose is to protect the four freedoms of free software: execution, copying, modification, and distribution. The GPL guarantees that users of the software can keep access to the source code even in modified versions of it. This protection of free software is called copyleft *as* opposed to copyright, which does not protect the common good. In the 2000s, this innovation was extended to other media such as scientific and artistic works under the term "Creative Commons."

We can see here a trajectory that starts from computer tinkering to social reinvention (Broca, 2013).

Following the information commons, other commons have been identified and studied: cultural, health, neighborhood, global, infrastructure, urban commons and so forth. Hess proposes to name these different commons under the generic term of "new commons" (Hess, 2008). The concept of "new commons" has the advantage of drawing attention to their respective specificities and the need to define them. According to Hess, the multiplication of the number of new commons identified in the literature testifies to a strong expectation in our societies to find adapted responses to the phenomena of globalization, commodification, and privatization. For Bollier (2014), it is in fact a question of freeing ourselves from the fundamental presuppositions of the market economy to promote new epistemological categories of knowledge. To achieve this, the commons rely on a bundle of distributed rights to qualify and protect the emerging collective uses intended by the commons to prevail (Orsi, 2015).

Within the new commons, the concept of urban commons allows for a different approach to preexisting spaces (Eynaud et al., 2018). These can be places as different as buildings, squares, shared gardens, sidewalks, and tourist areas. While physical commons are rather focused on the conservation of resources, urban commons are primarily oriented toward the development of new uses (Coriat, 2015). Thus, sidewalks can become commons if residents are given the freedom to autonomously manage certain green spaces in the street. A private building can become commons if it is acquired by a residents' cooperative with the aim of removing it from the pressure of the real estate market and maintaining affordable rents within it. The ecological transition can also become an urban common, as shown by the example of Totnes in England, which has launched the Cities in Transition[4] program (Eynaud, 2016). The objective of the initiatives of this international program is to encourage the citizens of a town, a district, or a village to engage in simple and concrete actions to

[4] The Transition movement was born in 2006 in Totnes, Great Britain, driven by Rob Hopkins. The movement is international with more than 2000 initiatives worldwide and 50 countries involved. http://www.entransition.fr/

face the challenges of climate change. These examples show that the urban commons can be born in the city around original collaborations between institutions and inhabitants, some of which can take the form of a new collective entrepreneurship (Aufrère et al., 2018).

The concept of solidarity economy differs from the social economy by inserting the political dimension in its analysis grid from the beginning. From the 1970s onward, the solidarity economy has been challenging a social economy that was too concerned with managerial respectability and ideological neutrality. This critical perspective mainly concerns three points: the importance given to the object of production (including its aspects of social utility and social innovation), the mobilization of a plurality of economic principles (market, redistribution, but also reciprocity and domestic administration, to quote Polanyi), and, finally, the emphasis placed on the political dimension (arguing that the formal equality guaranteed in the statutes should be extended by internal deliberative bodies and by participation in external public debates, in alliance with other struggles and movements). This is how solidarity economy organizations are envisaged (despite their private law status) as organizations voluntarily engaged in forms of public action (Laville & Salmon, 2015b). For this, two observations can be made. The first concerns the denunciation of what Polanyi called the economist fallacy, that is, the reduction of the economy to market exchanges alone. By proposing a substantive definition of the economy based on a diversity of principles in which exchange logics coexist with domestic logics, redistribution, and reciprocity (Polanyi, 1977), the solidarity economy thus provides itself with a framework of analysis that makes it possible to give visibility to the actions carried out by the organizations that claim to be part of it. The second observation concerns the deliberative spaces necessary for the implementation of a democratic approach. The solidarity economy approaches democracy in its citizen space and thus refuses to confine it to the analysis of internal instances of organizations. As Nyssens and Petrella (2015) point out, social utility is generally multidimensional because it is played out around a project in connection with a mode of organization. Collective benefits are not "a phenomenon induced (an externality) by economic activity, but a dimension claimed by their promoters" (Laville & Nyssens, 2001). Consequently, the democratic mode of organization of an association is not a plus. It has an intrinsic utility. The concept of critical public space developed by Habermas makes it possible to link the question of deliberative spaces and the action of associations (Habermas, 1991). It is a question of seeing how a communicative action can develop around a solidarity project and be expressed in a public space of proximity (Laville, 2011).

If we trace the historical roots of the solidarity economy back to the associationist authors of the nineteenth century, it is possible to say that the solidarity economy bases its project in the democratization of the economy (Laville, 2010). In a pragmatic approach, the solidarity economy seeks to preserve institutional diversity by valuing hybrid forms (Nyssens Petrella, 2015). In this, it is close to the theory of the commons. However, the solidarity economy has its own characteristics. It recognizes the diversity of stakeholders and values heterogeneous actor collectives. It also recognizes the role of the state in defending the general interest and is part of co-production and co-creation strategies with the public authorities. Finally, solidarity economy organizations rely on a diversity of public, market, and voluntary funding which allows them to hybridize their resources.

5.2.4 Toward a Pluralist Synthesis

The theory of the commons and the solidarity economy can be seen as two entry points to the same topic. On the side of the commons, three criteria are essential (Coriat, 2015): resources, a system for distributing rights and rules, and a wide variety of governance arrangements. This positions the question of governance at the heart of the commons. On the side of the solidarity economy, what is most important is an analytical grid for another economy associated with a reflection on the pluralism of forms of public action and democracy. The question of governance is a relatively recent issue for the solidarity economy, and it has been motivated by the need to understand the modes of organization of hybrid multi-stakeholder forms (Borzaga & Depedri, 2015). We thus note the commons' strong capacity to favor locally self-organized forms around shared resources and forms related to peer-to-peer in the digital space.

The solidarity economy, on the other hand, has a conceptual reflection more oriented around public action and the political dimension constructed in the interaction of civil society actors with the State. The two analyses can therefore be enriched (Eynaud & Sultan, 2014). For Bauwens (2015), the convergence between commons and the solidarity economy is strong. It can be expressed through the creation of global and open cooperatives based on a new ownership model and multi-stakeholder governance. The goal of these cooperatives is to co-produce the commons (Bauwens, 2015; Bauwens & Lievens, 2016).

Having excluded the state as a governance actor from her analytical grid, Ostrom needs the concept of polycentric governance to manage to connect the local to the global (Ostrom, 2010b). However, the objective of polycentric governance is first and foremost to secure the agreements made by local actors (Nyssens & Petrella, 2015). For Ostrom, the construction of the commons is necessary under certain specific conditions and for certain specific goods. Her analysis does not question the rationality of markets or the state. Dardot and Laval (2014) point out that a system of norms is always the object of conflict and that law is therefore an area of struggle. These authors thus consider that Ostrom cannot reflect on the possible political constitution of the commons as a generalizable alternative rationality. These conceptual oppositions pose challenges within each school of thought and beyond, when it comes to linking different schools.

5.3 Epistemology and Methodologies for a Different Management

If *gestão social* and management of the commons are two very different fields of practice and knowledge, they seem to us, however, to be complementary, first of all by their origins. The first one arises in the study of solidarities between men, while the second one is interested in the solidarities between men and nature. If we follow Polanyi in characterizing the substantive economy by the manifest dependence of man on nature and his fellow men in order to obtain his subsistence (Polanyi, 1977), the two frameworks of analysis thus combine to form the foundations of a substantive management. They are then combined by the orientations given to their research. *Gestão social* delves into the question of democratic solidarity, while management of the commons is interested in the institutional diversity of self-organized forms. The two approaches thus complement each other to help us rethink emancipation in renewed organizational contexts, such as those opened by Guerreiro Ramos' para-economy. But these two approaches are not only complementary. It seems to us that in many aspects they converge and that bridges can be built between them. This possibility exists notably in the reflection on a common epistemological position and on the sharing of methodologies.

5.3.1 Epistemology for the Other Management

Solidarity is a flexible concept that has the particularity of being able to blend with many disciplines and schools of thought (Musso, 2015). Therefore, this concept calls fully on the interdisciplinarity of management sciences. As we have seen, solidarity and organization each have to deal with history, anthropology, sociology, and psychology. Taken together and in their transdisciplinarity, these two concepts lead us to re-question the formal economy and to consider an extension toward the substantive economy. From this enlargement, a different attitude can emerge, one that is likely to revisualize the contribution of solidarity organizations and improve our understanding of them.

The first foundation of this position is political. It is expressed in the refusal of any sectorization of solidarity organizations. By privileging the link over goods, citizenship over consumption, the solidarity economy is "a militant dynamic and not an economic sector" (Dacheux & Goujon, 2016; page 203). We can deduce from this first foundation that all organizations can seize the solidarity issue to transform themselves into actors of the ecological and social transition. There are no prerequisites in terms of activity, even if the logic of commitment may appear easier in some sectors than in others.

The second foundation lies in the public dimension of this posture. Solidarity initiatives have this capacity to serve the general interest. This is why they seek to develop and promote spaces for exchange and discussion that can be defined as public spaces of proximity (Eme & Laville, 1994). These spaces are the places where the dimensions of solidarity action participating in public action can be discussed (Laville & Salmon, 2015a). In a multi-stakeholder logic, they participate in the implementation of participatory democracy and the strengthening of solidarity in a co-construction and co-decision process. Solidarity management can thus initiate an intrinsically democratic organizational model where it is a question of "reconciling the citizen, the employee and the consumer" to engage in "deliberalism" (Dacheux & Goujon, 2016; page 204). In other words, it is a question—behind the play on words liberalism-deliberalism—of constructing an organizational model that distances itself from the postulates of liberalism without giving the latter the exclusive right to make a claim on freedom.

The third foundation is the pragmatic affirmation of a commitment to action. It is about working with ordinary people to "shape their practices and desires" and to expand the scope of commonly accepted skills in order to break with a logic of assistance (Frère, 2015; page 390). With Dewey and against Lippman, it is a question of opposing the figure of the dominating expert. This attitude is accompanied by the refusal of a dualistic view of the world. It is opposed to "the ambition to build social sciences by importing into them the methods that have proven themselves in the natural sciences" (Génard, 2015; page 55). On the contrary, it is a matter of preferring the concern for the understanding of meaning, dear to Dilthey, against the causal vision of the world resulting from the natural sciences and to the "great division between nature and culture" (Ibid.). Behind these choices, the challenge is to move toward a sociology capable of progressing toward a new politics of emancipation. Taking into account the devastating effects on society of the commodification of labor, money, and nature, Burawoy calls for sociologists to cooperate directly with society before its complete demise in a "public sociology" approach (Burawoy, 2013). It seems to us that there is no reason why this idea should not be extended to the discipline of management science. Indeed, managers can initiate public-oriented management by establishing close and direct collaboration with associations, movements, and publics. Faced with the threats arising from the waves of commodification, such management can engage with the actors in society to promote a reflexive process of re-integration. In this configuration, social science "does not confine itself to simple empathy" but "positions itself in the struggles waged by actors" (Laville, 2015; page 426).

Faced with these postulates of the primacy of politics, of the public dimension and of pragmatism, Sousa Santos' epistemology of the South appears to be a particularly suitable reflexive framework. Starting from the observation that the world is deformed by relations of domination, it proposes a decentering of thought in order to engage another relation to the world. As Sousa Santos rightly reminds us, the understanding of the world far exceeds the Western understanding of the world (Sousa Santos, 2014). The epistemology of the South proposed by Sousa Santos focuses on deconstructing the claim to universality of ethnocentrism and the denial of certain parts of reality that follows (Laville, 2015). It notes that there has been a theft of history by the West (Goody, 2012). But the value of the proposal is that it does not seek to replace one monological system of thought with another, but rather to "promote a conversation with many voices" (Laville, 2015). Thus, Sousa Santos invites us to seek a new articulation between the principles of equality and difference (Sousa Santos, 2014). To do this, he hypothesizes the existence of equal differences allowing for an ecology of differences including mutual recognition. The epistemology of the South should therefore not be understood in an opposition between the North and the South in an approach that would only be geographical. The epistemology of the South postulates that there is a South in the North and a North in the South. From then on, this epistemology indeed invites us to a dialogue between the visible and invisible part of our worlds.

From the critical perspective of Bloch (1995), Sousa Santos rejects the concepts of "everything" and "nothing" in favor of the category of the possible that alone can reveal the inexhaustibility of the world. For him, the "not yet" is a way of inscribing the future in the present and enlarging the present (Sousa Santos, 2014). Indeed, Sousa Santos' "not yet" contains and reveals both potential and power. From this primary idea, he deduces two types of sociology that escape a logic of determination and seek to implement an axiology of care: the sociology of "absences" and the sociology of "emergences." In doing so, Sousa Santos points to two particularly rich directions of work because they are open to a recomposition of time. With Guerreiro Ramos, he opposes "the monoculture of linear time" (Sousa Santos, 2014). For him, the plurality of times is a condition for understanding the world because the silent language of cultures is above all a temporal language. His proposal is simple: To extend the present, we need a sociology of absences; to contract the future, a sociology of emergences. Let us now detail these proposals.

The sociology of absences starts from the observation that what does not exist is in fact actively seen as nonexistent. From then on, the nonexistent is either ignored or thought of as a non-credible alternative to what is supposed to exist (Sousa Santos, 2014). The nonexistent is then "held to be retrograde, inferior, local and particular, unproductive and sterile" (Laville, 2015; page 427). On a methodological level, the goal of the sociology of absences is to liberate social practices from their status as residuals, to transfer to them their own temporality and, in this way, to open up the possibility of autonomous development (Sousa Santos, 2014). Thus, the sociology of absences has the power to play on temporalities so that practices and sociabilities become credible and intelligible objects of argument and political debate. To use the metaphor of the person who has lost his keys at night, Sousa Santos invites us to search for the missing keychain not directly under the streetlight and in its light, but to venture into the dark areas where the keys have in fact slipped. This initial effort is an indispensable precaution to escape the epistemological trap of a world marked by a hegemonic logic.

The sociology of emergences, on the other hand, is about replacing the emptiness of the future with a future of plural and concrete possibilities, utopian and realistic at the same time and constructed in the present by means of caring activities (Sousa Santos, 2014). The sociology of emergences thus proposes to break the straightjacket of linear time. It extends the present "by adding to existing reality the future possibilities and the hopes that these possibilities raise" (Laville, 2015; page 427). This sociology aims to reinforce the emancipatory nature of experiences in order to consolidate their visibility and credibility. In refusing a simple critical analysis, it seeks to strengthen initiatives rather than weaken their foundations (Frère, 2015). To this end, it refuses to believe that practitioners are abused by the standards. In any case, it does not infer an inability to engage in social resistance (Laville & Salmon, 2015a). It opens up a space for dialogue and action with practitioners in an approach of radical democracy and social inquiry (Dewey, 2008) where the researcher and the practitioner are on an equal footing to understand and solve the problems of collective action.

The epistemology of the South is particularly adapted to the study of solidarity organizations. It helps us to decentralize our vision. The associationist imaginary of the solidarity economy has its roots in the libertarian revolutionary movements and thoughts of the mid-nineteenth century (Frère, 2009; Chanial, 2010; Cefaï & Chanial, 2000). These movements, which distinguished themselves from both the market economy and the dictatorship of the proletariat, were the bearers of genuine alternatives for social organization. However, pioneer associationism has been despised by both liberal and Marxist authors. Nevertheless, there is a big difference between the image it has been given and the real content of its ideas.[5] If we look at this pioneer movement through a critical analysis, we find ideas that have not lost their strength. Associationism strives to extend political democracy into social life, and in this way it goes against any separation between politics and economics (Laville, 2018, 2023). As Abensour notes, the impulse is inherently democratic, and utopia is a condition for emancipation (Abensour, 2013). This primacy of democracy allows for the defense of equal rights and a logic of mutual aid in opposition to the logics of charity and benevolence. The claim is that of reciprocity. There is in this project an intention of social transformation. In a nonlinear time approach, we can think that the contemporary solidarity economy (with experiences like social currencies, proximity services, short circuits, fair trade) is less an emergence than a resurgence (Laville & Salmon, 2015a). The sociology of absences helps us to realize that not only ideas but also achievements are passed over in silence. Thus, the French Revolution is mainly known through the events of 1789. The work of contemporary historians converges to reveal how the 1848 revolution in France has been forgotten because of its foundations similar

[5] On this subject, the special issue of *La Revue du M.A.U.S.S.*(*Mouvement anti-utilitariste dans les sciences sociales*) n° 16 « *L'autre socialisme: entre utilitarisme and totalitarisme* » (2nd sem. 2000)

to that of solidarity associations (Riot-Sarcey & Gribaudi, 2008; Gribaudi, 2014; Riot-Sarcey, 2016; Hayat, 2014; Chanial, 2003).

In the end, the two approaches to the epistemology of the South complement each other. The sociology of absences invites us to return to the forgotten history of organizational solidarity and to rediscover forgotten histories that will help us readjust our vision of the present. The epistemology of emergence argues for a valorization of current experiences and is perfectly in keeping with a sociological or public management approach. In doing so, a reflection on the methodologies that can be mobilized can be started.

5.3.2 The Contribution of Anthropology to the Other Management

The work in solidarity management mobilizes a wide repertoire of knowledge and scientific disciplines. Including management in social sciences is a strong principle for the reaffirmation of the project of another management. The Other Management wants to explore the diversity of meanings associated with practices. Reflexivity is a constant exercise in this other way of doing management. In this field, the contribution of anthropology is particularly important not only in terms of reflection but also in guiding the practices of an alternative management. Anthropological knowledge was built as a science of otherness with the ambition of understanding the other, the other society, the other culture. For anthropologists, knowledge is built through the understanding and recognition of difference, so it is therefore less a matter of defining a research object than a method. Anthropology is shaped through its approach reality and its capacity for immersion in the field, as shown by ethnographic practice. Training in anthropology consists in exercising another way of looking at the world, and the experience of this exercise reveals itself as an intercultural experience. The effort to perceive the Other in his or her difference produces a reflexive effect in the direction of oneself, one's culture, one's society. According to Laplantine and Olievenstein (1993), the perplexity or "feeling of strangeness" that is born of the encounter of cultures is inherent to anthropological training. This authorizes the modification of one's view of oneself. Fieldwork induces personal transformations that go far beyond the framework of a professional practice or a scientific training project. It sets in motion a process of existential learning.

From the Other Management to the Management of the Other

We have defined the Other Management as a management that is different in its methods, principles, and rationality. The contribution of anthropology allowed us to clarify the definition. Other Management is a management of difference. In so doing, it asserts a political dimension in the sense of Arendt, taking into account people and not man (Arendt, 1970). It is a management that expresses itself with and in Otherness. The question of recognition occupies a central place. The Other Management takes into account the quest for recognition by proposing: another economic institutionality (beyond the market economy), other forms of organization (beyond the principle of the company), other territories (beyond the urban market spaces), and other publics (beyond those already covered). Thus, it is situated in the recognition of another culture of living together (beyond individualism). It looks for what is not clearly seen, what is invisible in everyday life, what emerges. In this, the anthropological approach goes hand in hand with the dual sociological perspective proposed by the epistemology of the South (Sousa Santos, 2014). It is necessary for the Other Management to assume the challenge of diversity and intercultural dialogue. From this perspective, the epistemology of the South can be relevant because it renounces the monopoly of the dominant visions of Western modernity to incorporate subaltern and silenced versions (Ibid).

The question of recognition has always been at the heart of human societies in that it refers to the problem of the relationship to difference. Historically, two social answers have prevailed according to Todorov (1993): the inferiorization and then the subordination of certain social groups by a hierarchical system, and the assimilation of these same groups to obtain the dissolution of the problem. Contemporary societies do not escape this tension. Nevertheless, we observe that some of them bet on keeping the difference without losing social cohesion, that is, they try to manage the difference without pretending to neutralize or dissolve it (Barbosa & Veloso, 2009). Thus, the problem of recognition becomes a central issue in the debate on multiculturalism. This concept, which appeared in the mid-1970s, was intended to provide the governments of countries such as Canada and Australia with keys for action in order to define policies adapted to the cultural minorities and ethnic pluralism that characterize these societies (Barbosa & Veloso, 2009). The aim was to overcome assimilationist policies that were considered morally questionable. The aim was to maintain the cultural identities of minorities and to foster both a sense of pride in cultural differences and a sense of belonging to a larger whole. As a political doctrine, multiculturalism supported policies that recognized minority rights and cultural identities and advocated for cultural diversity (Barbosa & Veloso, 2009).

Since the early 2000s, numerous studies on this topic have helped the evolution of multicultural thinking (Barbosa & Veloso, 2009) by identifying two different perspectives. The first is supported by Charles Taylor (1992) and Will Kymlicka (1997) who argue that difference is the intrinsic value of a multicultural society. For them, difference presupposes its recognition without the requirement of overcoming it by building a common whole. To "recognize" means to accept the existence of the Other without compromise. Syntheses are then produced between the differences. The second perspective is supported by authors such as Fraser and Honneth (2003). They consider that the recognition of the existence of a difference is insufficient if society does not know how to deal with it (Barbosa & Veloso, 2009). For Fraser, the difficulty of dealing with the Other refers to a deep dilemma: how to offer recognition without redistribution of resources and without social justice? For Honneth and Joel (1998), it is a question of bringing together, around the notion of recognition, both the cultural aspects valued by Taylor (1992) and Kymlicka (1997) and a moral and ethical imperative allowing for a higher level of consensus and unity (Barbosa & Veloso, 2009). The question posed by Honneth could well be this: how to offer recognition without social esteem? With this author, "to recognize" the Other is verified only when we establish links of mediation based on solidarity (Honneth & Joel, 1998). Social esteem for Honneth refers to the existence of moral links between socially and culturally different individuals. Unlike a simple "acceptance of the Other," Honneth suggests "appreciation of the Other" through the establishment of a sociability based on reciprocity (Barbosa & Veloso, 2009).

Cultural, Economic, and Organizational Anthropology

Today, more than ever, societies are confronted with the relationship to difference. The increase of migratory flows in the world and conflicts of all kinds testify to the importance of the problem. The increase in inequalities makes it difficult to recognize differences. Cultural diversity questions our practices and presupposes a change in our forms of socialization: How can we offer recognition if we do not collectively cultivate an interest in the Other? How can we offer recognition if we do not collectively organize active solidarity? These questions underline the importance of following the comprehensive and substantive approach of Polanyi and Guerreiro Ramos. How to offer recognition without a solidarity economy? Understanding this sociability of solidarity is one of the important tasks necessary to define the contours of an Other Management.

In the quest for knowledge of the solidarity-based sociability suggested by the Other economy, economic anthropology constitutes a privileged source. We have seen in the previous chapters how another view of the economy (carried by studies of history and anthropology) allows us to better approach the diversity of the institutional principles of human societies. The economic anthropology approach provides answers and avenues for reflection on contemporary issues. It allows us to benefit from a broader view of the economy, and it opens the analysis to history and to other cultures. Anthropology is particularly useful because of the decentering of the vision it proposes. What does the past teach us? What does the culture of ancestral peoples transmit to us? Economic anthropology is not the expression of a nostalgia for ancient times but is rather a privileged source of inspiration to find in the study of cultural diversity the new paths of a management capable of facing contemporary challenges.

Finding the anthropological foundations of the Other Management, leads us to make a detour through two fundamental fields of knowledge: cultural diversity and the diversity of economic forms. From then on, the affirmation of recognition becomes a major principle of the Other economy and consequently of the Other Management. A path is emerging.

Cultural and economic anthropologies are a prerequisite for organizational anthropology which assumes a link between culture and management. In the 1990s, this link was built through the concept of corporate culture and organizational culture. The expansion of the use of organizational anthropology then took place in a range of themes: ethnomarketing, diversity management, ethnic entrepreneurship, intercultural management. These works develop ethnographic research applied to management. However, organizational anthropology can be criticized for reducing its managerial questioning to performance expectations. A critical text by Chanlat (1991) suggests an anthropology of the human condition in organizations. In this approach, the author proposes a different vision of the human in organizations that goes beyond behaviorist perspectives. By denouncing the restricted nature of management training, Chanlat (1991) appeals to the multiple dimensions of the human being that should be the basis of an anthropological theory of organizations understood on several levels in interaction between the individual and society.

Alternative Management and Popular Education

Finding this human condition in organizations is undoubtedly the most important contribution of anthropology to alternative management. It allows us to situate the practices of the Other Management in the order of social mediation, whether between individuals, between institutions, or between individuals and institutions. This presupposes the effectiveness of an alternative viewpoint constructed in an anthropological stance. The Other view is placed ahead of others, of institutions, of society, and of life. The Other Management thus aims at getting closer to the needs or demands of the other. It is opposed to the self-centered character of market rationality and its management mode. Understanding the Other is the task of the Other Management. This presupposes a movement of decentering toward the Other which has to do with the perceptive experience of the world. As an experience, the Other Management is not realized without thinking about how it might be realized (praxis) around the meaning of work, of belonging to a group, of its relationship to the institution or to society. The Other Management brings together personal projects and the collective project. It can thus make it possible to rediscover the lost meaning of institutionalized projects and at the same time deal with individualistic drifts. Some actors may indeed be concerned with their professional careers and a form of material achievement. Giving meaning back to both actors and institutions is one of the vocations of alternative management. For this, the anthropological approach refers to the question of education. The role of the manager here is that of an educator of meaning according to Freire's proposal (1994). The requirement of social mediation in the Other Management brings out the need for dialogue. According to Freire, education is a liberating step played out in a relation of alternating roles between the one who educates and the one who is educated. This alternation is justified by the need to understand the world of the Other. According to Freire, one cannot build a learning process without reference to the context or the reality of the life of those involved. This is in contrast to classical learning where role alternation is not possible and where education is seen as a simple one-sided transfer of knowledge. In opposition to a "pedagogy of the oppressed," Freire (1994) puts forward the principle of dialogicity as the basis for a "pedagogy of liberation." Freire is internationally known for his literacy methods for youth and adults. They are characterized by a political praxis and a renewed awareness of the learning process. His ideas are the basis of a field of knowledge called popular education (PE).

According to Paludo (2015), PE is a field of knowledge related to educational practices engaged in permanent critique of the social system. The approach is counter-hegemonic and promotes another model of sociability. Originating from the popular struggles and resistance movements in Latin America, this concept closely links education and politics in a quest for emancipation. In Brazil, PE was born with the basic education and popular culture movements in the late 1950s and grew up in the popular resistance movements of the 1970s–80s as a set of ideas that were at once political, philosophical, and pedagogical (Gloria Gohn, 2013, 2015).

Among the different PE paradigms, Freire's method represents one of the most important in Latin America (Gadotti, 1999). It emerged as an emancipatory and progressive alternative to the prevailing school programs of the time. Since the end of World War II, these were mainly sponsored by North American agencies and consisted mainly in rural extension and community development programs. In contrast, Freire's method was multidisciplinary in nature and considered several dimensions including political education (Gloria Gohn, 2015). Indeed, Freire postulated a liberating education oriented toward the awareness and transformation of individuals and their social environment (Freire, 1979). One of the great innovations of his method is the fact that it is based on dialogue. For Freire, communication and reflexivity are major challenges in learning situations (Freire, 1994). The oppressed are only free when they acquire the capacity to reflect on the conditions of their own lives and conquer their autonomy in order to realize their historical destiny (Gloria Gohn 2015). Dialogue pedagogy redefines the pedagogical relationship. Freire sees the teacher as someone who seeks and learns by standing next to the student. The latter has an active position, and in doing so gains dignity in the educational process (Gloria Gohn 2015). In Freire's work, education is a practice of freedom that promotes awareness (Gloria Gohn 2015). It is also a political act, an act of knowledge, and an act of creation that posits that reality must be transformed. To be liberating, educators must be historically and politically aware. It is understandable that PE played a key role in the resistance movements of the 1970s and 80s. At that time in Latin America in general and in Brazil in particular, PE was synonymous with social movement. Subsequently, PE extended these practices to civil society organizations, universities, and certain public authorities, with the common goal of supporting marginalized populations or social groups.

It is precisely this work of mediation with an emancipatory aim between distinct social worlds and between different institutions that founds the field of the Other Management. The challenges of this mediation work are immense, and they outline a relevant agenda for the knowledge and practice of management. Nevertheless, we have to acknowledge the lack of cross-fertilization between PE and the management approach. This situation can be explained, as we have seen in a previous chapter, by the eviction of solidarity from the field of management sciences. However, the intersection makes sense and allows us to define the Other Management as an emancipating practice of social mediation working to build solidarity processes according to PE principles. We deduce that any form of management mobilizing PE in its operating modes is part of the Other Management. Initiating the Other Management presupposes an educational component and an anthropological posture. It is a matter of seeing reality differently and of having an ethical position that engages management and the manager. A certain number of principles and values are behind this approach: trust, respect, dialogue, solidarity, emancipation, otherness, listening, and social mediation. It leads to the possibility of ethno-accountability.

5.3.3 Ethno-accounting

For Cottereau, the starting point of ethno-accounting is found in the questioning of what matters in life (Cottereau, 2016, page 11). This primary question is fundamental because it proceeds from a practical and conceptual expansion. By asking what people care about, ethno-accounting puts people back at the heart of the analysis. In so doing, it extends the accounting approach to the notion of well-being. It does so through "the evaluation competence of the people concerned and not of the economist or statistician" (Cottereau & Marzok, 2012; page 17). The main idea of this approach in its analysis is not to dissociate what is economic and what reveals everyday life. "In life, people count and evaluate and investigating their ways of operating means not imposing a priori a separation between facts of an economic order and facts of another order" (Cottereau, 2016, page 11). Taking into account what people take into account "has the characteristics of a detoxification" (Cottereau, 2016, page 24) and implies freeing oneself from *homo economicus* in favor of *homo ethicus* (according to Walras' formula). This calls into question the usual disciplinary approach that reserves the modelable analysis of "the relationship of men to things" to economists and "the study of the social roots of economic life or the social meaning of money," or "the relationships between men about things" to the social sciences (Cottereau, 2016, page 11). Orléan sees the empire of value as a marker of orthodox economics' desire to dissociate itself from the rest of the social sciences. Thus, orthodox economics thinks it possible to obtain an objective measure of value when anthropology, history, and sociology refer it to human interactions and intersubjectivity (Orléan, 2011).

According to Orlean, the crisis thus stems from the fact that "valuation was left in the hands of the markets, while the markets practice a pathological form of valuation" (Orléan, 2012; page 21). This pathology is expressed in the confusion between measurement and evaluation. As Supiot reminds us, confusing measurement and evaluation condemns us to lose the meaning of measurement (Supiot, 2012). Indeed, to evaluate is not only to measure but to refer the measurement to a value judgment that gives it meaning (Ibid). To confuse measurement and evaluation is to crush the various judgments that may have been made as "suppressed purchasing power, price justice and injustice, freedom from bargaining guided by maximization alone, consideration for interlocutors, evaluation in relation to a life project, etc." (Cottereau, 2016, page 16). When measurement and evaluation are superimposed, only the prices remain visible. The social part at stake in the market exchange that may have led to a change in price is erased. Thus, the possible benefaction of the exchange is erased as well as "the evaluations that lead to a gift price" (Cottereau, 2016, page 16).

Therefore, refounding the economy implies working on the approach to value in order to recover its relational nature. For this, ethno-accounting proposes to count how people count. On a practical level, ethno-accounting is accompanied by a "survey device designed to make the so-called invisible economy visible" (Cottereau, 2016, page 17). It should be noted, however, that this "invisibility" is not total. The domestic economy put forward by Polanyi is above all invisible "in the eyes of institutions, of official recording devices, private and public" (Cottereau, 2016, page 17). By calling it an informal economy, these same institutions maintain it in an assumed invisibility that implies a certain discredit. The work of ethno-accounting then consists in describing what is not described, in accounting for the very precise forms taken by this supposedly informal economy, in giving it consistency and reality. To do this, the work of valuation consists of "treating households as producers," and analyzing "any manufacturing or service activity that brings in resources as if it were a business" (Cottereau, 2016, page 21). Ethno-accounting seeks to "take seriously the art of managing individuals and family units" (Cottereau, 2016, page 23) by paying as much attention to the "self-governance of life conducts" as it does to the "governance of businesses and other communities" (Cottereau, 2016, page 23). It is clear that this work is party to a sociology of absence.

Methodologically, ethno-accounting inquiry involves "collecting each member's assessment of their resources through a day-to-day ethnography of daily life and a collection of personal records collected on site, recorded in an extensive survey diary" (Pruvost, 2016; page 105–106). It is then a matter of "formalizing the actors' estimated evaluations of the costliness of elements of their lives or their incommensurability, by synthesizing the information into accounting tables, schedules or inventories, submitted to the respondents for correction" (Pruvost, 2016; page 105–106). The point is not to "convert the totality of exchanges into monetary equivalents or profitable calculations but to observe ordinary evaluation procedures, inseparable from broader arbitrations about what a good life is in terms of family, friends, activism and work" (Pruvost, 2016; page 106).

Ethno-accounting is defined as an "anthropology of valuation or contextual accounting" (Blavier, 2016; page 28). It proceeds in fact by meticulously counting, with the respondents, all the socioeconomic exchanges carried out within the household. In this, the work of the ethno-accountant mixes the usual qualitative ethnographic approach with objective quantitative measures to get closer to a "contextualized balance sheet of well-being" (Cottereau & Marzok, 2012; page 17). This allows for the study of intra- and interfamily solidarities that are overlooked by state statistics. The ethno-accounting approach shows that the purchase of a property is not sufficient to insert oneself "locally into a chain of benevolent solidarity (municipal, local, alternative, family)" and that it is also necessary to play on "a patient integration into different mutual aid networks" (Pruvost, 2016; page 118). Consistent with the direction given by the sociology of absences, ethno-accounting is interested in showing the invisible of the social relations that ground and organize the domestic economy. In the same spirit, ethno-accounting pays attention to the lives of the poorest and most destitute (Macchi, 2016). This rigorous analytical work makes it possible to move away from miserabilist approaches by highlighting the rigorous management of these families in the face of their constraints. It provides criteria for possible intervention within the framework of public policy and provides a better understanding of the art of living together (Guénée, 2016). It opens up perspectives on the co-construction of indicators of well-being and their discussion between very diverse citizens who do not share the same tastes or the same vision of the world and do not have the same interests. This process of communication beyond the indicators themselves thus makes it possible to forge links between citizens who do not have many opportunities to talk to each other or to meet (Renault, 2011). The problem is then how to instrumentalize these indicators.

5.3.4 The Instruments and Tools of Alternative Management

As we have seen previously, the history of management thinking is marked by its applied dimension. These concepts have a practical purpose. They seek to respond to the concrete problems of organizations and accompany the formulation and design of management tools. The focus on the private market enterprise as the primary—and almost unique—object of analysis is undoubtedly a factor of impoverishment. Thus, management seems to know only the universe of companies obeying market logic. Management education disseminates managerial thinking bathed in economic and financial concerns and illuminated by a Holy Grail: performance. This Grail is the focus of all attention. The manager's ambition is to master all of its characteristics and to serve it piously through an array of managerial technologies (França Filho, 2003). Although any action can be instrumentalized, action is nonetheless guided by principles. The formal and functionalist vision cultivated by management, however, tends to make us forget these values. As producers of measurement, management tools participate in a process of justification (Boltanski & Thévenot, 2006). The use of financial performance management tools in an organization is similar to a pledge given to formal rationality. This is done to the detriment of value-based rationality, as Guerreiro Ramos has clearly shown.

This situation is clearly detrimental to organizations that have management needs but whose rationality does not coincide with market rationality. We are thinking of course of public organizations, associations, cooperatives, mutuals, foundations, but also of family businesses and market businesses that want to take a step aside, as is the case with liberated businesses (Gilbert et al., 2017). All of these organizations, which are very diverse in their structures and purposes, have no management system that responds to their differences and specificities. The situation is serious because the extension of enterprise management thinking to all these organizations tends to be valued as a general progress (Eynaud & Mourey, 2015). Thus, introducing business management with its focus on margins into the public hospitals in charge of our health would be a good thing for the general interest. Rationalizing through costs a solidarity association that takes care of the most disadvantaged would participate in a professionalization of its management (Eynaud & Mourey, 2012). Subsidiarizing neighborhood social associations into a regional parent association would help improve service to users. Restoring the finances of a social center in the same way that one restores the accounts of an overindebted company would be a plus for the beneficiaries. We could multiply the examples over and over again. We will remember that this current situation shocks very few people. *Homo economicus* takes precedence over *homo ethicus*. We seem to be collectively stunned, and the monoculture of corporate management is barely denounced. Bonnafous-Boucher's (2005) remark on the need for organization theories rather than organization theory remains a dead letter, at least in management education. The reasons for this lack of consideration are undoubtedly to be found in Sousa Santos' analysis of the sociology of absences.

The field of management knowledge has thus left open an ocean of possibility for the proposal of another management, and a positive factor is the growth of a critical literature in the field of management (Dorion, 2017). This particularly stimulating literature reveals considerable advances in the diagnosis of reality. Nevertheless, it seems to us that a research agenda on the Other Management has yet to be made. This agenda needs to have exchanges with a wide variety of fundamental issues that emerge from the complex dynamics of contemporary societies. There is therefore a need to deepen our thinking by enriching it with contributions from the most diverse fields of the human and social sciences. Even more than formal management, substantive management has a crucial need to develop interdisciplinary approaches. Indeed, they are the only ones able to grasp the complexity of the issues at stake in collective action when it is not confused with the market. The strong point of this agenda is the possibility of linking theoretical knowledge in management with that which is invented every day in the field of action of the above-mentioned organizations. If their management is not the same as the management of a commercial enterprise, these organizations also need instruments for analysis, piloting, and decision-making. We can therefore ask ourselves the following question: What types of technologies does the Other Management need? How is the method of alternative management defined? How is the management of the Other economy done? What tools are necessary to build in practice the management of the demarketing of work, money, and nature? By their diversity, these general questions underline the broad scope of the agenda. From the perspective of alternative management, two things appear to be paramount: taking into account the particular context in which organizations operate and interacting and confronting regularly with the realities on the ground. The challenge for alternative management is certainly to be able to articulate the particular and the general and to have tools whose contours fit this need for connection.

The practice of incubation in the solidarity economy is particularly interesting in that it combines a space for research and a space for experimentation. In this way, it is an ideal field of work for the construction of tools adapted to the needs of the Other Management. The work undertaken on these solidarity practices allows us to highlight three main categories of tools: (a) tools for the management of each initiative (intra tool), (b) tools for the management of the solidarity network to which the initiative belongs (inter-intra tool), and (c) tools for the management of the relationship with distinct institutional actors (inter tool). Regardless of the category, the Other Management tools must demonstrate a greater requirement than that of the classic business management tools. Indeed, they are expected to be consistent with values such as solidarity, cooperation, and trust. In order to achieve this coherence, two paths can be followed, which we have already mentioned. The first refers to a social innovation approach that can guide the collective. The second is a work of re-signification of the relationship between science, technology, and innovation. In the first case, the construction of tools in itself represents an innovation process of a different nature (as we saw in the previous chapter). This is a promising field of research applied to the management sciences that opens up questions such as the following: What are the tools that are socially appropriate to the realities of organizations seeking to transform their environment? How to make these tools? How can they redefine the relationship between science, technology, and innovation? How can they be integrated into a transdisciplinary approach to knowledge in connection with an "ecology of knowledge" (Sousa Santos, 2014)?

From Financial Viability to Social Utility

The Brazilian context appears particularly emblematic because it benefits from a long experience of solidarity intervention in highly disadvantaged territories. The main challenge of an intervention with excluded people lies in understanding their background and the deficits they have accumulated. This is a prerequisite before thinking about any kind of reintegration. It seems difficult to envisage a reintegration project for people who are seriously excluded on the basis of financial viability alone. Indeed, solidarity economy initiatives respond to strong demands in terms of local needs and are of great importance in people's lives. The results obtained by these initiatives must be measured on a broad perimeter in order to understand what has changed in the lives of the people concerned (those who participate directly in the initiatives but also the beneficiaries, their families, and all the inhabitants). It is also important to distinguish between monetary and nonmonetary benefits attributable to the initiative. Within the framework of a territorial development strategy based on the strengthening of self-organization initiatives in local solidarity economy networks, three questions can guide the monitoring process in the agenda of another management: (a) How to build the sustainability of the initiatives? (b) How to plan the management of the initiatives? (c) How to evaluate the sustainability of the initiatives? This third question on the evaluation of sustainability seems to us to be of capital importance. We are now going to detail it.

For the Other Management, territorial anchoring raises a practical question about the means of evaluation. The principle of financial viability is not adapted to the innumerable initiatives that develop a broad approach to the economy. They do so in three different ways: by reshaping market practices through rules of cooperation and solidarity, by mobilizing nonmarket resources from partner institutions (public or nonpublic), or by encouraging the use of nonmonetary resources. From then on, alternative management needs to resort to hybrid financing modalities and to expanded institutional formats for the economic viability of initiatives. Thus, the question of sustainability needs to be (re) defined before considering its evaluation. Sustainability must be considered in relation to financial viability. In a market logic, the degree of sustainability of an initiative is essentially approached through its financial viability. The latter is seen as a means of generating the autonomy and self-sufficiency of the initiative in relation to its environment. For the Other Management, on the contrary, the sustainability of an initiative is not reduced to the problem of financial viability since both the purpose and the context of action of the initiatives go beyond the strictly commercial framework.

In fact, as we have seen above, initiatives that promote alternative management seek above all to satisfy local needs in a given territorial context. They tend to promote new ways of relating the economic and the social, or democracy and the economy. They also have a vocation to generate results both for the individual actors and for the local territory in which they are inserted. In this broader context, social utility replaces financial viability as the goal of the management method and leads to the formulation of new evaluation tools. As social utility is attached to human life, to the context of the project, to the necessity of the project in its context, the Other Management guided by social utility is not subordinated to financial viability. It presupposes a multidimensional perspective of sustainability based on the socioeconomic, the sociopolitical, the sociocultural, the socio-technological, and the socio-environmental. These five dimensions together translate, in a combined way, the meaning of social utility and its sustainability. The challenge of an evaluation tool is then to identify as well as possible this multidimensionality of sustainability in action in the practice of the Other Management. This is conceived as an evaluation of social utility.

Sustainable But Not Viable, the Challenge of Alternative Management
If the Other Management is formulated in the refusal of a sustainability reduced to financial viability, it has to face a choice that opens up a double perspective (França Filho, 2012). In the first, the solidarity initiative is financially viable but unsustainable because it generates negative externalities (socially unjust effects, harm to the environment). In the second, the initiative is sustainable and not financially viable, that is, the initiatives created have great strength in terms of legitimacy in the territory because of their great social utility, but they are not viable in the sense that they are not able to produce their self-financing through market activities. The Other Management approach rejects the first perspective (because of its lack of sustainability) and focuses on the second. In this case, it is a question of finding the means of support and the necessary supports to strengthen the solidarity initiative. Evaluation tools can make a positive contribution in this sense. They can in fact be seen as a means of bringing out what is not normally visible or is invisible in formal management. It is a matter of bringing to light substantial analytical results that have the power to indicate new paths on which managers can build another form of management. We will study and illustrate this with two examples, one Brazilian and one French.

Example 1: Social Utility Assessment Matrix and Self-assessment
The social utility assessment matrix was developed in Brazil. It is a tool designed to be used by an external actor to understand the degree of sustainability of solidarity economy initiatives. The tool seeks to explore five dimensions of sustainability in the dynamics of the initiative on a day-to-day basis: socioeconomic, sociopolitical, sociocultural, socio-technological, and socio-environmental. The socioeconomic dimension refers to the initiative's capacity to generate and mobilize the resources necessary to develop its activities. Focused on the resource, it emphasizes the organization's capacity to materially reproduce its conditions of survival, beyond financial resources alone. To do this, this dimension brings together distinct socioeconomic logics structured around three types:

market, redistributive (or nonmarket), and reciprocal (or nonmonetary). With the market logic, the capacity of the initiative is measured by its ability to generate financial income from commercial relationships. These are the usual economic practices related to buying and selling relationships in a market environment. In a nonmarket logic, the initiative's capacity is approached through the mobilization of resources via partnerships, agreements, and contracts with public actors. The nonmarket logic is noncompetitive. It is part of an exchange based on the nature of the social utility and the importance for the public actor to participate in it. Finally, the reciprocal logic refers to obtaining nonfinancial (or financial) resources through different and varied mechanisms of cooperation and according to principles of solidarity. This logic is expressed in a simple exchange of goods and services, the pooling of resources, production for self-consumption, and disinterested exchange. The Other Management is concerned with the balance of the three dimensions mentioned. To preserve the sustainability of the initiative, it is necessary to avoid one logic developing to the detriment of the other two. In terms of evaluation, it is a question of knowing whether the initiative is capable of mobilizing the resources necessary for its sustainability (by using the different logics) and whether there is a balance between these logics. The evaluation aims to see to what extent it is possible for the initiative to assert its inclusion in the field of a substantive economy and how it can develop a strategy adapted to its context of inclusion and its organizational nature to achieve this. The evaluation in connection with the Other Management will therefore ensure that market logics respect fundamental ethical and social principles and that mechanisms of solidarity with public actors and forms of mutualization of nonmonetary resources are present. The ability to act in a balanced way between these different economic logics demonstrates the vitality of the initiative.

The sociopolitical dimension refers to the capacity of a group of people to work together over a long period of time toward a common goal, that is, the self-organizing capacity of the initiative or the self-institutionalization of the organization. This is particularly important in an environment of social exclusion, when social ties are so weakened by the degradation of sociability mechanisms that the processes of human association are difficult. The challenge is to engage in a learning (or relearning) experience around the ability to work in a group. This implies the slow construction of a common democratic political culture. The sociopolitical dimension refers to two dimensions. The first relates to the degree of empowerment of the group of local actors in the process of managing the initiative. This involves assessing the degree of democratization of relations, the level of participation of the people, the level of autonomy of the initiative, and its decision-making profile. The second dimension concerns the promotion of a mode of public action through the practices undertaken locally. This dimension is linked to the level (and form) of participation of the people associated with the initiative, to the group's capacity to discuss common problems related to daily life, and to the necessary institutional contacts (with the public authorities, the different institutions, the different networks of civil society). This last aspect implies the drawing up of charters, pacts, alliances, agreements, or contracts. The form and nature of these links can determine the innovations achieved at the local level and the social transformations undertaken at the territorial level. In the end, the criteria that can guide the analysis of social utility in this sociopolitical dimension are the empowerment of participants, involvement in public action, and the development of institutional relationships.

The sociocultural dimension refers to the capacity of the initiative to create links between each member of the collective concerned but also with the actors of the territory in which it is placed. The production of links represents an important basis for the maintenance of the initiative. It is even a condition for its sustainability. These links can be both social and cultural. The initiative must be able to generate social inclusion, that is, offer opportunities for local actors traditionally excluded from the dynamics and processes of work, and it must also be a vector of social cohesion by strengthening the self-esteem of the people associated with the initiative. This requires the implementation of a culture of relationships based on cooperation and trust. The learning of such values represents an indispensable basis, in terms of social capital, for human development and the achievement of the initiative's objectives. From a cultural point of view, this dimension provides information about the degree to which people identify with the initiative and its territory. It allows us to understand the degree to which the activities undertaken are rooted in local cultural life. In terms of evaluation, it is a question of knowing whether the dynamics of the initiative are capable of producing human development, either by modifying the perception that the subjects have of themselves (work on self-esteem), or by introducing or reinforcing values such as cooperation and confidence in daily life. It is also a question of whether the initiative contributes to the strengthening of the local identity and culture. The relevance of this proposal for sustainability is measured by greater organizational stability. Thus, a solidarity initiative consolidates its sustainability by identifying itself with the territory in which it is located and developing roots based on a cultural commitment. In the end, the criteria that can guide the analysis of social utility in this sociocultural dimension are social inclusion, social cohesion, and cultural rootedness.

The socio-technological dimension refers to the group's capacity to generate and socialize knowledge around the work undertaken by the collective. The objective is to evaluate the extent to which the collective learning process at work is based on local technological solutions, that is, based on knowledge available in the local cultural heritage. The evaluation focuses on the way the initiative carries out its activities through the technological solutions it selects, and how it manages its own learning process while respecting the cultural autonomy of the group. In terms of sustainability and social utility, the relevance of this dimension is therefore based on the value of knowledge production, the learning process associated with it, and the capacity to generate local technologies. It is a question of seeing how the group learns from its experience and how it uses this learning to achieve its objectives. In the end, the criteria that can guide the analysis of social utility in this sociopolitical dimension are the production of knowledge, socialization, and the generation of locally developed technologies.

The socio-environmental dimension refers to the degree to which the initiative is linked to the environmental characteristics of its territory. It is thus a matter of evaluating the levels of the ecological impact of the action in its environment. These can be approached in terms of controlling negative externalities generated by the productive activity, or in terms of producing positive externalities. The aim is to recognize the level of reflection and practice of the initiative with regard to the environment and to understand how this attention is translated into the daily life of the collective. In terms of sustainability and social utility, the relevance of this dimension is based on a balanced relationship between the initiative and its natural environment and on the construction of an "ecological utility." In the end, the criteria that can guide the analysis of social utility in this sociopolitical dimension are the control of negative externalities and the production of positive externalities.

A game has been designed for groups formed around solidarity initiatives in order to help them engage in a process of meaning-making by carrying out a self-assessment of their conditions of sustainability. In this kind of approach, the questions and answers are made by the group involved in the solidarity initiative. The game uses the metaphor of the circle (Fig. 5.1) to raise awareness of the idea of a process with multiple, strongly intertwined dimensions. The game uses the socioeconomic,

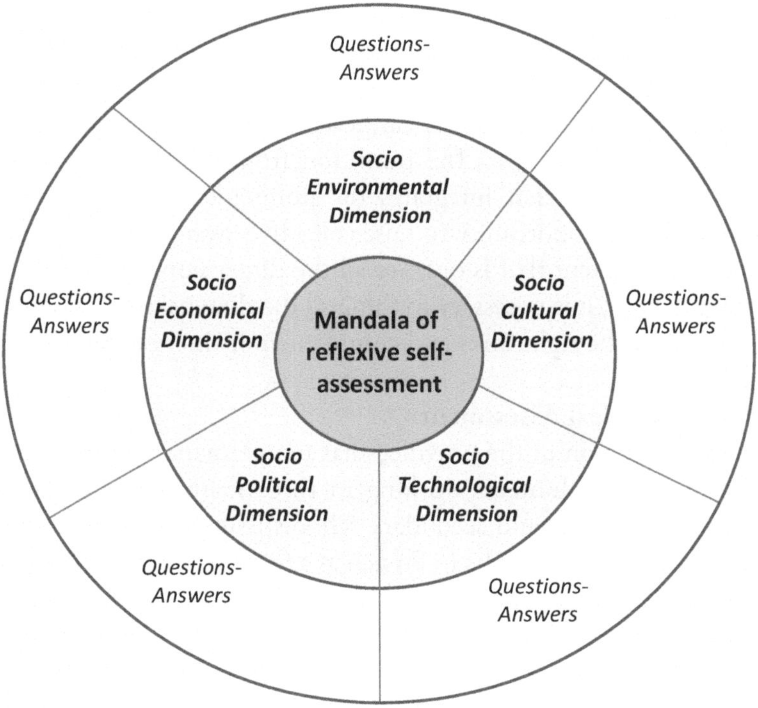

Fig. 5.1 Self-assessment mandala

sociocultural, sociopolitical, socio-technological, and socio-environmental dimensions mentioned above. Each dimension is questioned through categories and targeted evaluation criteria. The game thus invites participants to answer several sequences of questions. This process allows the members of the collective to judge the progress of their initiative or project. Throughout the game, collective members are encouraged to build a shared vision of their experience. New meanings emerge during the process, and this leads the members of the collective to reflect on the issues and challenges they face and on the possibilities of changes or shifts in the trajectory they are following. To facilitate the game, the group has tokens that they place on a mandala. For each criterion, the group has from zero to three tokens as an evaluation. At the end of the game, a picture is obtained of the group's situation on all the dimensions evaluated which gives a general overview of the initiative. It is important to emphasize that the evaluation process leads the group to consider solutions to certain shortcomings or deficits that it has identified. The typical ideal approach is to strike a balance between the various dimensions that will help the initiative to become sustainable. An imbalance (for example, the predominance of market resources) can lead the collective to question the invisible part of its action. The transition from an essentially market-based vision to one that integrates the nonmarket and nonmonetary aspects can be an opportunity to raise collective awareness of the importance of management that is open to all the dimensions of the solidarity initiative. Indeed, it is necessary to value all the dimensions of the project and to look for the right links and complementarities between them.

Example 2: Critical Assessment

A French association in the provinces has ten permanent employees and a hundred or so volunteers working in three main areas: support for schooling (in primary and secondary schools), support for parenthood, and literacy courses for adults in French as a foreign language (FFL). FFL activities are about teaching French to people whose native language is not French. The association observes that its institutional environment is evolving robustly (new measures, new rules, new modalities in the evaluation of actions). The old partnership with the public authorities has to be rebuilt. The future seems uncertain because the public financiers are now primarily interested in the proposed associative actions conforming with the national objectives of public policies. Any association project that does not fit into the analysis grid is eliminated. Moreover, the associative projects are not approached in a global way but are broken down activity by activity. An emblematic example of this new approach can be found in the willingness of public actors to make the financing of FFL activities conditional on a goal of professional integration and employment. However, the association's project is to support populations that do not quite fit into this single objective. Debates are taking place within the association. Some believe that the association's FFL activity can be brought into line with the new requirements of public funders. They plead for a rapprochement with the public finance contacts in order to find an arrangement. However, other members of the association feel that the representatives of the public funders have no room for maneuver and that there is a real threat to the survival of the association's project. Other associations in the city have already closed down, and it seems that this has not caused a great stir among the funders.

It turns out that the FFL activities started with the birth of the association. In a way, they illustrate the specific skills that the association has developed throughout its history. The FFL learning process is carried out in small groups, with the presence of many volunteer teachers. They engage with the learners in a relationship that goes beyond a teacher-student relationship. They seek to promote social integration by creating privileged relationships with (and between) the different participants in the workshops. The association's FFL action is in contradiction with usual practices which do not seek to combine language learning and social learning. The usual FFL actions place the learning relationship in a strictly professional dimension and exclude the family and domestic sphere from the learning sphere.

Within the framework of the new institutional environment, the public funders ask the association for monitoring indicators. They make the continuation of financial support for FFL conditional on the achievement of these indicators. However, the support of the public financer is essential for the maintenance of the FFL action. It allows them to pay for the premises where the courses take place. The funders asked for statistics on the number, age, and gender of the people taking FFL courses. Once the statistics were produced, the funders pointed out that the majority of those attending the courses were women. However, the priority of the public authorities is the fight against unemployment. They therefore believe that as part of their strategy, they should give priority to the FFL course for men, who are a priori more employable. The women who go to the courses are not looking for a job. Their main concern is to learn the French language so that they can help their children in the evening when they have to do their school work. The association passed on the request of the funders to the volunteers who provide the courses free of charge. It asked them to encourage men to attend the classes. The volunteers protested. They do not want to make a gender-based selection in their classes. They do not want to be the "minions" of public policy choices they do not agree with. The association is in crisis.

Faced with this situation, the members of the association seek to distinguish between measurement and evaluation. To this end, an extraordinary general assembly was convened. In order to distance themselves from the figures produced, the numerical information was discussed collectively and democratically. During the meeting, some people felt that the figures should not have been sent to the funder. Others replied that a solidarity organization must be absolutely transparent. Still others put forward the idea that the information should not have been transmitted alone but that it should have been accompanied by other more accurate indicators to express the nature of the work carried out by the association and thus better convey the quality of the service provided. The discussions continued, and one of the founders of the association spoke up. He said that, in his opinion, there was no opposition between the expectations of the funder and the objectives of the association. All eyes turned toward him. He added that the association had always aimed at professional integration and employment. However, it did so with a depth that is the fruit of time and its experience. By strengthening the mastery of French for mothers today, we increase the capacity of these women to help their children with their evening homework. This will improve the integration and employability of young people who will enter the job market in ten or twenty years' time. This remark allowed the debate to move forward by lifting the initial opposition between the funder's request and the association's project. It was decided collectively to argue with the public funder by pointing out that the short-term priority that they were asking for in terms of integration should not be to the detriment of the future employability of today's youth. The volunteers agreed on this principle with the employees and decide to mobilize as many people as possible around this idea in order to be successfully heard by the public financier. This example is a demonstration of the collective intelligence that can develop in an association practicing democratic management. The deliberation organized around the production of the figures made it possible to adopt a critical attitude. The result of this process was to give a new meaning to the figures. This meaning is all the stronger because it is linked to the history and experience of the association.

5.3.5 Another Idea of Action: Toward a Pragmatic Approach to Management

Confronted by the dangers that threaten him, man is bound to seek safety (Dewey, 2015). This compelling need engages him in a quest for certainty. Thus, modern man cannot be satisfied with an approximation. With the progress of science, he wants to be able to rely on factual elements that reassure him. He wants to be able to put figures on reality in order to evaluate it. However, Dewey warns us on this point. Certainty is not "the horizon of thought". Rather, it is "its cross, its burden, the risk it must avoid, the temptation from which it must depart" (Savidan, 2014, page 14). For Dewey, the lure of certainty is like a siren song. We must guard against it because "certainty is a repose that the intellect must never know" (Savidan, 2014, page 14). It distracts us from action and practice. Dewey shows that the natural man dislikes the discomfort that accompanies the experience of doubt and stands ready to seize anything that will put an end to it (Dewey, 2015). However, he warns against this love of certainty which takes the form of a desire not to be disturbed or disturbed. It leads to dogmatism, the internalization of beliefs out of respect for authority, intolerance and fanaticism on the one hand, and to a disempowering dependence and laziness on the other (Dewey, 2015). In this, Dewey's thought helps us to define the Other Management in an experiential approach that refuses the dogma of the market. Indeed, the pragmatist approach posits the primacy of life and human experience, proposes a model of analysis through social inquiry, and is rooted in a radical democratic approach.

Dewey's pragmatist thinking is particularly useful when related to the reflection on another management. It allows us to open up the ethical question and the reference to human life. The investigative approach advanced by Dewey thus puts "human intelligence at the service of life" (Savidan, 2014, page 15). He refuses the elitist posture of "those who place thought on the highest peaks only to be assured of not meeting the plebs there" (Savidan, 2014, page 16). He also rejects the age-old separation of theory and practice "by placing" action at the heart of ideas (Dewey, 2015). For Dewey, knowing is itself a kind of action (Dewey, 2015). With the Other Management, it is about reintroducing human feelings and especially solidarity into the order of priorities. Management decisions are not divorced from emotions and the relationship to others (as we have seen with ethno-accounting). It is about recognizing that desire, purpose, and planning have meaning only under conditions where something is at stake (Dewey, 2015). With the epistemology of the South, the pragmatist proposal opens to an "epistemology of emancipation that can lead democracy back to its powers of invention" (Savidan, 2014; page 17). Certainty gives way to an ethic "tending towards the progressive, melioristic demand for continuous political and social reform" (Savidan, 2014, page 15) as we have seen with the solidarity incubator approaches. Against orthodox economists who claim their scientificity through voluntary omission of human values, Dewey proposes to accept to lose in theoretical certainty if we gain in practical judgment (Dewey, 2015). This is exactly the ambition of an alternative management that tends to dissociate measurement and evaluation.

For Dewey thinking is "a practice turned toward solving concrete problems" (Savidan, 2014, page 15). Based on the premise that every true idea is an experimentally verified idea, he proposes to develop social inquiry (Dewey, 2008). For him, the social sciences must rely on social experience because there is an intimate connection between knowing and doing. Dewey thought of social inquiry as a means of increasing factual knowledge of situations and of considering the reversibility of the causalities brought to light by it. If social inquiry supposes an instrumentation and a technicality, Dewey identifies three stages in the experimental inquiry. The first stage of all, an ostensible action induces changes in the environment and in the relationship we have with it. The next stage is an activity conducted with reference to ideas satisfying the conditions of the identified problem. Finally comes a new empirical situation that is the result of the action conducted and in which objects find themselves differently related to each other (Dewey, 2015). This incessant chaining together of situations, problems, and results of action means action is at the heart of ideas (Ibid). Real-life operations give a new status to ideas. They are no longer abstract and no longer mere ideas but experimental and operative ideas that feed the intelligence. From then on, the full and final reality of knowledge is located at the level of the individual case, and not at the level of general laws (Ibid.). Here again, the contribution for the Other Management is important. Through the reversal of causalities, the collective process of social inquiry is intended to lead to a social transformation whose configuration is not given a priori but is constructed in the exchange.

In his speech "Creative democracy, the task before us" delivered in 1939, Dewey states: "Democracy in relation to other ways of life is the only one that sincerely believes in the process of experience as an end and as a means." His refusal of the expert and the overarching positions of actors places Dewey in a position close to the models of popular education. For Dewey, it is indeed a question of engaging in a creative democracy (Joas, 1996) without concession. The emphasis is on "the communicative dimensions of action and on the processes of imagining creative solutions to problematic situations through deliberation" (Renault, 2011; page 169). The interest of the pragmatist posture is that it makes it possible to envisage a deepening of democracy, or in other words the possibility of democratizing democracy (Callon et al., 2001). The creative dimension in the face of problems recalls the work of Follett, whose position was close to that of the pragmatists. Thus, for Follett, management is part of a permanent learning process, experimentation, and creative exchanges (Follett, 1924). In management situations, the actors are led to rub shoulders, influence each other, and even confront each other. For Follett, this is normal behavior, and conflict should not be avoided. It is constructive. Follett demonstrates that there are three ways to resolve a conflict: the domination of one actor over the other, negotiation followed by consensus, and recourse to creativity through the invention of a new solution. Follett calls this third option constructive conflict. In this case, it is a matter of avoiding both the maintenance of domination and the crisis resulting from the impossibility of consensus. Follett thus puts creativity at the service of conflict resolution and values internal debate as a producer of meaning (Follett, 1924).

5.3.6 Perspectives for the Other Management

In the end, the Other Management that we have tried to define around this panorama of proposals and methodologies participates in a renewal of organizational thought. To conclude this chapter, it is possible to propose several nonexclusive definitions of alternative management. We will discuss them in ten points: (1) substantive management, (2) democratic management, (3) management of the territory, (4) management of fictitious goods, (5) management of reconciliation, (6) management of social innovation, (7) management of the commons, (8) management of the Other, (9) experimental management, and (10) management of the good life.

1. The Other Management is opposed to the formal and functionalist model. It rejects calculative rationality in favor of a substantive rationality in value. The Other Management postulates that human needs are not unlimited and that scarcity does not guide all management decisions. The Other Management is in dialogue with the heterodox economy, expresses itself in the solidarity economy, and deploys itself in a plural economy. The Other Management is therefore first and foremost the management of the Other economy (Hart et al., 2010).
2. The Other Management approach places democracy at the heart of organizational issues which it aims to enrich within the framework of democratic governance. It is built around issues of inclusiveness and openness to all stakeholders. It places the broad and egalitarian sharing of decisions as a management principle. It practices informa-

tional transparency with all its stakeholders. It protects whistleblowers. The Other Management is a democratic management.
3. The Other Management engages a process of demarketing at multiple levels (institutional, sociopolitical, sociocultural, socioeconomic, socio-environmental) and on several scales (individual, community, network). This can only be done in reference to a territory in which solidarity initiatives are rooted. The Other Management is the management of a territory of solidarity.
4. We then showed that management could be successfully associated with the necessary process of demarketing fictitious goods. We described how social currencies (convertible or not) could be part of a work of re-signification of the economy and participate in a democratic reappropriation of the management of financial activities. We have witnessed the demarketing of the work carried out by the activity and employment cooperatives and the platform cooperatives. Behind these initiatives, the emancipating proposal of an associated work is brilliantly outlined. This consists in giving back autonomy and power to those who engage in an individual activity by proposing a collective framework of a cooperative type where they are associate members. As far as nature is concerned, we have seen how a solidarity incubator approach could lead to the preservation of the natural wealth and biodiversity of a village with the choice of a responsible and community-based tourism. This leads us to formulate another definition. The Other Management is the management of the demarketing of work, money, and nature.
5. The Other type of management opens up the possibility of a reconciliation between the economy and the social. It is built at the juncture of a management that participates in democratic governance and a management that is guided by a goal of social utility. The Other Management is the management of reconciliation.
6. To meet the challenges of the Other economy, the Other Management must therefore demonstrate social innovation. To be protected from possible instrumentalization, it must be territorially anchored and democratically managed. The Other Management is then the management of a social innovation of solidarity type.

7. The Other Management is built by and with self-managing and self-organized collectives. It is based on the mutualization and sharing of resources. It integrates the approach of free software and platform cooperatives and shares their culture. It innovates by producing its own rules in a deliberative process. The Other Management is the management of the commons.
8. The Other Management is part of comprehensive approaches nourished by the contributions of anthropology, ethnology, psychoanalysis, and educational sciences. From then on, alternative management is part of human life and of the ethical concerns that organize life in society. The Other Management is developed through an empathetic approach and a concern for humility and recognition of the other. The Other Management is a matter of popular education. It refuses the commodification of man and human relations. It is lived in the long-time of the convivial and friendly relation. The Other Management is the management of the Other.
9. Finally, the Other Management is about experimentation, creativity, and radical democracy. In this respect, the Other Management is strongly influenced by the pragmatist approach. It refuses the fixity of thought that the claim of certainty and the dualism of formal thought cover. It does so using a dual approach of reintegrating the economy into the social and of deepening democracy. It does so by collectively investigating the problems that arise and by experimenting with new solutions that are the fruit of constructive conflict. It develops its action patiently in a melioristic perspective. The Other Management is the management of experimentation and social investigation.
10. The Amerindian approach shares with pragmatist authors the Cartesian refusal of the ontological separation between man and nature. It is anchored in the respect of the balance of life and nature. The collective ideal of good living that it carries refutes the model of domination based on a private logic and opposes the appropriation of material wealth by a restricted group at the expense of the majority. The Other Management is anchored in social and democratic life. It is the management of the good life.

Faced with this diversity of definitions of alternative management, many perspectives are offered. They make it possible to define orientations for a future research program. Some of the criteria mentioned have already been established: "overcoming binary and reductive oppositions, deconstructing dominant managerial discourses, critically distancing oneself from the managerialist drift, from the increasing instrumentalization that accompanies it and from the harm it does to the organization, to the workers and to society, taking a conceptualized, longitudinal and historical approach to the phenomena studied in order to gain a better understanding of the mechanisms that are at work" (Dietrich et al., 2015; page 177). Other perspectives can be added. Among these, we would point out the following: (1) a reinvestment in multidisciplinarity, (2) the study of the foundations of substantive management, (3) the exploration of Other Management, (4) the preservation of Other Management, (5) new management indicators, (6) the links between management and public action, and (7) the opening of a North-South dialogue on solidarity management.

1. Although management sciences are relatively open to other disciplines, this openness is not equal according to the disciplines considered. Thus, the proximity with economics is much stronger than with sociology, anthropology, or ethnology. This difference is notable and leads to a reduction in the interest of management sciences in comprehensive and qualitative approaches. This imbalance of openness within the social sciences is accentuated by a weak dialogue with the humanities (particularly with history, as we saw in the first chapter of this book). The first step could therefore be to reinvest in multidisciplinarity by focusing on the less explored disciplines of the humanities and social sciences.
2. We have seen the importance of a substantive approach in order to be able to think about another form of management. This implies that the researcher in management sciences should develop the study of the logics brought to light by Polanyi, such as reciprocity, redistribution, and domestic sharing. Anthropological and ethnographic approaches are able to serve this project. They allow us to extend organizational research beyond formal management to substantive management.

3. We have noted that one of the limitations of management sciences is to confine the organizational question to the field of the firm. In so doing, management refers to a single theory of organizations rather than to theories of organization. It is desirable to open up and deepen organizational thinking beyond the firm. Interest should be shown in particular in noncapitalist organizations (associations, cooperatives, mutuals). This interest needs to be translated into dedicated research that is the only way to prevent the inappropriate reuse of corporate management concepts. The objective is therefore to develop a plurality of organizational conceptual approaches in close relation to the plurality of nonmarket organizational forms found in the field.
4. The analysis of these forms of organization will not be able to compensate for the hegemony of market forms of organization. Part of the research work on other nonmarket and nonmonetary organizational forms must therefore be devoted to ways of preserving the socio-diversity of our economic fabric. This can be done through the exploration of intersecting forms of democratic economic cooperation (combining the logics of reciprocity, redistribution, domestic sharing, and re-signified markets) in the service of social utility goals.
5. A review has been carried out among economists with, in particular, the work of the Stiglitz Commission on new wealth indicators in order to bring to light macro-economic approaches that are more faithful to social reality. The aim of this Commission was to develop a reflection that would go beyond strictly quantitative measures of collective performance. The same work must be undertaken in management sciences to produce new approaches to evaluation. It is a matter of deconstructing reductive approaches in terms of market performance and impacts. They are incapable of accounting for the richness of associative projects and run the risk of distorting them. On the contrary, we need to develop and promote approaches that distinguish measurement from evaluation in order to rediscover virtuous dynamics in terms of collective intelligence.
6. Management must be put at the service of the ecological and social transition. For this to happen, it is undoubtedly necessary to develop research in conjunction with practitioners of the social and solidarity economy in order to identify the lines of management oriented toward

public action. For the moment, management has been too closely linked to business management to be able to imagine such a role. A management conceptualized in the interaction with associations can notably allow it to envisage other horizons not reduced to the functional boundaries of market organizations. It is a question of analyzing how private organizations can be placed at the service of a renewed public action.

7. We have shown in this book the importance of a decentering in management analyses. This decentering can be achieved by the depth of the historical analysis. It can also be achieved by a geographical shift to the South. It is high time to move away from the North–North dialogue and to free management from the market analysis to which the Anglo-Saxon vision tends to confine it. To do this, a North–South dialogue around a management that is re-embedded in human life is necessary. This book, written in two voices and straddling two hemispheres, bears witness to this desire.

References

Abensour, M. (2013). *Le procès des maîtres rêveurs (followed by) Pierre Leroux et l'utopie*. Sulliver.

Arendt, H. (1970). *The human condition*. University of Chicago Press. 340 pages.

Aufrère, L., Eynaud, P., Gauthier, O., & Vercher-Chaptal C. (2018, Septembre). De l'entreprendre à l'encommuns : comment un processus entrepreneurial peut-il s'inscrire dans une perspective de création de communs ? WP23. *Entreprendre en communs*.

Barbosa, L., & Veloso, L. (2009). A cultura do outro: interculturalidade e dialogia nas empresas. In Barbosa (Ed.), *Cultura e diferença nas organizações*. Atlas.

Bauwens, M. (2015). Plan de transition vers les communs : une introduction. In Coriat (Ed.), *Le retour des communs : la crise de l'idéologie propriétaire* (pp. 275–290). Les liens qui libèrent.

Bauwens, M., & Lievens, J. (2016). *Sauver le monde : Vers une économie post-capitaliste avec le peer-to-peer*. Éditions Les Liens qui libèrent.

Blavier, P. (2016). Un couple espagnol dans la récession de 2008 : Composition et évaluation des revenus alternatifs. *Revue des politiques sociales et familiales, 123*, 27–40.

Bloch, E. (1995). *The principle of hope* (Vol. 1). The MIT Press. 528 pages.
Bollier, D. (2014). *La renaissance des communs, Pour une société de coopération et de partage*. Charles Leopold Mayer.
Boltanski, L., & Thévenot, L. (2006). *On justification: Economies of worth. (Princeton studies in cultural sociology)* (1st ed.). Princeton University Press. 400 pages.
Bonnafous-Boucher, M. (2005). *Anthropologie et gestion*. Economica. 169 pages.
Borzaga, C., & Depedri, S. (2015). Multi-stakeholder governance in civil society organizations: Models and outcomes. In J. L. Laville, D. Young, & P. Eynaud (Eds.), *Civil society, the third sector and social enterprise: Governance and democracy* (pp. 109–121). Routledge.
Broca, S. (2013). *Utopie du logiciel libre : du bricolage informatique à la réinvention sociale*. Le passager clandestin. 282 pages.
Burawoy, M. (2013). La sociologie publique face au marché. In I. Hillenkamp & J. L. Laville (Eds.), *Socioeconomie et démocracie : L'actualité de Karl Polanyi*. Eres.
Callon, M., Lascoumes, P., & Barthe, Y. (2001). *Agir dans un monde incertain : essai sur la démocratie technique*. Editions Seuil.
Cançado, A. C., Pereira, J. R., & Tenorio, F. G. (2015). Fundamentos teóricos da gestão social. *Desenvolvimento regional em debate, 5*, 4–19.
Cefaï, D. (2007). *Pourquoi se mobilise-t-on ? Les théories de l'action collective*. La Découverte, Mauss. 722 pages.
Cefaï, D., & Chanial, P. (2000). Politique de l'association. Une généalogie de l'associationnisme civique en France. *La revue du GERFA, 1*.
Chanial, P. (2003). *Les trésors perdus du socialisme associationnisme français* (Vol. 36). Hermes.
Chanial, P. (2010, January 30). La délicate essence du socialisme. *Revue du MAUSS permanente*.
Chanlat, J. F. (1991). Por uma antropologia da condição humana nas organizações. In J. F. In Chanlat (Ed.), *O indivíduo nas organizações - dimensões esquecidas*. Atlas.
Chanteau, J. P., & Labrousse, A. (2013). *L'institutionnalisme méthodologique d'Elinor Ostrom au-delà des communs : quelques enjeux et controverses*. Congrès de l'AFEP.
Coriat, B. (2015). *Le retour des communs : La crise de l'idéologie propriétaire*. Les liens qui libèrent.
Cottereau, A. (2016). Ne pas confondre mesure et évaluation: aspects de l'ethnocomptabilité. *Revue des politiques sociales et familiales, 123*, 11–26.
Cottereau, A., & Marzok, M. M. (2012). *Une famille andalouse : Ethnocomptabilité pour une économie invisible*. Editions Bouchene.

Dacheux, E., & Goujon, D. (2016). Les promesses théoriques des recherches sur les initiatives solidaires : L'exemple du délibéralisme. *Revue française de socio économie, 16*, 201–214.

Desroche, H. (1976). *Le projet coopératif.* Editions ouvrières.

Dewey, J. (2008). *Logic – The theory of inquiry*. Saerchinger Press. 844 pages.

Dewey, J. (2015). *The quest for certainty: A study of the relation of knowledge and action*. Andesite Press. 332 pages.

Dietrich, A., Pigeyre, F., & Vercher-Chaptal, C. (2015). *Dérives et perspectives de la gestion : échanges autour des travaux de Julienne Brabet*. Septentrion, Presses Universitaires. 180 pages.

Dorion, L. (2017). Construire une organisation alternative. *Revue Française de Gestion, 264*, 143–160.

Eme, B., & Laville, J. L. (1994). *Cohésion sociale et emploi*. Desclée de Brouwer.

Eynaud, P. (2016). Culture and civil society for a positive change in the EU urban agenda. In *Build the city: Towards a practice-based manifesto*. European Cultural Foundation (ECF).

Eynaud, P. (2018). Quand développement territorial rime avec économie solidaire. *Revue Diagonal, 203*, 12–14.

Eynaud, P., & Mourey, D. (2012). Professionnalisation et identité des associations du secteur social : chronique d'une mort annoncée. *Revue Politiques et Management Public, 29*(4), 671–693.

Eynaud, P., & Mourey, D. (2015). Apports et limites de la production du chiffre dans l'entreprise sociale. *Revue Française de Gestion*.

Eynaud, P., & Sultan, F. (2014, Février). Les associations et les communs : croiser les expériences. *Juris Associations, 501*, 19–20.

Eynaud, P., Juan, M., & Mourey, D. (2018). Participatory art as a social practice of commoning to reinvent the right to the city. *International Journal of Voluntary and Nonprofit Organizations, 29*(2), 1–16.

Follett, M. P. (1924). *Creative experience*. Nyc, Longman Green & Co. (reprinted in London, P. Owen Publ., 1951).

França Filho, G. C. (2003). Gestão Social: um conceito em construção. In *Anais do Colóquio Internacional sobre Poder Local* (Vol. 9). CIAGS/UFBA.

França Filho, G. C. (2012). Indicadores para a sustentabilidade em economia solidária: uma questão de utilidade social. In G. Kraychette (Ed.), *Economia popular e solidária: indicadores para a sustentabilidade* (pp. 27–34). Tomo Editorial.

França Filho, G. C., & de Freitas Boullosa, R. (2015). Gouvernance démocratique, social management et para-économie. In Eynaud (Ed.), *La gouvernance entre diversité et normalisation* (pp. 205–215).

Fraser, N., & Honneth, A. (2003). *Redistribution or recognition? A political-philosophical exchange*. Verso.
Freire, P. (1979). *Educação como prática da liberdade* (9th ed.). Paz e Terra.
Freire, P. (1994). *Pedagogia do oprimido*. Paz e Terra.
Frère, B. (2009). *Le nouvel esprit solidaire*. Desclée de Brouwer.
Frère, B. (2015). *Le tournant de la théorie critique*. Desclée de Brouwer.
Gadotti, M. (1999). *Convite à leitura de Paulo Freire*. Scipione.
Génard, J. L. (2015). Sociologie critique, sociologie morale. In Frère (Ed.), *Le tournant de la théorie critique*. Desclée de Brouwer.
Gilbert, P., Teglborg, A. C., & Raulet-Croset, N. (2017). L'entreprise libérée, innovation radicale ou simple avatar du management participatif? *Annales des Mines - Gérer et comprendre, 127*, 38–49.
Gloria Gohn, M. D. (2013). Educação Popular e Movimentos Sociais. In D. R. Streck & M. T. Esteban (Eds.), *Educação Popular: lugar de construção social coletiva*. Vozes.
Gloria Gohn, M. D. (2015). *A relação entre a educação popular e os movimentos sociais na construção de sujeitos coletivos*. Text presented at the XII Congresso Nacional de Educação (Educere), PUC/PR, 26–29.
Goody, J. (2012). *The theft of history*. Cambridge University Press. 352 pages.
Gribaudi, M. (2014). *Paris, ville ouvrière. Une histoire occultée : 1789–1848*. La Découverte.
Guénée, L. (2016). Désynchronisation des temps familiaux et coexistence solidaire : Enquête ethno-comptable des ressources d'une famille jordanienne. *Revue des politiques sociales et familiales, 123*, 91–103.
Habermas, J. (1991). *The structural transformation of the public sphere: An inquiry into a category of Bourgeois society*. The MIT Press. 301 pages.
Hardin, G. (1968, December). The tragedy of commons. *Science*.
Hart, K., Laville, J. L., & Cattani, A. (2010). *The human economy: A citizen's guide*. Polity Press.
Hayat, S. (2014). *1848: Quand la république était révolutionnaire. Citoyenneté et représentation*. Le Seuil.
Hess, C. (2008, July 14–18). Mapping the new commons. In *12th biennial conference of the international association for the study of the commons*. University of Gloucestershire.
Hess, C., & Ostrom, E. (2006). *Understanding knowledge as a commons: From theory to practice*. The MIT Press.
Hess, C. & Ruth, M. D. (2006). *The name change; or, what happened to the "P"? ibraries' and ibrarians'*. Publications paper 23.

Honneth, A., & Joel, A. (1998). *The struggle for recognition: The moral grammar of social conflicts*. MIT Press.

Joas, H. (1996). *The creativity of action* (1st ed.). Polity. 352 pages.

Kymlicka, W. (1997). *Multicultural citzenship: A liberal theory of minority rights*. Oxford University Press.

Laplantine, F., & Olievenstein, C. (1993). *Um olhar frances sobre São Paulo*. Brasiliense. 92 pages.

Laville, J. L. (2010). *Politique de l'association*. Seuil. 350 pages.

Laville, J. L. (2011). *L'économie solidaire*. les essentiels d'Hermès, CNRS Editions.

Laville, J. L. (2015). La théorie critique : de l'impasse au renouveau. In Frère (Ed.), *Le tournant de la théorie critique*. Desclée de Brouwer.

Laville, J. L. (2018). *L'association, sociologie et économie*. Fayard – Pluriel.

Laville, J. L. (2023). *The solidarity economy*. University of Minnesota Press.

Laville, J. L., & Nyssens, M. (2001). The social enterprise: Towards a theoretical socio-economic approach. In Borzaga & Defourny (Eds.), *The emergence of social enterprise* (pp. 312–332). Routledge.

Laville, J. L., & Salmon, A. (2015a). *Associations et Action Publique*. Desclée de Brouwer. 630 pages.

Laville, J. L., & Salmon, A. (2015b). Repenser la relation entre gouvernance et démocracie : le cadre théorique de l'économie solidaire. In P. Eynaud (Ed.), *La gouvernance entre diversité et normalisation* (pp. 175–189). Dalloz, Juris Editions.

Macchi, O. (2016). Portfolios of the poor how the world's poor live on $2 a day. *Revue des politiques sociales et familiales, 123*, 137–139.

Musso, P. (2015). La solidarité : généalogie d'un concept sociologique. In A. Supiot (Ed.), *La solidarité : enquête sur un principe juridique* (pp. 93–107). Collège de France, Edition Odile Jacob.

Nyssens, M., & Petrella, F. (2015). ESS et ressources communes : vers une reconnaissance d'une diversité institutionnelle. *Revue française de socio-économie, 15*, 117–134.

Olson, M. (1965). *Logic of collective action*. Harvard University Press.

Orléan, A. (2011). *L'empire de la valeur, Refonder l'économie*. Le Seuil.

Orléan, A. (2012). Repenser la valeur, refonder l'économie. *The AEGIS Libellio, 8*(3), 11–21.

Orsi, F. (2015). Revisiter la propriété pour construire les communs. In B. Coriat (Ed.), *Le retour des communs : la crise de l'idéologie propriétaire* (pp. 51–67). Les liens qui libèrent.

Ostrom, E. (2005). *Understanding institutional diversity*. Princeton University Press.

Ostrom, E. (2010a). *Governance of the commons: For a new approach to natural resources*. De Boeck.

Ostrom, E. (2010b). Beyond markets and states: Polycentric governance of complex economic systems. *American Economic Review, 100*(3), 641–672.

Ostrom, E., & Ostrom, V. (1977). Public goods and public choices. In E. S. Savas (Ed.), *Alternatives for delivering public services: Toward improved performance* (pp. 7–49). Westview Press.

Paludo, C. (2015). Educação Popular como resistência e emancipação humana. *Cad. Cedes, Campinas, 35*(96), 219–238.

Polanyi, K. (1977). In H. W. Pearson (Ed.), *The livelihood of man*. Academic Press.

Pruvost, G. (2016). Dépenser moins pour vivre mieux : Le cas de boulangers paysans vivant en yourte. *Revue des politiques sociales et familiales, 123*, 105–119.

Renault, M. (2011). Elaborer des outils pour construire une société plus conviviale : d'une expérience de terrain à un raisonnement théorique. In Caillé, Humbert, Latouche, & Viveret (Eds.), *De la convivialité : dialogues sur la société conviviale à venir* (pp. 167–187). La Découverte.

Riot-Sarcey, M. (2016). *Le procès de la liberté. Une histoire souterraine du XIX ème siècle en France*. La Découverte.

Riot-Sarcey, M., & Gribaudi, M. (2008). *1848 : la révolution oubliée*. La Découverte.

Savidan, P. (2014). *La quête de certitude ou les leçons d'une pratique, in Dewey, La quête de certitude : une étude de la relation entre connaissance et action*. NRF, Editions Gallimard. originale 1929.

Sousa Santos, B. D. (2014). *Epistemologies of the south: Justice against epistemicide*. Routledge. 284 pages.

Supiot, A. (2012). *The spirit of Philadelphia: Social justice vs. the total market* (1st ed.). Verso. 160 pages.

Taylor, C. (1992). *Multiculturalism: Examining the politics of recognition*. Princeton University Press.

Tenorio, F. G. (1998, set/out). Gestão social: uma perspectiva conceitual. *Revista de Administração publica, 32*(5).

Todorov, T. (1993). *Nós e os outros*. Zahar.

Vienney, C. (1994). *L'économie sociale*. La Découverte.

6

Managing for Solidarity, Sustainability, and the Commons

> Only the word, in its fragility, can bring together the crowd of men so that the outpouring of violence is transformed into convivial reconstruction (Illich, 1973; page 157)

> Utopia is not the unattainable but the unrealized Theodore Monot

Faced with the urgent issues raised by the changes in our world, this book aims to examine the relationship between solidarity and organization in an attempt to think of a different management approach. A review of the history of thought has shown us that although management has not been able to retain solidarity as a guiding principle, it has always underpinned management conceptualization. However, the weight of the Anglo-Saxon model on the discipline has, until recently, made invisible anything that did not fit with the presuppositions of a market economy. This is how generations of students learned that the objective of management is organizational performance with a view to maximizing profit. Formal management seems to unfold in a world without contradiction because it is without depth (Barthes, 2013). This instrumentalization of management in a market context has in turn favored calculative approaches and disqualified the more political questions posed in the

P. Eynaud, G. Carvalho de França Filho, *Solidarity and Organization*,
https://doi.org/10.1007/978-3-031-27568-5_6

introduction to this work, such as inequalities and environmental issues. The generalization of the contract in all areas of professional and personal life has had a profoundly "un-solidarity" dimension (Chauvière, 2007; p. 55). By its hegemonic character, the history of management thought and the management models have in a way relegated experiences from other geographical and cultural spaces to peripheral areas of knowledge, when it has not obscured them.

However, there is a little-known history of the relationship between solidarity and organization. It can be traced in the history of social and solidarity economy organizations. The latter owes a great deal to managerial inventions and organizational innovations that history has hardly remembered as such. A rereading of the history of management in the light of these organizations remains to be done. It would make it possible to bring out the forgotten and/or disqualified actors on these organizational issues. Among these are, of course, the authors of the associationist current, but also the entire history of the ancestral cultures of the peoples of the South, whose organizational processes have been marked by the relationship to solidarity. This narrative is not easy to construct because a large part of this memory resides in the oral culture. As such, the detour through the histories of the South is indispensable for acquiring fundamental knowledge, as Mauss (2000) has shown. In order to overcome the obstacle of what may appear to be unthought-of organizational theories, this critical historical work is, in our opinion, indispensable if we want to be able to rehabilitate and develop the organizational and economic question in a civic and social context. We have to note that the means can transform the ends and even subvert them. There are many examples of drift: "seeking money for money's sake, cultivating power for its own sake or conquering power to enjoy authority" (Chabot, 2015; p. 52). In a world that has become technical, vigilance about organizational choices is more necessary than ever. This vigilance can be maintained by cultivating the meaning that management sometimes lacks. Paraphrasing Rabelais, Naro ironically points out "that efficiency without consciousness, is only loss of meaning" (Naro, 2015; page 169).

In the course of this work, we have explored two paths. The first led us from organization to solidarity. We have shown that the organization of solidarity could not avoid questioning the definition of the economy. The reference to the Polanyian framework allowed us to lay the foundations of a substantive management likely to consider reciprocity, redistribution, and domestic sharing as principles alongside market exchange. This is how we have studied the possibility for this type of management to engage in a process of re-embedding fictitious goods. We have seen with Gueirrero Ramos that a management decision can be based on a substantive rationality, that is, on a rationality in value (Weber, 2019), and that it is necessary to rethink the question of time and space in order to hope to open up perspectives on a new theory of organizations. Guerreiro Ramos' thought thus completes the work initiated by Polanyi and extends it by questioning the fundamentals of organization theory.

The second path that the book has sought to explore is based on the opposite perspective. It has led us to question the means of solidarizing the organization. This time, the analysis raised questions related to democratic solidarity. To compensate for the corporatist mechanisms of community closure, Girard (1987) stated that solidary management can be read in the opening of the governance of organizations to multiple actors or stakeholders or in the inclusiveness of its approach. It thus leads to collective decision-making and evaluation, brings together the relevant actors in a given territory, and opens up proximity management (Bacqué et al., 2005). This complex task can only be solved by hybridizing resources, co-construction, and the inclusion of the organization in public action in the service of the general interest. From then on, the questions that arise are those of democratic governance, solidarity-based territories, the reconciliation of the economic and the social, and social innovation.

Once linked together reciprocally, the two concepts of solidarity and organization are the vectors of the Other Management. The latter finds expression in two particularly interesting schools of thought, which differ in their starting point. In the indirect lineage of the works begun in the 1950s by Gueirrero Ramos, the Brazilian school defines the dimensions of an open *gestão social* through a redefinition of the economy and a democratization of organizations. These organizations are not closed on themselves but considered in their relation with the public sphere. They are also considered in the intersubjectivity of their stakeholders, thus guaranteeing the possibility of their emancipation. In terms of sustainable management, the work of the Ostrom school is particularly relevant because it began with the preservation of the natural commons. The strength of this school of thought was that it did not stop there, and it opened up the question of the commons to resources other than natural ones. In particular, the merging of analysis with free software actors has allowed this theoretical framework to develop valuable thinking on self-organization and the management of new forms of collective property in relation to the digital (Eynaud & Sultan, 2014; Broca, 2017). These two schools of thought should not be thought of as competing. They are complementary and their approaches congruent. Both share the idea that the economic equation cannot be reduced to a market-state dichotomy. Both envisage the possibility of collective entrepreneurship. Finally, both open up the prospect of an open, emancipating, and democratic solidarity.

Questioning the combined links between solidarity and organization augurs an important change for researchers in organization theory. Indeed, "by recognizing the role of organizational phenomena in the construction of the world, it is then up to researchers to rethink the ethics of collective activity" (Vaujany et al., 2016; p. 20) and to "propose management and organizational models that are more respectful of human beings" (Chanlat, 2013; p. 18). This new ethic implies other methodologies, other epistemological stances, and no doubt other connections between researchers and field actors. This calls for a renewed critical theory (Laville, 2015). This effort is part of a new look at emergences. As Sousa Santos suggests, a sociology of absences can occur in the order of knowledge by substituting ecologies for monocultures (Sousa Santos, 2014).

Following the example of permaculture, which articulates agriculture and permanence, we need to build a "permanagement" that combines management and sustainability. On the political level, the urgency is there. Faced with the predicted catastrophe, we must accept our limits (Boeuf et al., 2017) and come to rest somewhere (Latour, 2017). Since we only have one planet, the defense of biodiversity and socio-diversity must be considered as one and the same fight. Indeed, an essential and profound link "makes energy and democratic transitions mutually supportive" (Chabot, 2015; p. 135). Faced with the threat of a technocratic apocalypse, we can oppose the convivial society (Illich, 1973; Caillé et al., 2011; Manifeste convivialiste, 2013). Faced with the hegemony of the market enterprise model and its amoral individualism, we can make the choice of democratic organization and pay renewed attention to solidarity-based organizational forms.

References

Bacqué, M. H., Rey, H., & Sintomer, Y. (2005). *Gestion de proximité et démocratie participative : une perspective comparative*. La découverte. 314 pages.

Barthes, R. (2013). *Mythologies* (2nd ed.). Hill and Wang. 288 pages.

Boeuf, G., Swynghedauw, B., & Toussaint, J. F. (2017). *L'homme peut-il accepter ses limites*. Quae éditions. 192 pages.

Broca, S. (2017). Le digital labor, extension infinie ou fin du travail ? Tracés. *Revue de sciences humaines, 32*, 133–144.

Caillé, A., Humbert, M., Latouche, S., & Viveret, P. (2011). Vers le convivialisme. In *De la convivialité : dialogues sur la société conviviale à venir* (pp. 15–24). La Découverte.

Chabot, P. (2015). *L'âge des transitions*. Puf.

Chanlat, J. F. (2013). Les études critiques en management : Un rappel historique. *Communication, Information médias théories pratiques, 31*(1).

Chauvière, M. (2007). *Trop de gestion tue le social : Essai sur une discrète chalandisation*. Alternatives sociales. Editions La Découverte.

Eynaud, P., & Sultan, F. (2014, Février). Les associations et les communs : croiser les expériences. *Juris Associations, 501*, 19–20.

Girard, R. (1987). *Things hidden since the foundation of the world*. Stanford University Press. 470 pages.

Illich, I. (1973). *La convivialité*. le Seuil.

Latour, B. (2017). *Où atterrir ? Comment s'orienter en politique*. La Découverte, Cahiers libres. 160 pages.

Laville, J. L. (2015). La théorie critique : de l'impasse au renouveau. In Frère (Ed.), *Le tournant de la théorie critique*. Desclée de Brouwer.

Manifeste convivialiste. (2013). *Déclaration d'interdépendence*. Le Bord de l'eau.

Mauss, M. (2000). *The gift: The form and reason for exchange in archaic societies*. W. W. Norton and Company. 184 pages.

Naro, G. (2015). Le new public management ou la gestion malade de la société. In Dietrich, Pigeyre, & Vercher-Chaptal (Eds.), *Dérives et perspectives de la*

gestion : échanges autour des travaux de Julienne Brabet. Septentrion, Presses Universitaires. 180 pages.
Sousa Santos, B. D. (2014). *Epistemologies of the south: Justice against epistemicide*. Routledge. 284 pages.
Vaujany, F. X. D., Hussenot, A., & Chanlat, J. F. (2016). *Théorie des organisations : nouveaux tournants*. Economica.
Weber, M. (2019). *Economy and society: A new translation*. Harvard University Press. 520 pages.

Bibliography

Abdelnour, S., & Lambert, A. (2014). L'entreprise de soi : un nouveau mode de gestion politique des classes politiques ? *Geneses, 95*(2), 27.

Abensour, M. (2013). *Le procès des maîtres rêveurs (followed by) Pierre Leroux et l'utopie*. Sulliver.

Acosta, A. (2014). *The Buen Vivir*. Utopia. 208 pages.

Aglietta, M., & Orléan, A. (1982). *La violence de la monnaie*. PUF. 324 pages.

Aktouf, O. (2000). *Management entre tradition et renouvellement*. Gaëtan Morin. 710 pages.

Albuquerque, P. P. (2003). Moeda social 2. In Cattani (Ed.), *A outra economia*. Veraz Editores.

Allard-Poesi, F., & Loilier, T. (2009). Qu'est-ce que la critique en sciences du management ? Que pourrait-elle être ? *Economies et Societes*, 1975–1999.

Andion, C. (2014). Inovação Social. In R. F. Boullosa (Ed.), *Dicionário para a formação em gestão social* (pp. 98–102). Ciags/UFBA.

ANPROTEC. (2008). *Associação Nacional de Entidades Promotoras de Empreendimentos Imovadores*. Perguntas e respostas. http://www.anprotec.org.br/publicacao.php?idpublicacao=117

Arendt, H. (1970). *The human condition*. University of Chicago Press. 340 pages.

Arnsperger, C. (2009). *Ethique de l'existence post-capitaliste : pour un militantisme existentiel*. Edition Cerf.

P. Eynaud, G. Carvalho de França Filho, *Solidarity and Organization*,
https://doi.org/10.1007/978-3-031-27568-5

Audier, S. (2010). *La pensée solidariste : aux sources du modèle social républicain*. PUF.

Aufrère, L., Eynaud, P., Gauthier, O., & Vercher-Chaptal C. (2018, Septembre). De l'entreprendre à l'encommuns : comment un processus entrepreneurial peut-il s'inscrire dans une perspective de création de communs ? WP23. *Entreprendre en communs*.

Azam, G. (2015). *Osons rester humain : les impasses de la toute-puissance*. Les liens qui libèrent.

Bacqué, M. H., Rey, H., & Sintomer, Y. (2005). *Gestion de proximité et démocratie participative : une perspective comparative*. La découverte. 314 pages.

Barbezieux, P., & Herody, C. (2016, February). *Report to the Prime Minister on the collaborative economy*. 94 pages.

Barbosa, L., & Veloso, L. (2009). A cultura do outro: interculturalidade e dialogia nas empresas. In Barbosa (Ed.), *Cultura e diferença nas organizações*. Atlas.

Barthes, R. (2013). *Mythologies* (2nd ed.). Hill and Wang. 288 pages.

Bauman, Z. (2000). *Liquid modernity*. Polity.

Bauwens, M. (2015). Plan de transition vers les communs : une introduction. In Coriat (Ed.), *Le retour des communs : la crise de l'idéologie propriétaire* (pp. 275–290). Les liens qui libèrent.

Bauwens, M., & Kostakis, V. (2017). *Cooperativism in the digital era, or how to form a global counter-economy*. Opendemocracy.net.

Bauwens, M., & Lievens, J. (2016). *Sauver le monde : Vers une économie post-capitaliste avec le peer-to-peer*. Éditions Les Liens qui libèrent.

Bayle, E., & Dupuy, J. C. (2012). *Management des entreprises de l'économie sociale et solidaire : identités plurielles et spécificités*. Editions De Boeck. 334 pages.

Beau, R., & Larrère, C. (2018). *Penser l'Anthropocène*. Presses de Sciences Po. 554 pages.

Béji-Bécheur, A., Codello, P., & Château-Terrisse, P. (2018). *Gestion des entreprises sociales et solidaires*. Editions Ems, Management et société. 259 pages.

Bernet, J., Eynaud, P., Maurel, O., & Vercher, C. (2016). *La gestion des associations*. Eres édition.

Berry, M. (1983). *Une technologie invisible : l'impact des systèmes de gestion sur les comportements humains*. École polytechnique, report for the Ministère de la Recherche et de la Technologie. http://crg.polytechnique.fr/incunables.

Birchfield, V. (2014). La contestation de l'idéologie de marché : articuler Polanyi et Gramsci. In I. Hillenkamp & J. L. Laville (Eds.), *Socioéconomie et Démocratie : L'actualité de Karl Polanyi* (pp. 65–88). Eres Editions.

Blais, M. C. (2007). *La solidarité : histoire d'une idée*. NRF, Editions Gallimard.

Blanc, J. (1998). Les monnaies parallèles : évaluation du phénomène et enjeux théoriques. *Revue d'économie financière, 49*, 81–102.

Blanc, J. (2011). Classifying "CCs" – Community complementary and local currencies' types and generations. *International Journal of Community Currency Research, 15*, 4–10.

Blavier, P. (2016). Un couple espagnol dans la récession de 2008 : Composition et évaluation des revenus alternatifs. *Revue des politiques sociales et familiales, 123*, 27–40.

Bloch, E. (1995). *The principle of hope* (Vol. 1). The MIT Press. 528 pages.

Blondiaux, L. (2008). *Le nouvel esprit de la démocratie. Actualité de la démocratie participative*. Seuil, coll. La république des idées. 109 pages.

Boeuf, G., Swynghedauw, B., & Toussaint, J. F. (2017). *L'homme peut-il accepter ses limites*. Quae éditions. 192 pages.

Bollier, D. (2014). *La renaissance des communs, Pour une société de coopération et de partage*. Charles Leopold Mayer.

Boltanski, L. (2015). Situation de la critique. In B. Frère (Ed.), *Le tournant de la théorie critique* (pp. 189–217). Desclée de Brouwer.

Boltanski, L., & Thévenot, L. (2006). *On justification: Economies of worth. (Princeton studies in cultural sociology)* (1st ed.). Princeton University Press. 400 pages.

Bonnafous-Boucher, M. (2005). *Anthropologie et gestion*. Economica. 169 pages.

Borzaga, C., & Defourny, J. (2001). *The emergence of social enterprise*. Routledge.

Borzaga, C., & Depedri, S. (2009). Working for social enterprises: Does it make a difference? In A. Amin (Ed.), *Social economy. International perspectives on economic solidarity* (pp. 82–114). Zed Press.

Borzaga, C., & Depedri, S. (2015). Multi-stakeholder governance in civil society organizations: Models and outcomes. In J. L. Laville, D. Young, & P. Eynaud (Eds.), *Civil society, the third sector and social enterprise: Governance and democracy* (pp. 109–121). Routledge.

Bouchard, M. J. (1999). *Recherche en sciences humaines et sociales et innovations sociales, Contribution à une politique de l'immatériel*. Conseil québécois de la recherche sociale (CQRS), Québec, les Publications du Québec.

Bouquin, S. (2010). Harry Braverman face à la sociologie du travail. *L'homme et la société, 4*(178), 159–179.

Bourgeois, L. (2015). *Solidarité*, Ed. originale A. Colin 1896. Bibebook Free Edition. 158 pages.

Braverman, H. (1998). *Labor and monopoly capital: The degradation of work in the twentieth century*. Review Monthly Press.

Broca, S. (2013). *Utopie du logiciel libre : du bricolage informatique à la réinvention sociale*. Le passager clandestin. 282 pages.

Broca, S. (2017). Le digital labor, extension infinie ou fin du travail ? Tracés. *Revue de sciences humaines, 32*, 133–144.

Bucolo, E., Eynaud, P., & Haeringer, J. (2015). La gouvernance des associations en pratiques. In P. Eynaud (Ed.), *Gouvernance entre diversité et normalisation*. Collection Hors Série Juris Association, Editeur Dalloz.

Burawoy, M. (2013). La sociologie publique face au marché. In I. Hillenkamp & J. L. Laville (Eds.), *Socioeconomie et démocracie : L'actualité de Karl Polanyi*. Eres.

Bureau, M. C., & Corsani, A. (2015). Les coopératives d'activité et d'emploi : pratiques d'innovation institutionnelle. *Revue Française de Socio-Économie, 15*, 213–231.

Búrigo, F. L. (2002). *Moeda social e circulação de riquezas na economia solidária*. Disponível em: http://money.socioeco.org/documents/67pdf_Moeda.pdf. Acesso em ago 29, 2010.

Burnham, J. (1941). *The managerial revolution: What is happening in the world?* John Day Company.

Cadalen, P. Y. (2018). Les temps conflictuels du commun en Equateur et en Bolivie. *Revista de economia solidaria, 11*, 79–97.

Caillé, A. (1994). In Coll. Recherches, Série Bibliothèque du Mauss (Ed.), *Don, intérêt et intéressement : Bourdieu, Mauss, Platon et quelques autres*. La Découverte.

Caillé, A. (2002). *Antropologia do Dom: o terceiro paradigma. Petrópolis* (pp. 7–139). Vozes.

Caillé, A. (2005). *Dé-penser l'économique : contre le fatalisme*. La découverte, Mauss. 307 pages.

Caillé, A., & Laville, J. L. (1998). Une seule solution, l'association ? Socio-économie du fait associatif. *Revue du Mauss, 11*.

Caillé, A., Humbert, M., Latouche, S., & Viveret, P. (2011). Vers le convivialisme. In *De la convivialité : dialogues sur la société conviviale à venir* (pp. 15–24). La Découverte.

Cailluet, L., Lemarchand, Y., & Chessel, M. E. (2013). *Histoire et sciences de gestion*. Vuibert, coll. Fnege.

Callon, M. (2006). *What does it mean to say that economics is performative?* Csi working papers, series 005.

Callon, M., Lascoumes, P., & Barthe, Y. (2001). *Agir dans un monde incertain : essai sur la démocratie technique*. Editions Seuil.

Calvo, S., & Morales, A. (2017). *Social and solidarity economy: The world's economy with a social face* (1st ed.). Routledge. 384 pages.
Cançado, A. C., Tenorio, F. G., & Silva, J. T., Jr. (2012). *Gestão social: aspectos teóricos e aplicações*. Editora Unijui.
Cançado, A. C., Pereira, J. R., & Tenorio, F. G. (2013). *Gestão social: epistemologia de um paradigma*. Editora CRV.
Cançado, A. C., Pereira, J. R., & Tenorio, F. G. (2015). Fundamentos teóricos da gestão social. *Desenvolvimento regional em debate, 5*, 4–19.
Casilli, A. (2013). Contre l'hypothèse de la fin de la vie privée. *Revue française des sciences de l'information et de la communication, 3*.
Casilli, A. (2015). *Digital labor: Work, technologies and conflictualities*. https://halshs.archives-ouvertes.fr/halshs-01145718
Cefaï, D. (2007). *Pourquoi se mobilise-t-on ? Les théories de l'action collective*. La Découverte, Mauss. 722 pages.
Cefaï, D., & Chanial, P. (2000). Politique de l'association. Une généalogie de l'associationnisme civique en France. *La revue du GERFA, 1*.
Chabot, P. (2015). *L'âge des transitions*. Puf.
Chambon, J. L., Davis, A., & Devevey, J. M. (1982). *Les innovations sociales*. PUF. Collection Que sais-je?
Chancel, L. (2017). *Insoutenables inégalités : pour une justice sociale et environnementale*. Editions Les petits matins.
Chandler, A. D. (1992). Managerial enterprise and competitive capabilities. *Business History, 34*(1), 11–41.
Chanial, P. (2003). *Les trésors perdus du socialisme associationnisme français* (Vol. 36). Hermes.
Chanial, P. (2010, January 30). La délicate essence du socialisme. *Revue du MAUSS permanente*.
Chanlat, J. F. (1991). Por uma antropologia da condição humana nas organizações. In J. F. In Chanlat (Ed.), *O indivíduo nas organizações - dimensões esquecidas*. Atlas.
Chanlat, J. F. (2013). Les études critiques en management : Un rappel historique. *Communication, Information médias théories pratiques, 31*(1).
Chanteau, J. P., & Labrousse, A. (2013). *L'institutionnalisme méthodologique d'Elinor Ostrom au-delà des communs : quelques enjeux et controverses*. Congrès de l'AFEP.
Chauvière, M. (2007). *Trop de gestion tue le social : Essai sur une discrète chalandisation*. Alternatives sociales. Editions La Découverte.

Chauvière, M., & Godbout, J. T. (1992). *Les usagers entre marché et citoyenneté.* L'Harmattan.

Chaves, R., & Demoustier, D. (2015). *The emergence of the social economy in public policy: An international analysis.* edited by CIRIEC.

Chomsky, N. (2017). *Who rules the world?* Penguin Books Ltd. 336 pages.

Coase, R. (1937). *The nature of the firm.* Blackwell Publishing.

Colliac, S. (2005). Monnaies parallèles provinciales et fédéralisme budgétaire en Argentine. *Revue d'économie financière, 81*, 1–20.

Colliot-Thélène, C. (2011). Retour sur les rationalités chez Max Weber. *Les Champs de Mars, 22*(2), 13–30.

Conaty, P., & Bollier, D. (2014, August 27–28). *Toward an open co-operativism: A new social economy based on open platforms, co-operative models and the commons.* Report on a commons strategies group workshop, Berlin, Germany.

Coraggio, J. L. (2004). *La gente o el capital. Desarollo local y economia en trabajo.* Espacio Editorial.

Corbett, S., & Walker, A. (2013). The big society: Rediscovery of 'the social' or rhetorical fig-leaf for neo-liberalism? *Critical Social Policy, 33*(3).

Coriat, B. (2015). *Le retour des communs : La crise de l'idéologie propriétaire.* Les liens qui libèrent.

Cottereau, A. (2016). Ne pas confondre mesure et évaluation: aspects de l'ethno-comptabilité. *Revue des politiques sociales et familiales, 123*, 11–26.

Cottereau, A., & Marzok, M. M. (2012). *Une famille andalouse : Ethno-comptabilité pour une économie invisible.* Editions Bouchene.

Courtel, Y. (2010). La lutte pour la reconnaissance dans la philosophie sociale d'Axel Honneth. *Revue des sciences religieuses, 82*(1).

Coutrot, T. (2002). *Critique de l'organisation du travail.* La Découverte.

Coutrot, T. (2018). *Libérer le travail : Pourquoi la gauche s'en moque et pourquoi cela doit changer.* Edition Seuil. 303 pages.

Crozier, M. (1964). Le phénomène bureaucratique. Essai sur les tendances bureaucratiques des systèmes d'organisation modernes et sur leurs relations en France avec le système social et culturel. *Revue française de science politique, 14*(5), 991–997.

Cummings, S., Bridgman, T., Hassard, J., & Rowlinson, M. (2017). *A new history of management.* Cambridge University Press.

Dacheux, E., & Goujon, D. (2016). Les promesses théoriques des recherches sur les initiatives solidaires : L'exemple du délibéralisme. *Revue française de socio économie, 16*, 201–214.

Dardot, P., & Laval, C. (2014). *Commun : Essai sur la révolution au XXIème siècle*. La Découverte.
David, A., Hatchuel, A., & Laufer, R. (2012). *Les Nouvelles fondations des sciences de gestion : éléments d'épistemologie de la recherche en management*. Presses des mines Paris Tech.
Debord, G. (2002). *The society of the spectacle*. Black and Red Publisher. 132 pages.
Dellemotte, J. (2009). La main invisible d'Adam Smith : pour en finir avec les idées reçues. *L'économie politique, 44*, 28–41.
Delvolvé, N., & Veyer, S. (2009). *De la coopérative d'activités et d'emploi à la mutuelle de travail : produire du droit pour accompagner un projet politique d'économie sociale*. Juin.
Demoustier, D., Rousselière, D., Clerc, J. M., & Cassier, B. (2003). L'entreprise collective : unité et diversité de l'économie sociale et solidaire. *Recma, 290*, 56–73.
Desroche, H. (1976). *Le projet coopératif*. Editions ouvrières.
Dewey, J. (2008). *Logic – The theory of inquiry*. Saerchinger Press. 844 pages.
Dewey, J. (2015). *The quest for certainty: A study of the relation of knowledge and action*. Andesite Press. 332 pages.
Dewey, J. (2016). *The public and its problems: An essay in political inquiry*. Swallow Press. 304 pages.
Diamond, J. (2005). *Collapse: How societies choose to fail or survive*. Penguin Books.
Dietrich, A., Pigeyre, F., & Vercher-Chaptal, C. (2015). *Dérives et perspectives de la gestion : échanges autour des travaux de Julienne Brabet*. Septentrion, Presses Universitaires. 180 pages.
Dockès, P. (2005). Léon Walras et la conciliation des vérités. *Cahiers du CERAS*. April, HS N°4.
Dorion, L. (2017). Construire une organisation alternative. *Revue Française de Gestion, 264*, 143–160.
Douglas, M. (1986). *How institutions think*. Syracuse University Press. 158 pages.
Dowbor, L. (2007). *Democracia econômica: um passeio pelas teorias*. BNB.
Dowbor, L. (2008). *Democracia econômica: alternativas de gestão social*. Vozes.
Dowbor, L. (2017). *A era do capital improdutivo - Autonomia Literária*. Outras Palavras.
Draperi, J. F. (1998). L'économie sociale, un ensemble d'entreprises aux formes infiniment variées. *Recma, 268*.
Drucker, P. (1954). The practice of management. 280 pages.
Drucker, P., & Maciarielo, J. A. (2008). *Management* (revised ed. 1973). Collins.

Dujarier, M. A. (2014). *Le management désincarné*. La Découverte.

Duncan, W. J. (1989). *Great ideas in management: Lessons from the founders and foundations of managerial practice*. Jossey-Bass.

Dupuy, J. P. (2002). *Pour un catastrophisme éclairé : quand l'impossible est certain*. Editions Points, Collection Essais. 216 pages.

Durkheim, E. (1975). *Textes. 1. Eléments d'une théorie sociale*. Collection Le sens commun, Paris Éditions de Minuit. 512 pages.

Durkheim, E. (2014). *The division of labor in society*. Free Press. 416 pages.

Durkheim, E. (2016). *De la division du travail social*. PUF.

Eme, B., & Laville, J. L. (1994). *Cohésion sociale et emploi*. Desclée de Brouwer.

Emery, F. E., & Trist, E. L. (1960). In C. W. Churchman (Ed.), *Socio-technical systems, management sciences models and techniques*. Pergamon.

Endenburg, G. (1988). *Sociocracy as social design*. Eburon.

Engels, F. (2015). *Socialism: Utopian and scientific* (1st ed.). CreateSpace Independent Publishing Platform. 70 pages.

Enriquez, E. (2003). *L'organisation en analyse*. PUF. 334 pages.

Eynaud, P. (2015). *Gouvernance entre diversité et normalisation*. Collection Hors Série Juris Association, Editeur Dalloz.

Eynaud, P. (2016). Culture and civil society for a positive change in the EU urban agenda. In *Build the city: Towards a practice-based manifesto*. European Cultural Foundation (ECF).

Eynaud, P. (2018). Quand développement territorial rime avec économie solidaire. *Revue Diagonal, 203*, 12–14.

Eynaud, P., & Gérome, F. (2014, Février 19). Faire face aux défis. *Juris Associations, 492*.

Eynaud, P., & Guibert, G. (2012, Novembre). La course à la taille dans le secteur associatif des musiques actuelles : de la crise de sens à la proposition alternative d'une plateforme collaborative. *Revue RECMA, 326*.

Eynaud, P., & Laville, J. L. (2018). Joining the commons with social and solidarity economy research: Towards the renewal of critical thinking and emancipation. *Revista de Economia solidaria, 11*. A Economia solidaria e os comuns.

Eynaud, P., & Mourey, D. (2012). Professionnalisation et identité des associations du secteur social : chronique d'une mort annoncée. *Revue Politiques et Management Public, 29*(4), 671–693.

Eynaud, P., & Mourey, D. (2015). Apports et limites de la production du chiffre dans l'entreprise sociale. *Revue Française de Gestion*.

Eynaud, P., & Schmidt, G. (2012). Le monde associatif en mutation : Restructuration, Les singularités du secteur. *Juris Associations, 465*, 30–32.

Eynaud, P., & Sultan, F. (2014, Février). Les associations et les communs : croiser les expériences. *Juris Associations, 501*, 19–20.

Eynaud, P., Juan, M., & Mourey, D. (2018). Participatory art as a social practice of commoning to reinvent the right to the city. *International Journal of Voluntary and Nonprofit Organizations, 29*(2), 1–16.

Fábián, A. (2010). New public management and what comes after. *Current Issues of Business and Law, 5*, 41–56.

Farah, I., & Gil, M. (2012). Modernidades alternativas: una discusión desde Bolívia. In P. H. Martins & C. RoDrigues (Eds.), *Fronteiras abertas da América Latina*. Editora da UFPE.

Feher, M. (2017). *Le temps des investis: essai sur la nouvelle question sociale*. Editions la Découverte.

Fischer, R. M., & Comini, G. (2012). Sustainable development: From responsibility to entrepreneurship. *Revista de Administração da USP. São Paulo, 47*(3), 363–369.

Fitoussi, J. P. (2004). *La démocratie et le marché*. Biblio Essais, Le livre de poche.

Flores, E. C. (2015). O conceito de "comunidade humana universal" na obra de Guerreiro Ramos. *Cadernos Ebape.Br, 13*, 573–592.

Follett, M. P. (1924). *Creative experience*. Nyc, Longman Green & Co. (reprinted in London, P. Owen Publ., 1951).

Fondation et renouveau (n.d.). (pp. 315–323).

França Filho, G. C. (2002). Terceiro setor, economia social, economia solidária e economia popular: traçando fronteiras conceituais. In *Bahia Análise e Dados* (Vol. 12). SEI/Governo da Bahia.

França Filho, G. C. (2003). Gestão Social: um conceito em construção. In *Anais do Colóquio Internacional sobre Poder Local* (Vol. 9). CIAGS/UFBA.

França Filho, G. C. (2006). Políticas públicas de economia solidária no Brasil. In França Filho, Laville, Medeiros, & Magnen (Eds.), *Ação Pública e economia solidária - uma perspectvia internacional* (pp. 259–267). EDUFBA/EDURGS.

França Filho, G. C. (2007). Teoria e prática em economia solidária: problemática, desafios e vocação. *Civitas-Revista de Ciências Sociais, 7*(1), 155–174.

França Filho, G. C. (2008). Definindo gestão social. In Silva Jr., Mâsih, Cançado, & Schommer (Eds.), *Gestão social: práticas em debate, teorias em construção* (pp. 26–37). Imprensa Universitária.

França Filho, G. C. (2010). Economie populaire et solidaire au Brésil. In Laville, Magnen, França Filho, & Medeiros (Eds.), *Action Publique et Economie Solidaire - Une Perspective Internationale* (pp. 75–90). Eres.

França Filho, G. C. (2012). Indicadores para a sustentabilidade em economia solidária: uma questão de utilidade social. In G. Kraychette (Ed.), *Economia popular e solidária: indicadores para a sustentabilidade* (pp. 27–34). Tomo Editorial.

França Filho, G. C. (2013). *Bancos Comunitários de Desenvolvimento (BCD's) como expressão de Finanças Solidárias: por uma outra abordagem da inclusão financeira* (1st ed.). Arte Visual.

França Filho, G. C., & Cunha, E. V. (2010, Out./Dez). Incubação de redes locais de economia solidária: lições e aprendizados a partir da experiência do projeto Eco-Luzia e da metodologia da ITES/UFBA. *Revista Organizações & Sociedade (O&S-EAUFBA), 16*(51).

França Filho, G. C., & de Freitas Boullosa, R. (2015). Gouvernance démocratique, social management et para-économie. In Eynaud (Ed.), *La gouvernance entre diversité et normalisation* (pp. 205–215).

França Filho, G. C., & Laville, J. L. (2004). *Economia solidária: uma abordagem internacional.* Editora da UFRGS.

França Filho, G. C., & Silva, J., Jr. (2009). Bancos Comunitários de Desenvolvimento (BCD). In Cattani (Ed.), *Dicionário Internacional da Outra Economia* (pp. 31–37). Edições Almedina.

Fraser, N., & Honneth, A. (2003). *Redistribution or recognition? A political-philosophical exchange.* Verso.

Freire, P. (1979). *Educação como prática da liberdade* (9th ed.). Paz e Terra.

Freire, P. (1994). *Pedagogia do oprimido.* Paz e Terra.

Freire, P., de Oliveira, W. F., & Freire, N. (2009). *Pedagogia da solidariedade.* Paz e terra.

Frère, B. (2009). *Le nouvel esprit solidaire.* Desclée de Brouwer.

Frère, B. (2015). *Le tournant de la théorie critique.* Desclée de Brouwer.

Gadotti, M. (1999). *Convite à leitura de Paulo Freire.* Scipione.

Gadrey, J. (2010). *Adieu à la croissance : Bien vivre dans un monde solidaire.* Les petits matins.

Gardin, L., & Laville, J. L. (2017). L'économie solidaire. In D. Nyssens (Ed.), *Economie sociale et solidaire : socio économie du 3ème secteur* (pp. 187–219). Editions Deboeck.

Gattes, B., & Kiviat, B. (2008, Jul 31). Making capitalism more creative. *TIME Magazine.* 4p. Disponível em: http://content.time.com/time/magazine/article/0,9171,1828417,00.html. Acesso em de novembro de 28, 2013.

Gaulejac, V. D. (2005). *La société malade de la gestion : idéologie gestionnaire, pouvoir managérial et harcèlement social.* Editions Points.

Génard, J. L. (2015). Sociologie critique, sociologie morale. In Frère (Ed.), *Le tournant de la théorie critique*. Desclée de Brouwer.

Georges, G. (1968). La multiplicité des temps sociaux. In Sorbonne (Ed.), *La vocation actuelle de la sociologie* (pp. 325–430). PUF.

Gide, C. (2010). *The works of Charles Gide* (Vol. XI). L'Harmattan. 273 pages. Texts presented and annotated by Patrice Devillers. Paris, Comité pour l'édition des œuvres de Charles Gide.

Gilbert, P., Teglborg, A. C., & Raulet-Croset, N. (2017). L'entreprise libérée, innovation radicale ou simple avatar du management participatif? *Annales des Mines - Gérer et comprendre, 127*, 38–49.

Girard, R. (1979). *Violence and the sacred*. John Hopkins University Press. 352 pages.

Girard, R. (1987). *Things hidden since the foundation of the world*. Stanford University Press. 470 pages.

Gloria Gohn, M. D. (2013). Educação Popular e Movimentos Sociais. In D. R. Streck & M. T. Esteban (Eds.), *Educação Popular: lugar de construção social coletiva*. Vozes.

Gloria Gohn, M. D. (2015). *A relação entre a educação popular e os movimentos sociais na construção de sujeitos coletivos*. Text presented at the XII Congresso Nacional de Educação (Educere), PUC/PR, 26–29.

Godbout, J. T. (1987). *La démocratie des usagers*. Les Éditions du Boréal Express. 192 pages.

Goody, J. (2012). *The theft of history*. Cambridge University Press. 352 pages.

Gorz, A. (2004). *Critique of economic reason* (2nd ed.). Verso. 256 pages.

Gorz, A. (2010). *The immaterial*. Seagull Books.

Gorz, A. (2018). *Ecologica*. Seagull Books. 186 pages.

Graeber, D. (2015a). *Bureaucracy*. Editions Les liens qui libèrent. 300 pages.

Graeber, D. (2015b). *The utopia of rules: On technology, stupidity and the secret joys of bureaucracy*. Melville House. 272 pages.

Granovetter, M. (2000). *Le marché autrement, Sociologie économique*. Desclée de Brouwer. 239 pages.

Granovetter, M. (2007). Ação econômica e estrutura social: o problema da imersão. *RAE eletrônica, 6*(1).

Gras, A. (2003). *Fragilité de la puissance : se libérer de l'emprise technologique*. Editions Fayard.

Gribaudi, M. (2014). *Paris, ville ouvrière. Une histoire occultée : 1789–1848*. La Découverte.

Guénée, L. (2016). Désynchronisation des temps familiaux et coexistence solidaire : Enquête ethno-comptable des ressources d'une famille jordanienne. *Revue des politiques sociales et familiales, 123*, 91–103.

Guérin, I., Hersent, M., & Fraisse, L. (2011). *Femmes, économie et développement : de la résistance à la justice sociale*. Eres Editions.

Guerreiro Ramos, A. (1981). *The new science of organizations: A reconceptualization of the wealth of nations*. University of Toronto Press. 210 pages.

Gurvitch, G. (1968). La multiplicité des temps sociaux. In Sorbonne, *dans La vocation actuelle de la sociologie* (pp. 325–430). Paris, Puf.

Habermas, J. (1991). *The structural transformation of the public sphere: An inquiry into a category of Bourgeois society*. The MIT Press. 301 pages.

Hardin, G. (1968, December). The tragedy of commons. *Science*.

Harribey, J. M. (2009). Ambivalence et dialectique du travail : Remarques sur le livre de Moishe Postone, Temps, travail et domination sociale. *Contretemps. Nouvelle série, 4*, 137–149.

Hart, K., Laville, J. L., & Cattani, A. (2010). *The human economy: A citizen's guide*. Polity Press.

Hayat, S. (2014). *1848: Quand la république était révolutionnaire. Citoyenneté et représentation*. Le Seuil.

Herreros, G. (2012). *La violence dans les organisations : plaidoyer pour des organisations réflexives*. Eres Editions.

Hess, C. (2008, July 14–18). Mapping the new commons. In *12th biennial conference of the international association for the study of the commons*. University of Gloucestershire.

Hess, C., & Ostrom, E. (2006). *Understanding knowledge as a commons: From theory to practice*. The MIT Press.

Hess, C. & Ruth, M. D. (2006). *The name change; or, what happened to the "P"? ibraries' and ibrarians'*. Publications paper 23.

Hillenkamp, I. (2013). Le principe de householding aujourd'hui. Discussion théorique et approche empirique par l'économie populaire. In I. Hillenkamp & J.-L. Laville (Eds.), *Socioéconomie et démocratie. L'actualité de Karl Polanyi*. Erès.

Hillenkamp, I., & Laville, J. L. (2014). *Socio-économie et démocracie: L'actualité de Karl Polanyi*. Eres Editions.

Honneth, A. (2000). *La lutte pour la reconnaissance*. du Cerf. (ed. or. Kampf um Anerkennung, 1992). 232 pages.

Honneth, A., & Joel, A. (1998). *The struggle for recognition: The moral grammar of social conflicts*. MIT Press.

Horkheimer, M. (1947). *Eclipse of reason*. Oxford University Press.

Huault, I. (2008). Les approches critiques en management. In G. Schmidt (Ed.), *Le management*.
Illich, I. (1973). *La convivialité*. le Seuil.
IPBES-IPCC. (2021). *Scientific outcome of the IPBES-IPCC co-sponsored workshop on biodiversity and climate change (report)*.
IPCC. (2022, September). *AR6 synthesis report: Climate change*.
Jappe, A. (2003). *Les aventures de la marchandise*. La Découverte. 350 pages.
Jappe, A. (2017). *La société autophage : capitalisme, démesure et auto-destruction*. Editions la découverte.
Joas, H. (1996). *The creativity of action* (1st ed.). Polity. 352 pages.
Jonas, H. (1984). The imperative of responsibility. In *Search of ethics for the technological age (translation of Das Prinzip Verantwortung)*. University of Chicago Press. 255 pages.
Juan, S. (2011). *La transition écologique* (3e ed.). Eres éditions. Juris editions. 372 pages.
Klein, N. (2015). *Everything can change: Capitalism and climate change*. Actes Sud/Lux. 623 pages.
Klein, J. L., Laville, J. L., & Moulaert, F. (2014). *Innovation sociale*. Eres Edition. 246 pages.
Kraychette, G., Lara, F., & Costa, B. (2000). *Economie dos setores populares - entre realidade e utopia*. Editora Vozes.
Kripalani, K. (1958). *All men are brothers: Life and thoughts of Mahatma Gandhi as told in his own words*. UNESCO. 196 pages.
Kropotkine, P. (1902). *Mutual aid: A factor of evolution*. McClure Phillips and Co.
Kymlicka, W. (1997). *Multicultural citzenship: A liberal theory of minority rights*. Oxford University Press.
Laborde, J. P. (2015). La solidarité entre adhésion et affiliation. In A. Supiot (Ed.), *La solidarité : enquête sur un principe juridique* (pp. 109–123). Collège de France, Edition Odile Jacob.
Lacan, A. (2006). Léon Walras et les sociétés d'assurance mutuelles. *RECMA, 299*, 68–82.
Lallement, J. (2012). Les économistes et les pauvres : de Smith à Walras. *L'économie politique, 55*(3), 43–66.
Lallement, M. (2015). *L'âge du faire. Hacking, travail, anarchie*. Editions Le Seuil. 448 pages.
Laloux, F. (2014). *Reinventing organizations: A guide to creating organizations inspired by the next stage in human consciousness*. Nelson Parker. 382 pages.
Laplantine, F. (1988). *Aprender Antropologia*. Brasiliense.

Laplantine, F., & Olievenstein, C. (1993). *Um olhar frances sobre São Paulo*. Brasiliense. 92 pages.
Larrère, C., & Larrère, R. (2015). *Penser et agir avec la nature : une enquête philosophique*. Editions la Découverte. 330 pages.
Latour, B. (2017). *Où atterrir ? Comment s'orienter en politique*. La Découverte, Cahiers libres. 160 pages.
Laurent, S. (2016). *La couleur du marché : Racisme et Néoliberalisme aux Etats Unis*. Editions Seuil.
Laurent, B., Baker, M., Baudoin, V., & Raulet-Croset, N. (2018). *Innovation et participation: approches critiques*. PSL, Presses des Mines. 282 pages.
Lautier, B. (1994). *L'économie informelle dans le tiers monde*. La Découverte. (Collection Repères).
Laville, J. L. (1994). *L'économie solidaire : une perspective internationale*. Desclée de Brouwer.
Laville, J. L. (2000). *Qu'est-ce que le tiers secteur ? La Revue du MAUSS* (Vol. 16). La Découverte.
Laville, J. L. (2009). Economia plural. In Cattani (Ed.), *Dicionário Internacional da Outra Economia* (pp. 145–149). Editora Almedina.
Laville, J. L. (2010). *Politique de l'association*. Seuil. 350 pages.
Laville, J. L. (2011). *L'économie solidaire*. les essentiels d'Hermès, CNRS Editions.
Laville, J. L. (2014). Convivialisme, luttes sociales et économie solidaire. *Revue du Mauss, 43*, 93–102.
Laville, J. L. (2015). La théorie critique : de l'impasse au renouveau. In Frère (Ed.), *Le tournant de la théorie critique*. Desclée de Brouwer.
Laville, J. L. (2017). *L'économie sociale et solidaire*. Seuil.
Laville, J. L. (2018). *L'association, sociologie et économie*. Fayard – Pluriel.
Laville, J. L. (2023). *The solidarity economy*. University of Minnesota Press.
Laville, J. L., & Glémain, P. (2010). *L'économie sociale et solidaire aux prises avec la gestion*. Desclée de Brouwer. 480 pages.
Laville, J. L., & Hoarau, C. (2013). *La gouvernance des associations*. Editions Erès. 368 pages.
Laville, J. L., & Nyssens, M. (2001). The social enterprise: Towards a theoretical socio-economic approach. In Borzaga & Defourny (Eds.), *The emergence of social enterprise* (pp. 312–332). Routledge.
Laville, J. L., & Roustang, G. (1996). *Vers un nouveau contrat social*. Desclée de Brouwer.

Laville, J. L., & Sainsaulieu, R. (1997). *Sociologie de l'association : Des organisations à l'épreuve du changement social.* Desclée de Brouwer, Collection Sociologie économique. 403 pages.

Laville, J. L., & Salmon, A. (2015a). *Associations et Action Publique.* Desclée de Brouwer. 630 pages.

Laville, J. L., & Salmon, A. (2015b). Repenser la relation entre gouvernance et démocracie : le cadre théorique de l'économie solidaire. In P. Eynaud (Ed.), *La gouvernance entre diversité et normalisation* (pp. 175–189). Dalloz, Juris Editions.

Laville, J. L., & Salmon, A. (2016). Les associations et leur contribution à la démocratie : un défi contemporain. In R. Lafore (Ed.), *Refonder les solidarités : les associations au cœur de la protection sociale* (pp. 147–162).

Laville, J. L., Young, D., & Eynaud, P. (2015). *Civil society, the third sector, social enterprise: Governance and democracy.* Routledge Publisher. April, paperback.

Le Méner, E. (2016). Au nom du fils : Ethno-comptabilité d'une famille de sans-papiers hébergée en hôtel social. *Revue des politiques sociales et familiales, 123*, 41–55.

Leroux, P. (1860). *Quelques Pages de vérités.* NTU Librairie Editeur.

Leroux, P. (2016). *De l'humanité, de son principe et de son avenir où se trouve exposée la vraie définition, Tome 1: de la religion & où l'on explique le sens, la suite & l'enchaînement du mosaïsme & du christianisme.* Hachette Livre BNF. Edition originale 1840. 508 pages.

Lévesque, B. (2000). Innovation sociale et innovation technologique: l'apport de la recherche en science sociale et humaine. *Report to the Conseil de la Science et de la Technologie du Québec.* Bibliothèque Nationale du Québec, Bibliothèque Nationale du Canadá. www.cst.gouv.qc.ca

Lévesque, B. (2002). *Les entreprises de l'économie sociale, plus porteuses d'innovations sociales que les autres ?* Cahiers de l'ARUC-ÉS.

Lévesque, B. (2009). Contribuição da nova sociologia econômica para repensar a economia no sentido do desenvolvimento sustentável. In A. C. B. Martes (Ed.), *Redes e Sociologia Econômica* (pp. 107–127). Editora UFSCAR.

Lévesque, B., & Mendell, M. (1999). L'économie sociale au Québec : éléments théoriques et empiriques pour le débat sur la recherche. *Lien social et Politiques, 41*, 105–118.

Lévesque, B., & Ninacs, W. (2000). The social economy in Canada: The Quebec experience. In Shragge & Fontan (Eds.), *Social economy. International debates and perspectives* (pp. 112–129). Black Rose Book.

Lietaer, B., & Kennedy, M. (2010). *Monedas regionales: nuevos instrumentos para una prosperidad sustentable*. La Hidra de Lerna Ediciones.

Limeira, T. (2015, junho). *Empreendedorismo social no Brasil: estado da arte e desafios*.

Luhmann, N. (2018). *Organization and decision*. Cambridge University Press. 418 pages.

Lynch, E. C. (2015, Jan./Apr). Teoria pós-colonial e pensamento brasileiro na obra de Guerreiro Ramos: o pensamento sociológico (1953-1955). *Cadernos CRH, 28*(73).

Macchi, O. (2016). Portfolios of the poor how the world's poor live on $2 a day. *Revue des politiques sociales et familiales, 123*, 137–139.

Mance, E. (2000). *A revolução das redes*. Vozes.

Mance, E. (2002). *Redes de colaboração solidária*. Vozes.

Mance, E. (2003). *Como organizar redes solidárias*. DP&A, Fase, IFIL.

Manifeste convivialiste. (2013). *Déclaration d'interdépendence*. Le Bord de l'eau.

Marcelo Maia, J. (2015). História dos intelectuais no terceiro mundo: reflexões a partir do caso de Guerreiro Ramos. *Cadernos Ebape.Br, 13*, 550–559.

Marival, C., Petrella, F., & Richez-Battesti, N. (2015). Coopérer : entre économie d'échelle et reconquête du fait associatif ? In *XVes Rencontres du RIUESS - La créativité de l'économie sociale et solidaire est-elle soluble dans l'entrepreneuriat ?*

Martins, P. H. (2014). La nature symbolique des usages politiques du bien vivre. *Revue du Mauss, 43*, 75–87.

Marx, K. (1992). *Capital: Volume 1: A critique of political economy*. Penguin Classics. reprint, 1152 pages.

Maucourant, G. (2005). *Avez-vous lu Polanyi ?* Champs Essais. 262 pages.

Maurel, L., & Aufrère, L. (2018). *Pour une protection sociale des données personnelles*. https://hal.archives-ouvertes.fr/hal-01903526

Mauss, M. (2000). *The gift: The form and reason for exchange in archaic societies*. W. W. Norton and Company. 184 pages.

Mayntz, R. (1965). The Weberian ideal type of bureaucracy and the sociology of organizations. *Zeitschrift für Soziologie und Sozialpsychologie, 17*, 493–502.

Mazuir, F. (2004). Le processus de rationalisation chez Max Weber. *Sociétés, 86*(4), 119–124.

Melo Neto, J., & Magalhães, S. (2005). *O poder do circulante local: a moeda social no Conjunto Palmeiras*. Palmas.

Melo Neto, J., & Magalhães, S. (2006). *Bancos comunitários de desenvolvimento: uma rede sob controle da comunidade*. Instituto banco palmas de desenvolvimento e socioeconomia solidária.

Menezes, M., & Crocco, M. A. (2009). Sistemas de moedas locais: uma investigação sobre seus potenciais a partir do caso do Banco Bem, em Vitória/ES. *Economia e Sociedade, 18*(2), 36.

Menger, C. (2002). In O. Meuwly (Ed.), *Grandsätze der Volkwirtschaftslehre*. Liberté et société. Original edition 1923. 264 pages.

Michels, R. (2016). *Political parties: A sociological study of the oligarchial tendencies of modern democracy*. Martino Fine Books. 380 pages.

Moulaert, F., Martinelle, F., Gonzáles, S., & Swyngedouw, E. (2007). Introduction: Social innovation and governance in European cities. *European Urban and Regional Studies, 14*(3), 195–209.

Murray, R., Caulier-Grice, J., & Mulgan, G. (2010). *The open book of social innovation*. ESTA/The Young Foundation.

Musso, P. (2015). La solidarité : généalogie d'un concept sociologique. In A. Supiot (Ed.), *La solidarité : enquête sur un principe juridique* (pp. 93–107). Collège de France, Edition Odile Jacob.

Naro, G. (2015). Le new public management ou la gestion malade de la société. In Dietrich, Pigeyre, & Vercher-Chaptal (Eds.), *Dérives et perspectives de la gestion : échanges autour des travaux de Julienne Brabet*. Septentrion, Presses Universitaires. 180 pages.

Nikitin, M. (2003, Décembre). De la science des affaires aux sciences de gestion : un siècle de tâtonnements ? *Revue Gérer et Comprendre, 74*.

Novy, A., & Leubolt, B. (2005). Participatory budgeting in Porto Alegre: Social innovation and the dialectical relationship of state and civil society. *Urban Studies, 42*(11), 2023–2036.

Nyssens, M., & Petrella, F. (2015). ESS et ressources communes : vers une reconnaissance d'une diversité institutionnelle. *Revue française de socio-économie, 15*, 117–134.

OECD. (1997). *Oslo manual*.

Ogien, A. (1995). *L'esprit gestionnaire : une analyse de l'air du temps*. Editions de l'EHESS. 226 pages.

Oliveira, L. L. (1995). *A sociologia do guerreiro*. Editora UFRJ.

Oliveira, F. R., & Vaasconcelos, J. J. (2011). Os desafios da gestão nos negócios sociais e inclusivos: marco regulatório. In Instituto Walmart (Ed.), *Mapa de soluções inovadoras - tendências de empreendedores na construção de negócios sociais e inclusivos* (Vol. 4). Instituto Walmart/Ashoka. Gestão de negócios sociais e inclusivos, 24p.

Olson, M. (1965). *Logic of collective action*. Harvard University Press.

Orléan, A. (2011). *L'empire de la valeur, Refonder l'économie*. Le Seuil.

Orléan, A. (2012). Repenser la valeur, refonder l'économie. *The AEGIS Libellio, 8*(3), 11–21.

Orsi, F. (2015). Revisiter la propriété pour construire les communs. In B. Coriat (Ed.), *Le retour des communs : la crise de l'idéologie propriétaire* (pp. 51–67). Les liens qui libèrent.

Ostrom, E. (1990). *Governing the commons: The evolution of institutions for collective action (political economy of institutions and decisions).* Cambridge University Press. 298 pages.

Ostrom, E. (2005). *Understanding institutional diversity.* Princeton University Press.

Ostrom, E. (2010a). *Governance of the commons: For a new approach to natural resources.* De Boeck.

Ostrom, E. (2010b). Beyond markets and states: Polycentric governance of complex economic systems. *American Economic Review, 100*(3), 641–672.

Ostrom, E., & Ostrom, V. (1977). Public goods and public choices. In E. S. Savas (Ed.), *Alternatives for delivering public services: Toward improved performance* (pp. 7–49). Westview Press.

Ostrower, F., & Stone, M. (2015). Governing boards and organizational environments: Growing complexities, shifting boundaries. In J.-L. Laville, D. Young, & P. Eynaud (Eds.), *Civil society, the third sector and social enterprise: Governance and democracy* (pp. 75–90). Routledge.

Paludo, C. (2015). Educação Popular como resistência e emancipação humana. *Cad. Cedes, Campinas, 35*(96), 219–238.

Parodi, M. (2008, Octobre). *L'économie sociale et solidaire, une alternative à l'économie capitaliste.* Colloque de l'Addes.

Passos, O. A. (2008). *Explorando novas práticas organizacionais em economia solidária: conceito e características dos bancos comunitários.* Anais do V Encontro Nacional de Estudos Organizacionais.

Pénin, M. (2006). Charles Gide est-il toujours d'actualité ? *Revue internationale de l'économie sociale*, (301), 65–81.

Pérez, R. (2009). *La gouvernance de l'entreprise.* La Découverte. 128 pages.

Perret, B. (2014). Transition écologique et choc de la finitude? "Du convivialisme comme volonté et comme espérance". *Revue du Mauss, 43*, 35–40.

Perroux, F. (1993). *œuvres complètes* (6 volumes). Presses universitaires de Grenoble.

Pessis, C., Topçu, S., & Bonneuil, C. (2015). *Une autre histoire des trente glorieuses.* La Découverte. 309 pages.

Peters, T. (1993). *L'entreprise libérée - Liberation management.* Dunod.

Piketty, T. (2015). *The economics of inequality*. Belknap Press. 160 pages.

Pol, E., & Ville, S. (2009). Social innovation: Buzz word or enduring term? *The Journal of Socio-Economics, 38*, 878–885.

Polanyi, K. (1977). In H. W. Pearson (Ed.), *The livelihood of man*. Academic Press.

Polanyi, K. (1983). *The great transformation, the political and economic origins of our time*. Gallimard. (original ed. 1944).

Polanyi, K. (1986, June). La fallace économiste. *Le Bulletin du Mauss, 18*. translation in French of an extract from "The Livelihood of Man".

Portal Negócios Sociais. (2013). *Conceito*. http://negociossociais.com/conteudo/?page_id=4

Postel, N., & Sobel, R. (2010). Le concept de marchandise fictive, pierre angulaire de l'institutionnalisme de Karl Polanyi ? *Revue de philosophie économique, 2*, 3–35.

Postone, M. (1996). *Time, labor, and social domination: A reinterpretation of Marx's critical theory*. Cambridge University Press. 440 pages.

Prates Junqueira, L. A., et al. (2013). *Gestão social: mobilizações e conexões*. LTCE Editora.

Primavera, H. (2003). Last Tango in Buenos Aires. Paris. *Revue du MAUSS, 21*, 113–118.

Pruvost, G. (2016). Dépenser moins pour vivre mieux : Le cas de boulangers paysans vivant en yourte. *Revue des politiques sociales et familiales, 123*, 105–119.

Putnam, R. D. (1993). *Making democracy work: Civic traditions in modern Italy*. Princeton University Press.

Quéinnec, E., & Igalens, J. (2004). *Les organisations non gouvernementales et le management*. Editions Vuibert. 319 pages.

Razeto, L. (1991, Février). La veine populaire dans l'économie latino-américaine. *La Revue Nouvelle, 47*(2), 27–36.

Renault, M. (2011). Elaborer des outils pour construire une société plus conviviale : d'une expérience de terrain à un raisonnement théorique. In Caillé, Humbert, Latouche, & Viveret (Eds.), *De la convivialité : dialogues sur la société conviviale à venir* (pp. 167–187). La Découverte.

Rey, O. (2014). *Une question de taille*. Les essais.

Rigo, A. S. (2014). *Moedas Sociais e Gestão de Territórios: Aplicações e Implicações Teóricas e Práticas*. Tese (Administração) - Universidade Federal da Bahia.

Rigo, A. S., & França Filho, G. C. (2017). *Bancos Comunitários e Moedas Sociais no Brasil - Reflexões a partir da noção de economia substantiva*. Edufba. Coleção E-Livro.

Rigo, A. S., França Filho, G. C., & Leal, L. (2015). Moedas Sociais nos Bancos Comunitários de Desenvolvimento: a Experiência das Conchas em Matarandiba/BA. *Revista Interdisciplinar de Gestão Social (RIGS), 4*, 15–33.

Riot-Sarcey, M. (2016). *Le procès de la liberté. Une histoire souterraine du XIX ème siècle en France.* La Découverte.

Riot-Sarcey, M., & Gribaudi, M. (2008). *1848 : la révolution oubliée.* La Découverte.

Rosanvallon, P. (1979). *Le libéralisme économique.* Le Seuil.

Rosenberg, T. (2011, May 26). The path from charity to profit. *New York Times. Opinionator – The Opinion Pages.* 3p.

Rospabé, P. (1995). *La dette de la vie.* Éditions La découverte/Mauss.

Sachs, I. (2002). *Caminhos para o desenvolvimento sustentável.* Garamond.

Sachs, I. (2006). *Desenvolvimento includente, sustentável e sustentado.* Garamond.

Salomon, L., & Anheier, H. (1992). Search of nonprofit sector: The quest for definitions. *Voluntas: International Journal of Voluntary and Nonprofit Organizations, 3*(2), 267–311.

Samson, D. & Daft, R. L. (2012). *Management* (4th Asia Pacific ed.). Cengage learning.

Sangiorgio, J., & Veyer, S. (2009). Les coopératives d'activités et d'emploi : un exemple de construction d'une innovation sociale. *Projectics/Proyéctica/Projectique, 1*(1), 51–61.

Santos, M. (1993). *O espaço do cidadão.* Nobel.

Savidan, P. (2014). *La quête de certitude ou les leçons d'une pratique, in Dewey, La quête de certitude : une étude de la relation entre connaissance et action.* NRF, Editions Gallimard. originale 1929.

Scholz, T. (2013). *Digital labor: The internet as playground and factory.* Routledge.

Scholz, T. (2016). *Platform cooperativism: Challenging the corporate sharing economy.* Rosa Luxembourg Stiftung.

Scholz, T., & Schneider N. (Eds.). (2016, November). *Ours to hack and to own.* OR Books. 272 pages.

Schumpeter, J. (1935). *Theory of economic development.* Routledge. 234 pages.

Scott, J. (1998). *Seing like a state.* MIT Press.

Sennett, R. (2013). *Together: The rituals, pleasures and politics of cooperation.* Penguin. 336 pages.

Servet, J. M. (2010). *Le grand renversement : De la crise au renouveau solidaire.* Desclée de Brouwer. 264 pages.

Servigne, P., & Chapelle, G. (2017). *L'entraide, l'autre loi de la jungle.* Editions Les liens qui libèrent.

Silva, L. E. (2008, junho). Paulo Freire e Milton Santos: Um encontro em favor da cidadania e da solidariedade. *Revista e-Curriculum, 3*(2).

Simon, H. (1955). A behavioral model of rational choice. *The Quarterly Journal of Economics, 69*, 129–138.

Smith, A. (2013). *The wealth of nations*. CreateSpace Independent Publishing Platform. 426 pages.

Soares, C. (2006). *Moeda social: uma análise interdisciplinar das suas potencialidades no Brasil contemporâneo*. Tese (Doutorado) - Centro de Filosofia e Ciências Humanas, Universidade Federal de Santa Catarina.

Soares, C. (2009). Moeda social. In Cattani (Ed.), *Dicionário Internacional da Outra Economia* (pp. 255–259). Edições Almedina.

Sousa Santos, B. D. (2014). *Epistemologies of the south: Justice against epistemicide*. Routledge. 284 pages.

Steen-Johnsen, K., Eynaud, P., & Wijkström, F. (2011, September 1–11). On civil society governance: A new field of research. *Voluntas Journal*. Special thematic issue on Civil society organizations governance.

Stervinou, S., & Noël-Lemaître, C. (2008). Les coopératives d'activité et d'emploi (CAE) : un outil juridique au service d'un entrepreneuriat responsable. *Management & Avenir, 20*, 65–86.

Stiegler, B. (2010). *Economie de l'incurie et économie de la contribution*. Editions Galilée.

Subirats, J. (2013). Outra sociedade, outra democracia. In A. Luciano (Ed.), *Prates Junqueira et al, Gestão social: mobilizações e conexões* (pp. 21–40). LTCE Editora.

Supiot, A. (2012). *The spirit of Philadelphia: Social justice vs. the total market* (1st ed.). Verso. 160 pages.

Supiot, A. (2015). *La solidarité : enquête sur un principe juridique*. Collège de France, Edition Odile Jacob.

Swedberg, R. (2009). A Sociologia econômica do capitalismo: uma introdução e agenda de pesquisa. In A. C. B. Martes (Ed.), *Redes e Sociologia Econômica* (pp. 161–198). Editora UFSCAR.

Taylor, C. (1992). *Multiculturalism: Examining the politics of recognition*. Princeton University Press.

Tchernonog, V., & Prouteau L. (2019). *Le paysage associatif français - Mesures et évolutions*.

Tenorio, F. G. (1998, set/out). Gestão social: uma perspectiva conceitual. *Revista de Administração publica, 32*(5).

Théret, B. (2008). Os três estados da moeda: abordagem interdisciplinar do fato monetário. *Economia e Sociedade, Campinas, 17*(1), 1–28.
Thompson, E. P. (1966). *The making of the English working class*. Vintage. 864 pages.
Tiscoski, G., Rosolen, T., & Comini, G. (2013). Empreendedorismo Social e Negócios Sociais: Um Estudo Bibliométrico da Produção Nacional e Internacional. In *Encontro Nacional da ANPAD* (Vol. 27). Anais.
Tocqueville, A. D. (2002). *Democracy in America*. University of Chicago Press. 722 pages.
Todorov, T. (1993). *Nós e os outros*. Zahar.
Tönnies, F. (2021). *Community and society* (1st ed.). Mockingbird Press. 320 pages.
Toucas-Truyen, P. (2014). Les différents âges de la solidarité mutualiste en France : un concept singulier, des pratiques évolutives. *Vie sociale, 7*, 95–107.
Trist, E., & Bamforth, K. (1951). Some social and psychological consequences of longwall method of coalgetting. *Human Relations, 4*, 3–38.
Ulanowicz, R. E., Goerner, S. J., Lietaer, B., & Gomez, R. (2009). Quantifying sustainability: Resilience, efficiency and the return of information theory. *Ecological Complexity*, 27–36.
Utting, P. (2015). *Social and solidarity economy: Beyond the fringe* (1st ed.). Zed Books. 402 pages.
Valéau, P., Eynaud, P., Chatelain-Ponroy, S., & Sponem, S. (2018). Toward a reassessment of the role of rank-and-file stakeholders in nonprofit organizations. *Nonprofit and Voluntary Sector Quarterly*, 1–27.
Vandervelde, E. (1913). *Coopération neutre et socialiste*. Librairie Felix Alcan.
Vaujany, F. X. D., Hussenot, A., & Chanlat, J. F. (2016). *Théorie des organisations : nouveaux tournants*. Economica.
Viard, B., & Vaillancourt, Y. (2000). *Pierre Leroux : socialiste associatif, Actualités de 1848*. Thierry Quinqueton Editeur.
Vienney, C. (1994). *L'économie sociale*. La Découverte.
Vitari, C. (2013). *Slow management: Undertaking the transition*. Pearson.
Viveiros De castro, E. B. (2002). *A Inconstância da Alma Selvagem e Outros Ensaios de Antropologia*. Cosac & Naify. 552 pages.
Viveret, P. (2004). *Reconsidérer la richesse*. Editions de l'aube, Poche essai.
Walras, L. (1992). Etudes d'économie politique appliquée. In Auguste et Léon Walras (Ed.), *Œuvres complètes* (Vol. X). Economica. (collection of studies written between 1874 and 1898).

Weber, M. (2002). *The protestant ethic and the spirit of capitalism*. Penguin Books. translated by Peter Baehr and Gordon C. Wells.

Weber, M. (2019). *Economy and society: A new translation*. Harvard University Press. 520 pages.

Weiss, R. (1983). Weber on bureaucracy: Management consultant or political theorist? *Academy of Management Review, 8*(2), 242–248.

Williamson, O. E. (1985). *The economic institutions of capitalism*. Free Press.

Woodward, J. (1970). Technology, material control and organizational behavior. In J. P. Schwitte & A. R. Negandhi (Eds.), *Organizational behaviour models* (p. 21). Kent State University, Comparative Administration Research Institute.

Yunus, M. (2007). *Creating a world without poverty: Social business and the future of capitalism*. PublicAffairs.

Yunus, M. (2008). *Um mundo sem pobreza: a empresa social e o futuro do capitalismo*. Ática.

Yunus, M. (2010). *Criando um negócio Social: como iniciativas economicamente viáveis podem solucionar os grandes problemas da sociedade*. Elsevier.

Zask, J. (2011). *Participer : essais sur les formes démocratiques de la participation*. Editions le bord de l'eau.

Zelizer, V. (2005). *La signification sociale de la monnaie*. Seuil.

Index[1]

[1] Note: Page numbers followed by 'n' refer to notes.

P. Eynaud, G. Carvalho de França Filho, *Solidarity and Organization*,
https://doi.org/10.1007/978-3-031-27568-5

The manufacturer's authorised representative in the EU is Springer Nature Customer Service Centre GmbH, Europaplatz 3, 69115 Heidelberg, Germany. If you have any concerns regarding our products, please contact ProductSafety@springernature.com

Printed and bound by CPI Group (UK) Ltd, Croydon, CR0 4YY

01/10/2026

02225894-0003